CW01455397

The Collected Papers of Emı

This book is an engaging study, using Emmanuel Ghent's collected papers, of theoretical and personal origins of the relational turn in psychoanalysis. Emmanuel Ghent was one of the founders of relational psychoanalysis, and his ideas have been hugely influential. However, he published sparingly and his papers are scattered across a range of sources. In this book, his key writings are reproduced, along with analyses and critiques by major contemporary psychoanalytic writers.

This book provides a thorough examination of the key tenets of Ghent's thinking and illustrates the continued importance of his theoretical and clinical work for the next generation of psychoanalysts.

Victoria Demos is Supervisor at the Institute for Contemporary Psychotherapy, New York.

Adrienne Harris is Clinical Associate Professor of Psychology (Adjunct) and Clinical Consultant on the Postdoctoral Program in Psychotherapy and Psychoanalysis, New York University.

RELATIONAL PERSPECTIVES BOOK SERIES

LEWIS ARON & ADRIENNE HARRIS
Series Co-Editors

STEVEN KUCHUCK & EYAL ROZMARIN
Associate Editors

The Relational Perspectives Book Series (RPBS) publishes books that grow out of or contribute to the relational tradition in contemporary psychoanalysis. The term *relational psychoanalysis* was first used by Greenberg and Mitchell[1] to bridge the traditions of interpersonal relations, as developed within interpersonal psychoanalysis and object relations, as developed within contemporary British theory. But, under the seminal work of the late Stephen A. Mitchell, the term *relational psychoanalysis* grew and began to accrue to itself many other influences and developments. Various tributaries—interpersonal psychoanalysis, object relations theory, self psychology, empirical infancy research, and elements of contemporary Freudian and Kleinian thought—flow into this tradition, which understands relational configurations between self and others, both real and fantasied, as the primary subject of psychoanalytic investigation.

We refer to the relational tradition, rather than to a relational school, to highlight that we are identifying a trend, a tendency within contemporary psychoanalysis, not a more formally organized or coherent school or system of beliefs. Our use of the term *relational* signifies a dimension of theory and practice that has become salient across the wide spectrum of contemporary psychoanalysis. Now under the editorial supervision of Lewis Aron and Adrienne Harris, with the assistance of Associate Editors Steven Kuchuck and Eyal Rozmarin, the Relational Perspectives Book Series originated in 1990 under the editorial eye of the late Stephen A. Mitchell. Mitchell was the most prolific and influential of the originators of the relational tradition. Committed to dialogue among psychoanalysts, he abhorred the authoritarianism that dictated adherence to a rigid set of beliefs or technical restrictions. He championed open discussion, comparative and integrative approaches, and promoted new voices across the generations.

Included in the Relational Perspectives Book Series are authors and works that come from within the relational tradition, extend and develop that tradition, as well as works that critique relational approaches or compare and contrast it with alternative points of view. The series includes our most distinguished senior psychoanalysts, along with younger contributors who bring fresh vision. A full list of titles in this series is available at https://www.routledge.com/series/LEARPBS.

1 Greenberg, J. & Mitchell, S. (1983). *Object relations in psychoanalytic theory.* Cambridge, MA: Harvard University Press.

The Collected Papers of Emmanuel Ghent

Heart Melts Forward

Edited by Victoria Demos and Adrienne Harris

LONDON AND NEW YORK

First published 2018
by Routledge
2 Park Square, Milton Park, Abingdon, Oxon OX14 4RN

and by Routledge
711 Third Avenue, New York, NY 10017

Routledge is an imprint of the Taylor & Francis Group, an informa business

British Library Cataloguing in Publication Data
A catalogue record for this book is available from the British Library.

Library of Congress Cataloging in Publication Data
Title: The Collected Papers of Emmanuel Ghent
ISBN: 9781138926783 was successfully transmitted
to the Library of Congress.
Library of Congress Cataloging-in-Publication Data
Names: Ghent, Emmanuel, author. | Harris, Adrienne, editor. |
Demos, Victoria, editor.
Title: The collected papers of Emmanuel Ghent: heart melts forward/
edited by Adrienne Harris and Victoria Demos.
Description: Abingdon, Oxon; New York, NY: Routledge, 2018. |
Includes bibliographical references and index.
Identifiers: LCCN 2017009835| ISBN 9781138926783 (hardback) |
ISBN 9781138926790 (pbk.)
Subjects: LCSH: Psychoanalysis.
Classification: LCC BF173 .G479 2018 | DDC 150.19/5–dc23
LC record available at https://lccn.loc.gov/2017009835

ISBN: 978-1-138-92678-3 (hbk)
ISBN: 978-1-138-92679-0 (pbk)
ISBN: 978-1-315-68297-6 (ebk)

Typeset in Times New Roman
by Deanta Global Publishing Services, Chennai, India

For our most esteemed and much missed colleagues from

The First Generation

Stephen Mitchell, Emmanuel Ghent, Muriel Dimen, Ruth Stein

Contents

Acknowledgements

VD:
I thank Adrienne, who conceived of this project and invited me to climb aboard. For her consistently wise and generous collaboration.

To Laura Kressel, who performed minor and major miracles on a weekly basis, and for steering me to *The Years with Ross* by James Thurber.

To our writing group with Heather Ferguson and Susan Klebanoff, who provided their encouragement, support and enthusiasm.

My thanks to Tom Cawley, who encouraged me every step of the way, and provided my foundation, past and present. To my son Ryan, who provides my inspiration for the future.

AH:
I thank Victoria Demos for wonderful co-editing and collaboration. A labour of love to be sure. But labour!

Thanks to Karen Weiss for opening Mannie's office files, computers and other treasures.

To all the contributors who went deep into their precious memories and histories with Mannie.

To the many people at Taylor & Francis who work on our series and on this book, but in particular Kate Hawes, who steers the mother ship from her Oxford offices, and Charles Bath, who minds so many details.

To my fellow editors at the Relational Perspectives in Psychoanalysis: Lewis Aron, Steve Kuchuck and Eyal Rozmarin, dearest comrades in projects and struggles, over now the expanding decades.

Thank you to my family, who sustain me in so many ways, and always in loving memory of Robert Sklar.

Permissions acknowledgements

Psyche and Eye by Emmanuel Ghent, M.D. *McGill Medical Journal*, *19*(2), 1950, pp. 101–117. Permission to reprint has been kindly granted by Karen Weiss.

Relations: Introduction to the First IARPP Conference by Emmanuel Ghent, M.D. *IARPP eNews*, *1*(1), 2002, pp. 7–9. Permission to reprint has been kindly granted by The International Association for Relational Psychoanalysis and Psychotherapy (IARPP).

On Relational Psychoanalysis: An Interview with Dr Emmanuel Ghent/ Interviewer: Lewis Aron, Ph.D. (2000) Presented for the International Online Seminar, Psychoanalytic Connection. Permission to transcribe and reprint has been kindly granted by Lewis Aron and Karen Weiss.

The Photo of Emmanuel Ghent (2002) featured in the introduction to this book is kindly provided by photographer, Joelle Shefts. Reprinted with her permission and the permission of Karen Weiss.

The following eight articles are reused in this book with permission of Taylor and Francis LLC:

Countertransference: Its Reflection in the Process of Peer-group Supervision by Chaim F. Shatan, M.D., Benjamin Brody, Ph.D. and Emmanuel Ghent, M.D. *International Journal of Group Psychotherapy*, *12*(3), 1962, pp. 335–346. Also reprinted by permission of the American Group Psychotherapy Association.

Credo: The Dialectics of One-Person and Two-Person Psychologies by Emmanuel Ghent, M.D. *Contemporary Psychoanalysis*, *25*(2), 1989, pp. 169–211. Also reprinted by permission of the William Alanson

White Institute of Psychiatry, Psychoanalysis and Psychology and the William Alanson White Psychoanalytic Society.

Masochism, Submission, Surrender: Masochism as a Perversion of Surrender by Emmanuel Ghent, M.D. *Contemporary Psychoanalysis*, *26*(1), 1990, pp. 108–136. Also reprinted by permission of the William Alanson White Institute of Psychiatry, Psychoanalysis and Psychology and the William Alanson White Psychoanalytic Society.

Paradox and Process by Emmanuel Ghent, M.D. *Psychoanalytic Dialogues*, *2*(2), 1992, pp. 135–159. Also reprinted by permission of The International Association for Relational Psychoanalysis and Psychotherapy (IARPP).

Interaction in the Psychoanalytic Situation by Emmanuel Ghent, M.D. *Psychoanalytic Dialogues*, *5*(3), 1995, pp. 479–491. Also reprinted by permission of The International Association for Relational Psychoanalysis and Psychotherapy (IARPP).

Wish, Need, Drive: Motive in the Light of Dynamic Systems Theory and Edelman's Selectionist Theory by Emmanuel Ghent, M.D. *Psychoanalytic Dialogues*, *12*(5), 2002, pp. 763–808. Also reprinted by permission of The International Association for Relational Psychoanalysis and Psychotherapy (IARPP).

On What We Need: A Celebration of the Work of Emmanuel Ghent by Adam Phillips, Ph.D. *Psychoanalytic Dialogues*, *11*(1), 2001, pp. 1–21. Also reprinted by permission of The International Association for Relational Psychoanalysis and Psychotherapy (IARPP).

Heart Melts Forward: Emmanuel Ghent (1925–2003) by Adrienne Harris, Ph.D. *Psychoanalytic Dialogues*, *15*(2), 2005, pp. 211–221. Also reprinted by permission of The International Association for Relational Psychoanalysis and Psychotherapy (IARPP).

Contributors

Lewis Aron, Ph.D., is Director of the New York University Postdoctoral Program in Psychotherapy and Psychoanalysis. He has served as President of the Division of Psychoanalysis (39) of the American Psychological Association; founding President of the International Association for Relational Psychoanalysis and Psychotherapy (IARPP); and founding President of the Division of Psychologist-Psychoanalysts of the New York State Psychological Association (NYSPA). He is co-founder and co-chair of the Sándor Ferenczi Center at the New School for Social Research. He was one of the founders and is an associate editor of *Psychoanalytic Dialogues*, and is the series editor (with Adrienne Harris) of the *Relational Perspectives* book series (Routledge). He is the editor and author of numerous professional articles and books.

Ron Balamuth, Ph.D., is a psychologist-psychoanalyst in private practice in Manhattan. His early career in psychology began in the neurophysiology lab, where he studied the effects of morphine and other opiates on various brain structures. His interest in clinical psychology and psychoanalysis paralleled his interest in meditation and other contemplative practices from different ancient traditions. Currently, he integrates these two vital influences into a therapeutic sensibility that includes relational psychoanalysis, mindfulness and meditation, hypnosis and somatic experiencing. He specializes in the treatment of very young children, as well as individuals and couples. He has deep gratitude for Mannie Ghent, who nurtured and supported him in developing his own integration of his psychological and contemplative practices as one seamless whole.

Anthony Bass, Ph.D., is a supervising analyst and on the teaching faculty of several institutes and training programs, including the NYU Postdoctoral Program in Psychoanalysis and Psychotherapy, the Columbia University Center for Psychoanalytic Training and Research, the National Institute for the Psychotherapies National Training Program, the Institute for Relational Psychoanalysis of Philadelphia, and the Stephen Mitchell Relational Study Center, where he is also president. He is Editor-in-Chief of *Psychoanalytic Dialogues: The International Journal of Relational Studies*.

Jessica Benjamin, Ph.D., is a founding board member of the IARPP and the SMRSC, and a faculty member and supervisor at the NYU Postdoctoral Psychology Program in Psychotherapy and Psychoanalysis. She is the author of *The Bonds of Love* (Pantheon, 1988); *Like Subjects, Love Objects* (Yale University Press, 1995); and *Shadow of the Other* (Routledge, 1988). Her newest book, *Beyond Doer and Done To: Recognition Theory, Intersubjectivity and the Third*, will appear with Routledge in 2017.

Benjamin Brody, Ph.D., received his Ph.D. at the University of Chicago in 1949. He was a faculty member at the William Alanson White Institute, and Professor of Psychology at Adelphi University. He was the 1953 President of the Henry Stack Sullivan Society, and the author of numerous articles.

Victoria Demos, Ph.D., is Supervisor at the Institute for Contemporary Psychotherapy. She is a graduate of the NYU Postdoctoral Program in Psychoanalysis and Psychotherapy, and is a psychoanalyst and psychotherapist in private practice in New York City. Her current work on the intergenerational transmission of trauma and ripple effects of boundary violations has been presented at Division 39 and and recently published in *Psychoanalytic Psychology* in April 2017.

Muriel Dimen, Ph.D., was Adjunct Clinical Professor of Psychology at the NYU Postdoctoral Program Psychotherapy and Psychoanalysis, as well as Fellow of the NY Institute for Humanities, NYU, former Professor Emerita of Anthropology at Lehman College (CUNY) and a founding board member of IARPP. She was Editor-in-Chief of *Studies in Gender* and Associate Editor of *Psychoanalytic Dialogues* and Editor of *With Culture in Mind* (Routledge, 2011). She is author of *Sexuality, Intimacy,*

Power (Analytic Press, 2003, Goethe Award, Canadian Psychological Association); *Surviving Sexual Contradictions* (Macmillan, 1986); *The Anthropological Imagination* (McGraw-Hill, 1977). She is Co-editor of *Gender in Psychoanalytic Space* (with V. Goldner, Other Press, 2002); *Storms in Her Head* (with A. Harris, Other Press, 2001); and *Regional Variation Modern Greece and Cyprus* (with E. Friedl, NY Academy of Sciences 263, 1976). She died Feb 3, 2016.

Adrienne Harris, Ph.D., is Faculty and Supervisor at New York University Postdoctoral Program in Psychotherapy and Psychoanalysis. She is on the faculty and is a supervisor at the Psychoanalytic Institute of Northern California. She is an editor at *Psychoanalytic Dialogues* and *Studies in Gender and Sexuality*. In 2008, she, Lewis Aron and Jeremy Safron established the Sándor Ferenczi Center at the New School University. She, Lewis Aron, Eyal Rozmaren and Steven Kuchuck co-edit the *Relational Perspectives* book series, a series now with over seventy published volumes. She is a member of the NGO that the IPA developed to work with the UN, and she has worked in education and development on the problem of human trafficking. She is an editor of the IPA ejournal psychoanalysistoday.com, which is developing cross-cultural communications on the topics of violence and migration. She has written on topics in gender and development, analytic subjectivity and self-care, primitive states and the analytic community in the shadow of the First World War. Her current work is on analytic subjectivity, on intersectional models of gender and sexuality, and on ghosts.

Barry Magid, M.D., is a supervisor and faculty member at Stephen Mitchell Relational Study Center and the Institute for Contemporary Psychotherapy. He has served on the executive board of the International Association for Relational Psychoanalysis and Psychotherapy (IARPP). He is the founding teacher of the Ordinary Mind Zendo, President of the Lay Zen Teachers Association (LZTA), author of *Ordinary Mind: Exploring the Common Ground of Zen and Psychoanalysis* (Wisdom Publications, 2002); *Ending the Pursuit of Happiness* (Wisdom Publications, 2008) and *Nothing Is Hidden: The Psychology of Zen Koans* (Wisdom Publications, 2013); and editor of *Freud's Case Studies: Self Psychological Perspectives* (Analytic Press, 1993) and *What's Wrong with Mindfulness (And What Isn't)* (Wisdom Publications, 2016).

Adam Phillips is a member of the Site for Contemporary Psychoanalysis and is in private practice in London. His most recent book is *Unforbidden Pleasures* (Farrar, Straus and Giroux, 2015).

Chaim Shatan, M.D. (1924-2001), moved to New York City from Canada in 1949, after receiving his M.D. at McGill University Medical School. He was a faculty member at the William Alanson White Institute, and became interested in work with trauma and Vietnam War veterans in the 1960's. Shatan founded the Vietnam Veterans Working Group to promote the recognition of Post Traumatic Stress Disorder by the psychiatric community and his advocacy was instrumental in getting the Post Traumatic Stress Disorder into the 3rd Edition of the DSM (APA,1980). He was a founding member of the International Society for Traumatic Stress Studies. His most well-known publication is a New York Times' Op-ed titled "The Post-Vietnam Syndrome" (1972).

C. Seth Warren, Ph.D., is a clinical psychologist and psychoanalyst with more than 25 years of full-time clinical work with adults, children and couples in a private practice in New Jersey. He completed his Masters and Doctoral degrees in clinical psychology at Rutgers, The State University of New Jersey, and is a graduate of the Postdoctoral Program in Psychoanalysis and Psychotherapy at New York University. He has taught for many years as a Visiting Professor of Clinical Psychology at the Graduate School of Applied and Professional Psychology at Rutgers University, and has served as a supervising psychologist for numerous graduate psychology programs around the New York City area. He is former Director of the Center for Psychotherapy and Psychoanalysis of New Jersey, located in Madison, New Jersey, a post-graduate psychoanalytic institute with training programs in psychotherapy, psychoanalysis and couples therapy. He also serves there as a member of the faculty, and as Training and Supervising Psychoanalyst.

Introduction

Victoria Demos and Adrienne Harris

Photo of Emmanuel Ghent (2002) kindly provided by photographer, Joelle Shefts. Reprinted with her permission and the permission of Karen Weiss.

The work on this book has been a labor of love and a task filled with emotion for both of us. From the beginning of our collaboration, we were committed to bringing readers closer to the depth and richness of the work of Emmanuel Ghent. When Ghent introduced the first IARPP conference just months after Stephen Mitchell's death in 2001, he said, "My only wish is that Stephen would be here among us today and standing right here in my place welcoming you," and we would say the same thing now in relation to Emmanuel Ghent.

That day, Ghent (2002) went on to say some important things about the concept of *relational psychoanalysis*, such as:

> There is no such thing as a relational theory but there is such a thing as a relational point of view, a relational way of thinking, a relational sensibility, and we believe that it is this unique sensibility that underpins the sea change that many of us recognize as breathing fresh life into our field. (p. 7)

This is something we're thinking about very widely and carefully today—Is it a theory? Is it a point of view? Is it, as Tony Bass (2014) says, a tent, or as Adrienne Harris (2011) says, a landscape? So, whether insiders or outsiders to relational thought, as we continue to ask ourselves these questions, let us remember that Emmanuel Ghent was thinking of them right from the very beginning.

To approach his work, it became clear that we had to approach his personal life, his avocations and traits, as well as his publications. Emmanuel Ghent was an inspirational person, with an unusually wide range of capacities and interests. One might treat these traits and capacities as separate from his work. Indeed, Ghent himself often kept his vast array of interests quite separate. In this Introduction, we will argue for a more integrated and interdependent perspective on Ghent as person. Creator, teacher, healer. Ghent was scientific but also reflective and deeply meditative. He was as interested in high-end genetics as he was in Buddhist meditation. He was an intriguing person, with a prescient understanding of the direction in which the psychoanalytic and cultural worlds were headed. At times, Ghent could be quite geeky. Probably baptized in these forms of thought from his work at Bell Labs, he was a computer nerd before there were computers. The entry on Ghent in Wikipedia names him as one of the innovators, indeed a primary inventor, of electronic music, moving the emerging computer apparatuses from synthesizing data to synthesizing music, notes and sounds, and eventually sound, light and movement. Perhaps we can push on the links between the music-making Ghent and the psychoanalyst Ghent, creating clinical experiences as kinds of "sound baths," spaces of deep resonance and regression.

Although Ghent is recognized as a founding figure in the history of relational psychoanalysis as it developed at New York University in the 1980s and 1990s, his work and his writing actually predate the relational turn. Many of the ideas presented in his published papers, the majority of which were submitted in the 1990s, were actually developed during the 1970s. The time lag between Ghent's thought and his publication record can be explained, in part, by the fact that he caught fire as a psychoanalytic writer under the mentorship of a much younger man, Stephen Mitchell. That Ghent allowed himself to be mentored by someone twenty years his junior highlights, among many things, Ghent's openness to others' ideas. In addition, though, Ghent received a Guggenheim Fellowship to work at Bell Laboratories in New Jersey for a ten-year residency. The fellowship enabled him to adapt computer systems to produce electronic music that coordinated with lighting in theaters, to coordinate with dance performance. During this time, he saw patients only at night, when he returned to the city.

Similarly, Ghent's clinical style was decades ahead of his time. He integrated ideas from attachment theory, the study of regulation of affect, of self states, and of attention to deep affect in the service of getting away from dissociation, long before it was commonplace to work this way.

Each of the papers reprinted in this book offers theory and clinical insight, but they also provide a glimpse of what it was like to *be* with Ghent in analysis, in supervision, as a colleague, in the world, and in the classroom. It's impossible to neatly summarize Ghent's technique, personality and the quality of his presence in written form, but we hope that the papers reprinted here, and the accompanying commentaries by selected authors—analysts from different generations— bring the reader a bit closer to Ghent as an analyst, theoretician, inventor, intellectual and spiritual being.

Credo: The Dialectics of One-Person and Two-Person Psychologies (1989)

Credo is an unusual paper, and one that Ghent thought everyone should write, both at the beginning of their career and at its height. From the outset, this paper sets itself apart by invoking the concept of *belief*—a term that's rarely used in psychoanalysis. People talk about intellect, theory, the "way that we work," what theories we use, but *belief*—which is something closer to the idea of faith or a deeply held, personal way of working—is the way that Ghent talks about his personal credo. As the term *belief* suggests, Ghent viewed psychoanalysis as more than just an intellectual exercise. To Ghent, psychoanalysis was also a transformative, quasi-spiritual experience.

We can see a two-person, interpersonal bent early in Ghent's analytic path. Ghent went to McGill Medical School, where he studied medicine and the basic sciences, and along the way he discovered Freud, whose ideas intrigued him. This led him to the works of Erich Fromm and Harry Stack Sullivan, and eventually to the decision to enter the field of psychoanalysis. So, in the 1950s, Ghent came to New York with a good friend of his from Toronto, David Schecter, M.D. Together, Ghent and Schecter visited the two major analytic institutes in existence at the time, the New York Psychoanalytic Institute and the William Alanson White Institute. Ghent's response to each institute is telling. Ghent (1989) writes that, despite his respect for the intellectual rigor of the New York Psychoanalytic Institute, he felt that its emphasis on metapsychology was a mismatch with his personal belief system. At the White Institute, Ghent discovered interpersonal psychoanalysis, and felt that this was a much better fit for him.

While at the White, Ghent underwent his first analysis with Clara Thompson. Thompson, who had completed a long analysis with Ferenczi, and who has been identified as patient Dm. in his clinical diaries (Ferenczi, 1932/1995, pp. 2–3), was heavily influenced by Ferenczi's trauma work, his ideas about a mutual analysis, and his style of deep, affectively engaged analytic work (Aron and Harris, 1993). We can see these theoretical and stylistic transmissions directly and indirectly in Ghent's Credo. Central to Ghent's Credo is his emphasis on what can befall someone as a consequence of *gross empathic failure*. Ghent believed that it is tragic when traumatic things happen to a person, but if the trauma is not acknowledged, contained, or registered by an other, the consequences are magnified. Ghent was a strong carrier of that idea and although there were other portals of course, this is one generational line: Ferenczi, Clara Thompson, and then to Ghent.

Fairbairn's influence is also apparent in Ghent's beliefs about the profound effects of empathic failure on character formation. When a child is met either by rejecting, frustrating, or over-stimulating caretaking, s/he creates an internal world of part-objects and part-selves in order to manage the intolerability of loss or emptiness or the danger of a rejecting other (Fairbairn, 1943, 1952, 1993). Following from this, Ghent (1989) believed that character change is brought about by the analyst's empathic engagement with the patient's inner world of part-objects and selves. By "nourishing the undeveloped aspects of the self," the analyst facilitates the integration of self-fragments into a coherent self. In a Ghentian analysis, one seeks "to revisit painful experiences of early life so as to be able to integrate them" (p. 183).

Ghent did this by establishing a calm and transcendent place in the consulting room. His resonant voice created a kind of sound bath that provided affective resonance and enabled patients to reach deep affect. One might speculate that Ghent's relationship to music fueled the way he thought about what was happening in a clinical setting and implicitly informed his work. The idea of the vocal register—the sensory matrix of sound in which the patient, the infant, is bathed—was central to the experience of sitting with Ghent as an analyst (Benjamin, in this volume).

Although Ghent provided his patients with deep empathic immersion, there was also a sturdy psychoanalytic process beneath this, which unearthed powerful and profound memories, feelings, and self states. Ghent's analytic process was rigorous. This was by no means a "milk and cookies" approach to treatment. That phrase, a decidedly scornful epithet often applied to Winnicott and to the relational turn, caricatures these approaches as too gentle and devoted to providing support and care. To be sure, these approaches are all in the lineage of Ferenczi's idea of psychoanalysis as a cure by love (Thompson, 1944), itself a controversial concept. Jessica Benjamin (personal communication, 5/22/2013), who was in analysis with Ghent in the 1970s, recalls that a colleague with whom she was in training rejected Ghent as a training analyst because, after several consultations with him, she realized that Ghent's approach would evoke too much pain and sadness.

Ghent had a deep affinity for British object relations theories at a time when American ego psychology dominated the field (1970s and early 1980s). This was a time when there was a strong antagonism to the importance of the pre-oedipal years and relational matrices. Analysts like Winnicott and Fairbairn were just not considered central to a psychoanalytic project. George Makari (2008) and Emily Kuriloff (2013) propose that the dominance of ego psychology in America was due, in part, to the impact of trauma on the generation of European analysts who immigrated to the United States in the 1930s. European analysts arrived in America and retreated into a more cerebral and scientific kind of psychoanalysis. The relational turn is a direct response to this: part of the field's attempt to dig its way out of an intellectualized, emotionally detached way of working. This was a part of Ghent's project as well: to find his way to a more emotionally and relationally intricate experience.

In the context of belief and credo, it is important to recognize that Ghent himself was an immigrant—a searching and adventurous soul who, along with his comrades Chaim Shatan and David Schecter,[1] blew out of stuffy, often anti-Semitic, fractured, post-war Montreal to find politics, psychoanalysis and rebellion in New York City. As Beltsiou (2016) points out, the immigrant often leaves because he/she already feels other, and this almost certainly was true of Ghent and his cohorts. These friendships were therefore especially meaningful to Ghent, and the tragic loss of David Schecter to suicide in 1979 had a lasting impact on him. At his 75th birthday celebration (called *For Mannie who will be 75 in the year 2000*), Ghent wanted his audience to know that, amidst a deeply pleasant celebration, the loss of Schecter continued to be a deep and abiding source of grief for him.

An attunement to the intrapsychic is characteristic of Ghent throughout his writing and clinical career. The internal world of the patient and of the analyst remain compelling, important, transformative, as well as the between world. We might surmise that Ghent's continuing attention to object relations theory, to Winnicott and Fairbairn, and later to Bollas, are among the reasons that he left White for New York University. Part of that leaving is leaving a part of intersubjective theory that tended to underemphasize the intrapsychic. Curiously, at White, despite the backdrop of Sullivan and Ferenczi (people with big developmental theories), there was an anti-developmental tilt. Sometimes this appeared as a determination not to infantilize the patient and as an antagonism to regression. Ghent's trajectory both to New York University and to object relations was to be able to hold the intrapsychic, the internal world, its vitality, its terrors, its extremes, and its intricacy along with what is transacted, interactionally. It is also possible to see how much Ghent's interests link to contemporary work on archaic and primitive experience, and our much greater comfort with infant cognition and early dyadic development.

Masochism, Submission, Surrender: Masochism as a Perversion of Surrender (1990)

This is Ghent's most well-known paper, his most frequently cited paper, and the one with the most intense clinical impact. There is a lot of experience-near, phenomenologically rich thinking about the different states of being that constitute submission and surrender. Ghent takes terms that are typically used in a characterological and pathologizing sense—like masochism and sadism—and turns them inside out. His agenda is to recognize the health and the necessary force of sadism and masochism. Similar themes arise in Jessica Benjamin's (1990) work on doer/done-to, and this is not a coincidence. In the 1980s, Ghent and Benjamin were engaged in dialogue about the powerful dynamics of a sadism and masochism, and the use of each as an attempt to manage attachment and separation. It is likely that Ghent's long involvement with Buddhism and meditation also played a role in the evolution of these ideas as well.

Ghent (1990) begins this paper by defining the concept of surrender as the "obverse of resistance"—a yearning for the letting go of the false self, a return to wholeness, liberation and the expansion of mental freedom (p. 110). Surrender is a kind of release into an experience of safety. Developmentally, it is akin to the primary experience of "going on being," which requires an other who is containing and observing. Surrender is a regression, but it's an interesting kind of regression and it's certainly not something that you can design or plan for. Ghent was completely concerned with the process. He was very interested in emergence—in things that aren't pre-set but appear and evolve, whether it's in individual development or in an analytic process.

Ghent takes a Winnicottian perspective when examining the inherent two-person-ness of sadism and masochism. Briefly, the progression from object relating to object usage is absolutely essential for development, and requires that the child make a sadistic attack on the object and that the object survive the attack (Winnicott, 1969, 1971). Only when the child perceives that the object can survive the attack can s/he move from object relating to object usage. Sadism and attack are how a child finds boundaries and otherness. When the parent survives the attack, the child's relationship to reality changes. The child learns to accept that the other is *other*—"I wanted you dead and you're not." That incredible possibility—the possibility of psychic survival of the hated other—is in the analytic process as well. The analyst's survival of the patient's attack is key. Sadism viewed in this manner is an attempt to find an object. It's a way to get the analyst's attention, to find the analyst. In other words, *fierce impact*—having an impact on the other, even in a violent way—has a function, and our task in analysis is to understand its interpersonal and intrapsychic functions. The task of the analyst is to survive that sadistic attack and to be able to communicate about it.

The analytic encounter is therefore a risky prospect for both analyst and patient. What happens if the other does *not* survive the attack? If the other is destroyed in some way? The highway to change is fraught with risk, and masochism is one of the exit points from that highway. Put simply, if I've killed the other, then I'm going to do myself in; I'm going to retreat to masochism. This is not so different from the use to which Steiner has put the concept. For Steiner (1993), psychic retreat is a withdrawal that both shields and also damages the person's capacities. Sometimes psychic retreat may be undertaken in the wish to avoid destructiveness, yet it leads often to fragmentation and to the impairment of capacities to think and feel. These ideas are not so foreign to the way Ghent was deploying ideas about masochism.

When Ghent uses the term masochism he sees its protective, adaptive function: to prevent an experience that feels too frightening to engage in. Masochism is a response to the fear of change. It happens in the analyst and it happens in the patient. All of us make many subtle moves in order to stop a process of change that is felt to be fatal to our internal and interpersonal worlds. The idea that masochism is undertaken in order to ward off an inner sense of catastrophe, including the catastrophe of change, is incredibly helpful, clinically.

Ghent knew well of the fraught path towards transformation, even as it is an ideal to be sought. Much is at stake when we're confronted with the possibility of change, including the death of the internal object—the damaged and dying internal object, the mother. Part of the anxiety about change in us, the analyst, and in the patient, is that something is going to change irrevocably in terms of an internal object whom our charge was to keep alive at all costs (Rey, 1988). So, do you work for change? Do you do something so change might take shape in you? And, can you survive change? Can your internal objects survive your change? One knows in this very intuitive way that something is *about* to change. Ghent, brilliantly, thinks masochism is one of the exits in the conflict between change and stasis. Masochism is the psychic labor of warding off change in an attempt to manage something internally.

And, for the analyst, what does it mean to survive a sadistic attack? What constitutes survival? Definitely there is to be no retaliating. Certainly, it is important to be able to experience hate and sadistic attack and live through it and not collapse. We often have patients whose primary object did not survive psychically. Usually the patient believes that the primary object was destroyed by the child, and this is a very difficult matter to transcend. So sadism is both *to find* and *to keep alive* the object, and Ghent is arguing that the analyst must contain and survive this attack. The analyst also must acknowledge our compromised strategies for various false-self enactments as part of the survival.

Again, Ghent is talking about the intense, inevitable two-person-ness of this process; at times the analyst has to surrender, at other times the patient has to. The masochism and sadism flip over and over, and part of the analyst's task is to own our sadism. This is very difficult to acknowledge: *our* misuse of patients, even in the service of ethical aims. It is often difficult to see how anguishing change is, how much loss is entailed. Ghent's original work with masochism and sadism illuminates these difficulties for analysts and analysands.

In a curious way, Ghent is arguing that generative or mutative processes of development will involve attempts to surrender and violent attempts to survive. The very dangerous thing that exists between masochism and sadism is indifference. Growth entails transcending indifference. Ghent's paper moves back and forth between optimism and caution. The scale of work that is entailed in trying to help somebody evolve from a false self into something more authentic, more meaningful, more porous is enormously difficult. Ghent thinks of us—the analysts—as fighting our own fears and the patients' fears, continuously.

Something that is true of Ghent and Winnicott is that there is an optimism in their thinking, writing and working. There is an optimism that the false self can be repaired. There can be reparation, there can be some healing. This is quite different from Bion, for whom there's a more tragic vision. For Ghent, one cannot set an agenda to become real or meaningful, but the longing for a true self is pervasive and paramount.

Paradox and Process (1992)

"Paradox and Process" was first presented in 1990 and published in 1992. In this paper Ghent plays with the concepts of "paradox" and "process" in order to highlight the clinical value of the interplay between the two. A paradox is a confounding of different logical types, and process refers to the mental steps used to resolve the apparent contradiction embedded in the paradox. A paradox itself is paradoxical because it can both exist and not exist. Ghent argues that one mustn't choose one over the other (i.e. paradox over process, or vice versa), and that the urges to either accept the paradox or to resolve it too quickly foreclose on the opportunity for a new kind of mental understanding of experience. Instead, the interplay between paradox and process leads to heightened understanding and growth, and allows us to understand reality in new ways. Ghent then describes three such paradoxes related to the clinical and theoretical basis of psychoanalysis.

The first paradox that Ghent addresses concerns the seemingly mutually exclusive views of the patient from a drive/conflict model versus an object-relational model. Is there a baby inside the patient? The classical view of the patient privileges drives at the expense of object relations. There is no baby to be found in the patient. In contrast, object relational and contemporary relational writings privilege the baby inside of the patient, and seek to connect with that baby in order to promote healing and integration. In this more developmental/relational approach, the idea is really experiencing the fragments of childhood experience. The classical view of the patients is from the outside in, whereas the object-relational view of the patient is from the inside out. This leads to very different conceptions of the patient and of the psychoanalytic endeavor. Ghent is very careful to say that he's not privileging one over the other—that both are important. Just as a dream is a kind of path to self-integration and self-knowledge, both elements exist and you listen for certain things at certain moments.

In addition, he contrasts the concept of *need* from that of *neediness*. A need that comes from the "true self" is a genuine need that reveals the inner yearning of the patient. Ghent (1990, 1992) includes the longings for human warmth, empathic responsiveness, trust, recognition, faith, playful creativity, and love as genuine needs. These are the kinds of need that a child might require from a parent, or that a patient might require from an analyst. In contrast, neediness is a demonstration of false self, and could more accurately be termed demandingness. Neediness protects the self in the moment, but it usurps selfhood by concealing the genuine need of the true self. Ghent believed that there is always a genuine need underneath neediness, no matter how dissociated it might be and no matter how difficult it might be to see in the moment.

In other words, neediness is a defensive apparatus that protects the patient from experiencing the genuine underlying need of the true self. The issue for the analyst then is *not* about whether or not to gratify the need (i.e. the defense). Instead, the analytic work is an ongoing process that enables the analyst and analysand to see and experience the genuine feeling state without the defense; to recognize and experience the need that exists beneath the neediness of the false self. As parent or analyst, you try to validate the real need.

Ghent relates the concept of neediness to Balint's (1969, 1979) malignant regression, in which the patient demands something from the analyst (e.g. love). If the analyst views the need as a drive that could be gratified or not gratified, he will probably pull back from the patient. However, if the demand is viewed as a defensive structure that protects a real need of the true self, the analyst will engage with the patient in a way that permits access to the genuine need that lies beneath the demandingness. In other words, the patient's apparent demandingness actually reflects a dissociated need—the need to be recognized and to be found in his or her authenticity. This is close to Balint's idea of a benign regression.

An analytic training case that I (VCD) brought to Ghent many years ago illustrates how he used these ideas about needs and neediness in a clinical setting. At the time, I was working with a young woman in her twenties, who was struggling to have a relationship with a man and struggling to develop her sense of self. This young woman was raised by two highly successful parents, who were emotionally and physically neglectful of her from a very early age. Her parents divorced when she was an adolescent, and this young woman was essentially abandoned by her mother and lived with her father—a man who was physically neglectful. At some point, she fled from her father's home and went to live with her mother, who had accepted a prestigious job in another state and who, unbeknownst to this young woman, was living with an emotionally abusive man and had entered into a clinical depression that would devolve into a psychotic depression. Complete non-functioning. Crumbling.

At some point in the treatment, she entered into a relationship with a young man, and this was actually her first relationship to last more than a week or two. As the relationship progressed, she began to develop a sort of demandingness/neediness in relation to him. He had recently started a new job that required him to work long hours, and this made him somewhat less available to her. She found this intolerable, and would call him up and complain, "Where are you? I need you."

Ghent said that this woman was confusing need and neediness. The deprivation that she had experienced early in life led her to mask the genuine needs of her true self (i.e. needs for warmth, empathic responsiveness, trust, recognition, etc.) with a kind of angry demandingness. If she had not been in a needy state, she might have been able to express her genuine need with a direct statement such as, "I'd love to have you here to help me, but I see you've got some urgent business right now." That would have been expression of her needs.

Mannie believed that the degree of neglect and deprivation in childhood influences the degree to which genuine needs are masked with angry, retaliatory responses. Mannie noted that these patients are almost phobic about getting their real needs met. The irony, of course, is that this demandingness does not bring the person any closer to getting these needs met, and often elicits a rejecting response from the present object, turning him into the rejecting object from the past.

In this paper, Ghent also addresses the seemingly paradoxical idea that destruction creates reality (Winnicott, 1969, 1971). The child's efforts to destroy the object, and the object's ability to withstand the destruction, takes the child from the realm of object relating to the realm of object usage. Ghent wonders how destruction can co-exist with an experience of growth, expansion of mental capacities, and transcendence. And what if the object fails to survive in the moment? If the object fails to survive, the child does not discover externality and begins to feel destructive him/herself. The stage is set for sadism and ab-use of the object.

Interaction in the Psychoanalytic Situation (1995)

Ghent (1995) uses this paper to discuss the inner workings of change, and to ponder some of the factors that contribute to the "healing, wholing, and mending" of the human soul (p. 482). He further elaborates on the concept of *need*, which he equates with a motivational system, and the ways in which *dissociated* needs may be brought into awareness, often unwittingly, by the analyst's spontaneous behavioral response to the patient.

There are key points he makes about this process (i.e. the process by which dissociated needs are brought into awareness). First, Ghent notes that the relationship between perception and response is a *bidirectional* relationship. In other words, the conventional assumption that perception leads to response is sometimes reversed; there are instances in which response initiates perception. In each of the provided examples, the analyst's spontaneous behavioral response to the patient allows a dissociated need to come into the patient's awareness.

Second, this moment is not something that the analyst can plan for, and the dissociated need is not something of which the analyst or patient is even aware. The interaction brings to light a dissociated element of the patient's motivational system. This is somewhat akin to Bollas's (1987) *unthought known*, in the sense that an element of past experience is not consciously recollected but its presence is felt in the moment-to-moment interaction between patient and analyst. There is a conscious and contextualized relationship, what we would now call a bi-personal conscious and unconscious field, and what transpires in the field is revelatory.

In one of the examples Ghent provides, he is in session with a patient in a drafty office. Without hesitation, he stands up and places a Scottish throw over her lap. She begins to quietly sob. After a while, she relates to him that she wasn't aware of being cold and then begins to weep more deeply. Ghent's response changed her perception. His response made her aware of her pain, of her dissociated needs for recognition and tenderness. Ghent theorizes that his response brings out the yearning, the sadness, in the patient but as yet unknown to her. He describes her response as something that surprised him. He wasn't doing it as a way of doing something corrective or healing—it was just a kind of impulse. There is a kind of emergent experience—not unrelated to Ogden's idea of reverie—in which an unremarkable action brings to light something unbidden. A kind of "third" appears in the analytic space. When productive interpersonal psychic work is being done, a third will emerge.

Ghent also emphasizes the importance of action in this process of bringing dissociated need to light. The analyst has not simply made an interpretation, but he has *done something*, and it is the action itself that brings the patient's dissociated need into awareness. Today, we might think of this as akin to *mutuality* or a *mutual process*. Ghent contrasts this with trying to change people in an intellectual or an informational way instead of in a transformational way. The analyst throws in a different response, and this response changes the perception.

Wish, Need, Drive: Motive in the Light of Dynamic Systems Theory and Edelman's Selectionist Theory (2002)

Ghent's final paper, "Wish, Need, Drive: Motive in the Light of Dynamic Systems Theory and Edelman's Selectionist Theory," is a wide-ranging essay on the daunting topic of motivation. This paper was published in 2002, shortly after Stephen Mitchell's death. That death and Ghent's own aging form the poignant backdrop in which this paper was written. The essay has the feel of a summation. Ghent pulls together all of his ideas about motivation and grounds them in developmental theory, complexity theory, epigenetics, and in Edelman's (1987, 1989, 1992) work on neuronal group selection. Ghent elegantly integrates developmental theory and neuroscience, and situates them within the landscape of relational psychoanalysis.

Ghent attempts something very ambitious in this paper. He builds a motivational system that is *not* centered on the concept of drive/impulse. In doing so, he grapples with two questions. With what psychic elements do we replace the concept of drive? And, what are the working assumptions of such a motivational system?

Ghent (1992) commits to the idea of *need* as important elements in such a system, stating that "meaning [for a person] derives from what happens between people from earliest infancy on" (p. 205). Ghent specifies six organizing and emergent needs, including a need for protection of the self and for meaningful others in one's life; a need for a feeling of self-worth, dignity, and self-esteem; a need for the expansion of awareness, a sense of aliveness; a need for integration of the self—a yearning for surrender of the false self and a quest for wholeness; need for meaning, coherence, and significance; and a need for growth. One begins to see that some of these needs may work in opposition to each other. There's a need for growth and creativity, and also a need for protection. There is a need to maintain coherence and stability, and also a need for new experiences that expand the self.[2] These become increasingly complicated motivational systems.

In Ghent's motivational system, *process* is what is important, not structure. In contrast with the more canonical schools of psychoanalysis, which speak of static psychic structure, Ghent speaks of a complex system of motivation that is fluid, dynamically informed by context, and that is self-organizing. According to Ghent, this process may manifest in different ways—the process can be a violent undoing or it can be a making, a pulling together, and an evolving. In defining process as both constructive and destructive, Ghent maintains the Winnicottian project of the importance of agency, creativity, and destruction in psychic life and growth. Ghent increasingly starts to talk about the darker aspects of human nature—that creativity often includes destruction.[3]

One must reasonably ask, where is sexuality in this system? Where is aggression? Ghent uses the word *need* very explicitly, because it connotes intensity and the potential for a great violence. To Ghent, giving up drive theory is *not* giving up intensity. It is giving up the notion of an innate, biological, instinctual drive.[4]

If needs are not innate, then from where do they come? Ghent approaches this topic from the perspective of epigenetics—a model of thinking about evolution, developed in the 1980s, in which genetics and experience interact to produce outcomes. Ghent applies principles of epigenetics and the work of Edelman (1987, 1989, 1992) to tell us about the evolution of motivational systems from infancy into adulthood.

From the very beginning, the subject (i.e., the baby) has values—and by values, Ghent does not mean moral or ethical values, but tendencies (e.g. tendencies to turn towards warmth or light). Over the course of development, these tendencies become biases, standard ways of acting, and eventually motives. The nature of the environment/genetic interaction will determine how values turn into biases. And the system is *emergent*, meaning that something develops and the system reorganizes aspects of what it has generated (the principle of reentry). This is a fluid and endlessly changing system.[5]

Ghent also makes a distinction between motives that are about excitement and expansiveness (but with intensity and ferocity) and those that are directed towards safety, security, and coherence. There are the quiet motives and the noisy motives. Ghent wants us to hold on to both.

For Ghent, these motives are complicatedly interactive and layered. Sometimes one system defends against the needs of another. This might inform how we think about needs and neediness. There is the possibility that a system is designed to *not* get needs met. We may also think about submission and surrender in this way. The motive to hurt oneself, to repeat anguish, to self attack, may cover a longing for surrender. Sometimes what on the surface appears to be a violent attack or a masochistic submission may, in fact, conceal a motive that is harder to get to—a motive for coherence and integration, a motive *not to fall to pieces.*[6]

Conclusion

This Introduction has focused on a close reading of Ghent's major papers. It has also been designed to place Ghent in his social, intellectual and psychoanalytic context, and to draw lines and links between Ghent and other figures who come before and after him. His period of high productivity in psychoanalysis is relatively short: the 1990s. But it is an incandescent period, and his work is original and deeply helpful clinically and theoretically.

In the book we combine Ghent's papers with reminiscences, personal tributes and colleagues' assessments about the work. One of the intriguing experiences we have had in writing and editing is the complexity of what name to use: Ghent, Mannie, Emmanuel Ghent. In this Introduction, we have kept to the formality of last name or full name. But in the commentaries and reminiscences, we have given the authors freedom to find the many unique forms this man could take. It is in the spirit of this extraordinary man that the personal, the clinical, the intellectual, the creative, the sublime and spiritual are all alive and in contact.

Notes

1. These three, born two years apart (1924–26), grew up in Montreal, went to medical school at McGill, came to New York City, trained at and joined White in the 1960s, and engaged with politics and psychoanalysis in the 1970s.
2. Here we may think of the work of other motivational systems thinkers—specifically, self psychologists—who, like Ghent, reframe drive theory and propose different motivational systems of behavior (Lichtenberg, 2001/1989; Lichtenberg, Lachmann, & Fossage, 2014, 2001/1992, 1996).
3. The idea of destruction is an important part of contemporary brain science, and we hear its psychoanalytic echoes in Spielrein's (1912/1994) work on the inevitable interplay of creativity and destruction, in Freud's (1923) death drive and in the Kleinian perspective on the developmental potency of envy and aggression (Klein, 1957, 1975). Ghent is casting a wide net.
4. In hindsight, with newer work of Laplanche available in translations, we see an overlapping aspect of their work—both believe that a biological model of drive, a centering on the individual and the intrapsychic, is no longer an adequate account of a psychoanalytic theory of motivation.
5. This model of development and change is very compatible with the contemporary models in field theory (the Barangers and Pichon Riviere in particular), in which a spiral process, a dialectic of something emerging being reintegrated and transforming the interior process from which those events or actions emerged.

6. This is Winnicott making the same move: seeing in an antisocial, delinquent boy who steals, the presence of hope, of hope to be found. There is a kind of motive that has aggressive and intense, contactful impulses and there's also a motive to be coherent.

References

Aron, L. and Harris, A. (1993). Sàndor Ferenczi: Discovery and rediscovery. In L. Aron & A. Harris (Eds.), *The Legacy of Sàndor Ferenczi* (pp. 1–36). London, UK: The Analytic Press.

Balint, M. (1979). *The Basic Fault: Therapeutic Aspects of Regression*. London, UK: Tavistock. (Original work published 1969)

Bass, A. (2014). Three pleas for a measure of uncertainty, reverie, and private contemplation in the chaotic, interactive, nonlinear dynamic field of Interpersonal/ Intersubjective Relational Psychoanalysis. *Psychoanalytic Dialogues*, *24*(6), 663–675.

Beltsiou, J. (2016). Seeking home in the foreign: Otherness and immigration. In J. Beltsiou (Ed.), *Immigration in Psychoanalysis: Locating ourselves.* New York, NY: Routledge.

Bollas, C. (1987). *The Shadow of the Object* (pp. 200–236). New York, NY: Columbia University Press.

Corrigan, E.G. and Gordon, P.-E. (1995). *The Mind Object: Precocity and Pathology of Self-Sufficiency.* Northvale, NJ: Jason Aronson.

Edelman, G.M. (1987). *Neural Darwinism*. New York, NY: Basic Books.

Edelman, G.M. (1989). *The Remembered Present: A Biological Theory of Consciousness*. New York, NY: Basic Books.

Edelman, G.M. (1992). *Bright Air, Brilliant Fire: On the Matter of the Mind.* New York, NY: Basic Books.

Fairbairn, W.R.D. (1994). Repression and the return of bad objects (with special reference to the 'war neuroses'). *Psychoanalytic Studies of the Personality* (pp. 59–81). New York, NY: Routledge. (Original work written 1943, published 1952)

Ferenczi, S. (1993). *The Clinical Diary of Sàndor Ferenczi.* (J. Dupont, Ed.). Cambridge, MA: Harvard University Press. (Original work published 1932)

Freud, S. (1923). The ego and the id. *Standard Edition*, *19*, 3–68.

Ghent, E. (1989). Credo: The dialectics of one-person and two-person psychologies. *Contemporary Psychoanalysis*, *25*(2), 169–211.

Ghent, E. (1990). Masochism, submission, surrender: Masochism as a perversion of surrender. *Contemporary Psychoanalysis*, *26*(1), 108–136.

Ghent, E. (1992). Paradox and process. *Psychoanalytic Dialogues*, *2*(2), 135–159.

Ghent, E. (1995). Interaction in the psychoanalytic situation. *Psychoanalytic Dialogues*, *5*(3), 479–491.

Ghent, E. (2002). Wish, need, drive: Motive in the light of dynamic systems theory and Edelman's selectionist theory. *Psychoanalytic Dialogues*, *12*(5), 763–808.

Ghent, E. (2002). Relations: Introduction to the first IARPP Conference. *IARPP eNews*, *1*(1), 7–9.

Harris, A.E. (2011). The relational tradition: Landscape and canon. *Journal of the American Psychoanalytic Association*, *59*, 701–735.

Klein, M. (1975). Envy and gratitude and other works 1946–1963 (pp. 176–235). *The International Psycho-Analytical Library*, *104*, 1–346. London, UK: Hogarth Press and the Institute of Psycho-Analysis. (Original work published 1957)

Kuriloff, E.A. (2013). *Contemporary Psychoanalysis and the Legacy of the Third Reich: History, Memory, Tradition*. New York, NY: Routledge.

Lichtenberg, J.D. (2001). *Psychoanalysis and Motivation*. Hillsdale, NJ.: Routledge. (Original work published 1989)

Lichtenberg, J.D., Lachmann, F.M. and Fosshage, J.L. (1996). *The Clinical Exchange: Techniques Derived from Self and Motivational Systems*. Hillsdale, NJ: Routledge.

Lichtenberg, J.D., Lachmann, F.M., and Fosshage, J.L. (2001). *Self and Motivational Systems: Towards a Theory of Psychoanalytic Technique*. New York, NY: Routledge. (Original work published 1992)

Lichtenberg, J.D., Lachmann, F.M., and Fosshage, J.L. (2014). *A Spirit of Inquiry: Communication in Psychoanalysis*. New York, NY: Routledge.

Luna-Reyes, Luis Felipe, and Deborah Lines Andersen. (2003). Collecting and analyzing qualitative data for system dynamics: Methods and models. *System Dynamics Review 19*(4): 271–296.

Makari, G. (2008). *Revolution in Mind: The Creation of Psychoanalysis*. New York, NY: Harper.

Rey, J.H. (1988). That which patients bring to analysis. *The International Journal of Psychoanalysis*, *69*(4), 457–470.

Spielrein, S. (1994). Destruction as a cause of coming into being. *Journal of Analytical Psychology*, *39*, 155–186. (Original work published 1912)

Steiner, J. (1993). *Psychic Retreats: Pathological Organizations in Psychotic, Neurotic, and Borderline Patients* (pp. 1–13). New York, NY: Routledge.

Thompson, C. (1944). Ferenczi's contribution to Psychoanalysis. *Psychiatry*, *7*(3), 245–252.

Winnicott, D.W. (1971). The use of an object and relating through identifications. In *Playing and Reality* (pp. 115–127). New York, NY: Routledge. (Original work published 1969)

Part I

Core papers and commentaries

Chapter 1

Emmanuel Ghent and the origins of relational psychoanalysis

Anthony Bass

"Credo: The Dialectics of One-Person and Two-Person Psychologies" (1989) was the first of three groundbreaking papers, along with "Masochism, Submission, Surrender: Masochism as a Perversion of Surrender" (1990) and "Paradox and Process" (1992), that Emmanuel Ghent published in the dawning days of relational psychoanalysis. Each of these papers served as a linchpin to an emerging relational perspective as it moved from a comparative psychoanalytic scholarly project explicating links and complementarities between diverse theoretical perspectives to an increasingly coherent, integrative theoretical and clinical position in its own right.

It would be impossible to overstate Dr. Ghent's[1] role in initiating, inspiring and defining the relational perspective. He spearheaded a movement to create a space for its development at the New York University Postdoctoral Program in the 1980s. He was a key contributor as a theoretician of this new psychoanalytic perspective, as well as a beloved teacher, analyst, supervisor and mentor to several generations of analysts who would go on to make significant contributions to relational psychoanalysis in their own right. In addition, he was a prime mover, organizer and strategist. He led a group of faculty, graduates and candidates (among whom I was one) to form a "relational track" at the New York University Postdoctoral Program, an organized relational faculty and curriculum, that added a significant new and vitalizing dimension to the diverse mix of ideas at New York University, formerly having been represented solely by Freudian and Interpersonal orientations. Having succeeded in organizing a "Relational Track" at New York University, we could select a faculty and design a curriculum that reflected the kinds of integrative and synthetic interests in psychoanalytic theory and practice that would become the hallmark of the emerging relational tradition.

A volume bringing together Emmanuel Ghent's collected papers is cause for celebration. It brings to the reader an engaging, creative, sophisticated course of study in the theoretical and personal origins of the relational turn in psychoanalysis. Reading these papers again now transports me as through a time machine, returning me in a flash to my own training years at the New York University Postdoctoral Program between 1983 and 1989. These were exciting times in psychoanalysis at New York University, with Emmanuel Ghent, Stephen Mitchell, Philip Bromberg and others introducing ideas that would change psychoanalysis forever. There I had the extremely good fortune to meet, study and have supervision with Mannie. I was in my first year of training when Dr. Ghent delivered an early version of the "Masochism, Surrender and Submission" paper. Listening to his inspiring reading of that paper, I believed that I had found my psychoanalytic home, much as Mannie described in "Credo" his own experience of knowing that he had come to the right place when he began his studies at the White Institute some 30 years earlier.

That same year (1983), inspired by his talk, I took Ghent's course on the development of psychoanalytic theory,[2] in all of its diverse streams, a course that was so rigorous and comprehensive that I wasn't able to complete all of the readings (required and recommended) until I had graduated from the program, and was myself teaching "Introduction to Relational Theory" at New York University. By then, a relational orientation with its own course of study was underway. It seemed to me that the whole curriculum of this new orientation constituted an effort to give sufficient time and attention to a full range of relational ideas (what he in this paper describes as a combination of one- and two-person perspectives). The entire curriculum covered material that Professor Ghent had attempted to teach in a single course!

The combination of rigorous, comprehensive, penetrating and creative engagement with a wide range of theories, contextualized by a personal, direct expression of his own values, sensibilities, experiences and beliefs, was what made Ghent an inspiring, transformational teacher.

That Ghent was a lover of theory is evident in "Credo." The breadth and depth of his scholarship was astounding. But as he makes clear in this essay, theory for Mannie was a personal matter, not merely an intellectual pursuit. Rather, theory was an expression of the therapist's subjectivity, sensibilities and values. Did he choose his preferred theory, he wondered, or did his theory choose him? His own theoretical commitments, while deeply and rigorously thought through, were never unmoored from his personal values, aesthetics and the experiences with his own patients and analysts that shaped his way of approaching psychoanalysis. Like the artist he was (he was a musician, a composer, a computer scientist, an inventor, as well as a psychoanalyst), his papers were, equally, works of art.

One- and Two-Person Psychologies in Relational Psychoanalysis

"Credo" manages to be at one and the same time a declaration of one man's psychoanalytic belief system ("credo" is Latin for "I believe"), and a "state of the art" study of the importance of "one-person" and "two-person" orientations to psychology. Ghent uses the "Credo" paper to consider how these ways of parsing human experience inform psychoanalytic theory as well as the quotidian psychotherapeutic choices that shape our daily practice.

In so doing, he shines a light on how our personal beliefs are fundamental to the psychoanalytic theories that we hold. They provide an underpinning, a framework, though not always a conscious one, for the rigorous explication and scholarly investigation of central psychoanalytic frames of reference. The personal and the theoretical were two sides of the same coin. The rigor of systematic study and thought was important, but that rigor is informed by the subjective frame of reference of the thinker. The emphasis on the essential subjectivity guiding our work, in our theorizing and in our work with our patients, influenced me deeply as a student, and has continued to inform my way of thinking about psychoanalysis throughout my career. Mannie exemplified, in word and deed, how the value of rigorous, committed thought was enhanced and deepened when combined with the humility that comes of realizing that our beliefs are just that: beliefs. Mannie encouraged me to think deeply while never losing sight of my personal subjectivity and values. In describing his course at New York University, Mannie notes that,

> For many years, I have tried to persuade psychoanalytic candidates embarking on a course of study to commit to writing as much as they could articulate about the theoretical beliefs they thought they held and practiced; and then at the conclusion of the course to repeat the exercise. This paper represents my own efforts at articulating the

> beliefs (and uncertainties that currently form the matrix of my own psychoanalytic thinking and practice.
>
> (Ghent, 1989, p. 169)

I was one of the beneficiaries of taking on that exercise in my first class in psychoanalysis. That experience of self-reflection was so meaningful for me that I have carried the application of Mannie's pedagogical approach into my own teaching. And I have initiated a feature in *Psychoanalytic Dialogues*, a journal of which I am an editor, in which we invite analysts of different persuasions to write their own "credos," as a way of highlighting the personal beliefs and experiences behind the theories that they hold.

Dr. Ghent's paper is an excellent reminder that analytic theories are the belief systems that analysts live and work by. Such beliefs inform how we hear, what we hear, how we assemble what we hear and how we conduct ourselves in light of what we hear in the analytic situation:

> Our patients are there to help us if only we have ears to listen. If we remain attuned we will discover that all is not resistance; in fact, a fair share is counter-resistance, our own difficulties with having to re-evaluate our theories and expectations in the light of experience that we uneasily sense is not fitting with those theories and expectations.
>
> (Ghent, 1989, p. 170)

With this caveat in place, Dr. Ghent goes on to explicate the two broad theoretical orientations: one-person and two-person psychologies in a scholarly consideration of the history of psychoanalysis from the vantage point of these two broad but essential frames of reference.

> I plan to use this question of a one person as against a two person psychology as a scaffolding on which to paint the backdrop of the play called psychoanalysis.
>
> (Ghent, 1989, p. 172)

He traces the history of psychoanalysis, beginning with two-person psychology and its pre-dawn origins in Freud's seduction theory, and then moving to one-person psychology, which emphasizes instincts, drives and a cure based in the release of damned-up energy—catharsis and an emphasis on fantasies founded in the vicissitudes of drives. He considers Ferenczi's stark divergence from Freud in the 1930s, his revisiting the reality basis of trauma, and the ways in which analysts on both sides of the Atlantic (Horney, Fromm, Sullivan, Thompson, Balint, Winnicott, Fairbairn, and many others in the object relations schools) followed Ferenczi's lead. He shows how a two-person psychology began to take shape that credited experience over drives as a key source of the kinds of problems that people sought therapy to address.

The theoretical center of Ghent's "Credo" is to be found in his personal consideration of where he stands in relation to both two-person and one-person dimensions of human experience and development. We find that Ghent, through his appreciatively receptive engagement of a wide range of perspectives, reveals how one-person and two-person perspectives are complementary. Both points of view are required to grasp the mysteries and complexities of human experience.

Dr. Ghent makes a crucial, fateful distinction in his engagement of psychoanalytic theories, a distinction that is crucial to understanding the project of relational psychoanalysis. He shows that relational approaches have in common the stress on the experiential and relational aspects of human development, psychopathology and therapeutic action. He reveals that relational approaches follow the basic tenets of psychoanalysis, while eschewing the classical metapsychology of drives and their vicissitudes. These are essentially psychological rather than biological theories, emphasizing issues of motivation and meaning-making in the developing human being.

Dr. Ghent clarifies that what we commonly think of as intrapsychic experience, the experience of an inner world, refers to the way our experience in the world has been internalized and held. The internal world and the interpersonal world are, at bottom, transformations of one another. The world of internal relations is derived from interpersonal experience even as interpersonal experience is itself shaped, affected and distorted by expectations that have been internalized as part of the self.

The artful theoretical pivot that Dr. Ghent makes in this essay unmoors the intrapsychic world from Freud's theory of drives, with which it had for so long been associated.

> Unfortunately the term intrapsychic has been so long associated with drive theory and with the implicit notion that the contents of

> the unconscious are largely innate in their origin that it seems like a contradiction in terms to speak of interpersonal relations as the very stuff of the intrapsychic.
>
> (Ghent, 1989, p. 180)

The relational turn in psychoanalysis knitted together the tear that had developed between the intrapsychic and the interpersonal. It enabled analysts to think of the intrapsychic in interpersonal terms, and the interpersonal as deeply informed by the intrapsychic. Ghent averred, "I see no difficulty then for an interpersonalist to be as interested in the patient's inner world as in his externally observable interaction; they complement each other" (p. 181). In further critiquing the state of interpersonal psychoanalysis at that time, he noted that "it is unfortunate that interpersonalists cling to the inseparability of the intra-psychic, inner world, and drive theory, as if they were a hyphenated unit" (p. 181).

The Internal World and the Interpersonal World: Expanding Possibilities and Looking Toward the Future

In prying apart an appreciation for the internal world from the drive theory that restricted its possibilities and its uses in analysis, Dr. Ghent expanded the possibilities for dialogue and mutual appreciation for analysts emphasizing the internal world, and those emphasizing the interpersonal world. In so doing, he helped create a kind of integrative, middle space in which relational psychoanalysis came into being and has thrived.

Ghent's remarkable sense of the history of psychoanalysis, as well as its contemporary transformations, is on full display in "Credo." His grasp of the ebb and flow of theoretical emphases in our short history made for a heightened consciousness of the ways in which theory itself, and his own beliefs about it, were always in flux. And always subject to new learning. As he highlights at the end of his essay, quoting Eliot's "Little Gidding" to make the point most poetically: "For last year's words belong to last year's language. And next year's words await another voice" (p. 208). Of course, we have heard many new and powerful voices since Mannie said his last words in 2003. Yet, his modesty aside, I know that we still have a lot to learn from him. I believe that you will find his voice as powerful, resonant and inspiring as it ever was, as you read this wonderful, complex essay that set psychoanalysis on a course that we continue to chart.

Notes

1. I will refer to Emmanuel Ghent as Mannie when I am referring to him personally, as my mentor, teacher, supervisor, colleague and friend over the twenty years that I knew him until his death in 2003. That is what I called him and how I think of him. At other times, when I refer to his contribution as a prime theorist, and historic figure in the relational movement, I will refer to him as Dr. Ghent, or Ghent.
2. All courses at the New York University Postdoctoral Program are "elective" rather than required. Each candidate creates his or her own curriculum by taking the courses that are of most interest at any point during one's training. Taking Ghent's course during my first year of training set me on a course of study that I have sustained throughout my career.

Credo

The dialectics of one-person and two-person psychologies[1]

Emmanuel Ghent

For many years I have tried to persuade psychoanalytic candidates embarking on a course on psychoanalytic theory to commit to writing as much as they could articulate about the theoretical beliefs they thought they held and practiced by; and then at the conclusion of the course to repeat the exercise. The task proved daunting. This paper represents my own effort at articulating the beliefs (and uncertainties) that currently form the matrix of my own psychoanalytic thinking and practice. The paper has two goals, as reflected in its double title. The first, *Credo*, has as its focus the inevitability that every analyst theorizes, indeed thinks and practices on the basis of a belief system or credo. The second part of the title both points to the vehicle for containing and organizing the expression of this particular author's credo, and at the same time represents a study in its own right: the question of a one-person versus a two-person psychology.

I believe, *credo*, sounds cognitive, as if it were a close cousin to *I think*, and in practice the words are often used interchangeably. In fact, however, the word believe, stemming from the Indo-European root *leubh*, is much closer in origin to words like *love* or *beloved*, words meaning to hold dear, to trust, to have faith in, and to *libido*, Latin for desire.

In our field where hard facts are hard to come by, beliefs are often transacted as if they were facts. Belief plays an immensely important role in psychoanalysis but it is seldom spoken about. Usually we grace our beliefs by calling them theories, thereby giving them the stamp of cognitive approval. In addressing similar concerns, Arnold Cooper (1985) wrote:

> The analyst does his best to understand the patient's communications as the patient intends them to be, but both patient and analyst

> are heavily influenced by a theory … used by both parties. For example, patients have theories about the nature of responsibility and the causal agents of behavior, and these theories may range from extremes of conviction that "everything is my fault" to "nothing is my fault" … Patients have theories about the nature of their motivation; some are convinced that all their actions are altruistic, while others believe that their most innocent thoughts are evidence of their murderous intent … All human beings weave their experience and their capacities into a holistic way of understanding themselves and their world and create a theory that provides some degree of comfort. At high levels these theories may be philosophies, religions and life attitudes.
>
> (p. 1385)

In fact at high levels they also become analytic theories. And the paradigm—ultimately a *belief* system that the analyst lives and works by (and there is no assurance that the analyst has full conscious access to the system under which he or she is really operating)—makes a very significant difference as to how one hears, what one hears, how one assembles what is heard, and how one conducts oneself in the analytic setting.

Particularly because there is a paucity of validating strategies in psychoanalysis it behooves us to keep abreast of continuing developments both in our own discipline and in related areas, such as the currently exploding field of infant development. But even more important: our patients are there to help us if only we have ears to listen. If we can remain attuned we will discover that all is not resistance, in fact a fair share is counter-resistance, our own difficulties with having to re-evaluate our theories and expectations in the light of experience that we uneasily sense is not fitting well with those theories and expectations. And if the rewards are not sufficiently inviting, then we need heed the penalties that so often otherwise accrue. When interpretations begin to sound like clichés (Casement, 1986) we are well on the way to the analytic "burnout syndrome" (Cooper, 1986) where the analyst finds himself or herself discouraged and no longer intensely involved in the process; he or she is beset by boredom and a feeling of deadness if not outright anger and sarcasm; playfulness has disappeared and given way to an aura of cynicism and nihilism. Even under the best of circumstances we all feel, or ought to feel, vaguely insecure about the lack of reliable data affirming the superiority of one theory or theoretical approach over another. Burnout intensifies the tendency to seek refuge in defensive behaviors such as clinging rigidly and dogmatically to a particular theoretical belief, or becoming disillusioned with all theory, even anti-intellectually pretending to be theory-free, or yet again under the guise of ecumenicism, making a salad of bits and pieces of all manner of theories, unburdened by a need for coherence.

In psychoanalysis beliefs appear in many guises, sometimes explicit, sometimes as axioms, and most often by implication. How frequently we read and hear sentences that begin with "I believe that ..." or some such locution. A few illustrations that have relevance to this paper:

> Christopher Bollas (1986) began a recent paper with "Sometime in the early 1960s Heinz Kohut lost his *belief* (italics mine) in the rhetoric of [classical] psychoanalysis," and continued with a quotation illustrating the point.
>
> Daniel Stern (1986): "The idea of a period of undifferentiation that is subjectively experienced by the infant as a form of merger and dual unity with the mother is very problematic. ... Ultimately this kind of notion is a statement of belief about whether the essential [or original] state of human existence is one of aloneness or togetherness."
>
> (p. 240)
>
> Many classical analysts believe that interpretation, alone, is the key to psychoanalytic cure.

Even strongly held beliefs may change in time, and dramatically. To some readers it may come as a surprise that Sullivan (1938) once wrote (and clearly believed):

> The method of free association is the technique *par excellence* for the study of the subjective sequence of events. Free associations enables data to appear at the focus of waking attention which are otherwise barred from consciousness. The new data supply the individual with indispensable clues to the nature of his deeper motivating impulses. It is quite possible that many psychoanalytic theories will be tried and found wanting as research moves ahead; but there is no reasonable doubt that

> competent exercise of the free association technique is profoundly valuable for gradually acquiring the self-knowledge adequate for objectivity. (p. 138)

Just as we have come to re-evaluate in a new light some of Freud's repudiated *beliefs* (like the traumatic theory of neurosis) so too may we re-evaluate in a new light some of the early *beliefs* of Sullivan. Here I refer not only to issues such as the utility of the technique of free association, but more centrally to the kind of issue recently brought forward by Wolstein (1987). After presenting three reasons in support of his view (belief) on the importance of a selfic center, Wolstein (pp. 631–632) says: "All three suggest (another version of "I believe") the growing acceptance of a new clinical observation: a psychic point of origin, an internal source of agency, a unique sense of self that each participant must place before the other during some phases of their psychoanalytic experience. This is the psychic center of the self, which I distinguish from the interpersonal ego." Clearly this is a statement of belief, unquestionably based on observations and an expanded understanding, but nonetheless a belief, in this instance a belief in the central significance of the self, a belief which I happen to share, as will presently become evident.

I come now to the second goal of this paper. As the paper began to write itself I became aware of a dialectical pattern in the evolution of my own psychoanalytic thinking, particularly with regard to the question of a one-person versus a two-person psychology; then I realized that this pattern bore a certain relation, a loose parallel, to the overall evolution of psychoanalysis. Finally to my surprise and amusement I noticed that even my choice of analysts likewise paralleled that evolutionary sequence. It became clear that whatever I might say about what I believe, can at best, only be true in this moment. I take comfort in recalling what Erich Fromm once said to me about himself, "Every five years when I look back on the work I was doing five years earlier, I am horrified. How could I have practiced, understanding so little by comparison with what I have come to understand now?"

I plan to use this question of a one-person[2] as against a two-person psychology as a scaffolding from which to paint the back-drop for the production of the play called psychoanalysis. Needless to say only a few of the many possible scenes will be touched on; but the very choices[3] I make will in themselves reflect my own version of "I believe."

How does one choose one's theory? Or, is it that, unbeknownst to ourselves, we are chosen? Silone (1955), the Italian author, writing on the choice of comrades, once said,

> One fine Sunday some of us stopped going to Mass, not because Catholic dogma seemed to us, all of a sudden, false, but because the people who went began to bore us and we were drawn to the company of those who stayed away. ... The choice once made, the rest, as experience shows, follows automatically. ... The choice is emotional, beyond logic. ... We proclaim ourselves revolutionaries or conservatives for motives, often ill-defined, that are deep within us, and before choosing, we are, unknown to ourselves, chosen. As for the new ideology, *that* we learn at the schools of the [group] to which we have already pledged allegiance by an act of faith.
>
> (p. 12)

How then, way back in the 1940's and 1950's did I get to become an interpersonal analyst, or perhaps "relational analyst," rather than a Freudian? My undergraduate work was almost exclusively in hard science: chemistry, physics, biochemistry. I remember sitting in on a few lectures in sociology and psychology at McGill and leaving each one with the reaction of "How can anyone listen to that moosh?" In medical school although I was by now teaching biochemistry I became interested in psychoanalysis and found Freud wonderful to read. The almost diagrammatic logic appealed very much to my "scientific mind." Yet somehow, the formulations, as tempting as they were, seemed to me almost too neat, as if everything had to fit the diagram or else it didn't exist. Then, one day, on the recommendation of a few friends, comrades shall we say, I read Erich Fromm's *Escape from Freedom* (1941). The book lit a fire. Then a year or two later came another recommendation—Harry Stack Sullivan's *Conceptions* (1940/1953). Although at first I found his language all but incomprehensible, it gradually began to feel like I had landed on a newly discovered planet full of marvels and fresh clear air. I could no longer construct the neat diagrams in my head; equations and formulas didn't work and that left me feeling rather naked. That was 1947 or 1948. Then, in 1950 David Schecter and I came to New York to meet with some faculty from the New York Psychoanalytic Institute and the William Alanson White Institute.

Perhaps because, unbeknownst to us, we were already "chosen," we both chose for the latter. While we admired and respected the rigor of the people we met from the New York Psychoanalytic Institute, we found them rather grim and dour, somehow doctrinaire and without excitement. To our innocent eyes they seemed more interested in diagrams—my private word for metapsychology—than in people. On the other hand our enthusiasm for the White Institute was dampened by the fact that Sullivan had died the year before, and Fromm was about to move to Mexico. But probably even more important, was the distress we both felt that perhaps the tide of the new ideas in psychoanalysis had already reached its high point, was played out, so to speak, and what would follow would be its institutionalization. We sensed even then that instead of a continuing development of the new thinking there was what we took to be a defensive posture—a tendency to focus on what was wrong with Freudian thinking.

One-Person versus Two-Person Psychology

In the pre-dawn of psychoanalysis the emphasis was clearly on a one-person psychology. The essential pathology was seen as a kind of affect obstruction, the cure for which was the release of the dammed-up affect, a "catharsis." At its true dawn, however, psychoanalysis was interpersonal. With the seduction or traumatic theory, it was explicitly a two-person psychology in which prime responsibility fell on the adult and secondary responsibility fell on the child who had developed secret and unacceptable wishes, and fears in response to those wishes.

When Freud discovered that his patients' memories of seduction were not true, he assumed (1) that they were fantasies, and (2) that the fantasies stemmed from wishes that were derivatives of an innately unfolding program. It remains difficult to see why Freud, a man of such perspicacity, never seemed to have entertained the other logical possibility, that indeed the memories were not literally true, but that the fantasies were nonetheless symbolically reflective of some truth. Is it possible that such a hypothesis might have been even more disquieting to bourgeois Vienna and perhaps to Freud himself, than the horrifying notion that sexual events take place rather frequently between adult caretakers and children? The implication would be that the parents, although themselves unaware of it, were in some way destructive (as well as loving) to their children, and that literal seduction was only a special case of a far more general issue: aggression[4] (in its connotation of destructiveness, not assertion).

With the repudiation of the seduction theory Freud went on to build, in successive stages, the towering edifice of psychoanalytic theory. The revisions and emendations notwithstanding, the structure all stood on the firm foundation of a one-person psychology fully supplanting the original two-person psychology.

Winds of change were already discernable in the early 1930's. Ferenczi's (1933/1955) focus on the reality aspect of children being traumatized by adult misunderstanding of their meaning, anticipated by 30 years the notion of the pathogenicity of gross empathic failure. His efforts to redress the balance in favor of a two-person psychology led to an enormous rift with Freud.

Meanwhile in America, the work of Horney, Fromm, Sullivan, and Clara Thompson, who incidentally, at Sullivan's suggestion, was analyzed by Ferenczi, led to a radical break with the Freudian establishment and to the development of a thoroughgoing two-person psychology. Two other analysands of Ferenczi, Sándor Rado and Franz Alexander did not go that far, but nonetheless repudiated the primacy of drive theory. In 1939 the splintering began that ultimately led to the founding of the White Institute, the Horney Institute, the Flower and Fifth Institute, and under Rado, the Columbia Institute where there has remained a certain receptivity to a two-person psychology. Alexander in Chicago clearly moved to a position of apostasy with his version of a two-person psychology, the celebrated corrective emotional experience. Perhaps it is no accident that Chicago was the city that gave birth to Kohut a generation later. The question as to whether Kohut's system is a two-person or a one-person psychology is, however, complex, and I will return to it later.

This sketchy historical overview is intended as background for my own view (belief) that after witnessing the dialectical shift from two-person to one-person then again to two-person psychology, and more recently, as I will try to show, the reintroduction of a one-person psychology in the form of emphatic focus on the self, that we may be on the way to an enlarged theory that does not yet exist, one that will encompass an integration of both one-person and two-person psychologies. The state of flux in whose midst we are currently living, and the relative acceptability of theoretical pluralism may herald the advent of some new synthesis, but clearly that has not yet arrived. Meanwhile, as a relational analyst I would like to examine where I stand in relation to Sullivan, British object relations theory, and to Kohut.

Sullivan had two interrelated goals in creating a theory of interpersonal relations. One was to restrict himself to a theory that was designed not as a theory of personality, but as a theory of therapy for what he pragmatically referred to as problems in living. The other was to discover how far a thoroughgoing exploration of purely interpersonal factors could go in creating such a coherent and inclusive theory. Levenson (1983) states the case for an extreme version of a two-person psychology with engaging lucidity. His elegant prose, derivative of Sullivan's, points again to the impossibility of using the kind of "diagrams" that has for many made drive theory appealing.

> Our patients are disabled not by their drives or inadequate defense but, rather, by an inability to read and interpret the world, to grasp nuance, and to operate with sufficient skill to affect the people around them (p. 40). … People do not run into difficulty because terrible things were done to them, or because they distort ordinary experience into terror, but because they are tangled in an elusive semiotic web of omissions, simulacrums, and misrepresentations. The problem with narcissism is not so much that it is depriving, which it certainly is, but that it is confusing. A deprived child can, often does, turn elsewhere—a sibling, to the other parent, to a friend's parent. But the confused child stays put, wondering why the love does not satisfy.
>
> (p. 45)

After recognizing and acknowledging the enormous contribution Sullivan has made, several questions present themselves: How fully has an exclusively two-person theory succeeded in explaining human psychology? And secondly, What is its relation to other essentially two-person theories?

Relational Theories

The variety of approaches which collectively I will refer to as relational theory, have in common the stress on the experiential and relational aspects of human development, of psychopathology, and of the therapeutic efforts at relieving psychopathology. These approaches represent a genus of psychoanalytic theories and therapies that hold to the basic clinical tenets of psychoanalysis, but eschew the classical metapsychology of energy discharge, and of instincts or drives and their vicissitudes. These species of the genus "relational psychoanalysis" are essentially psychological rather than biological or quasi-biological theories, and therefore, have as their focus issues of motivation and meaning and their vicissitudes in the developing human being. Each of these theories approaches and describes the human being from a different angle, and often with distinctly different emphases. Each in its own way is critical of classical theory, and each proposes solutions some of which are uncompromisingly antithetical to classical theory, where others are at pains to maintain conciliation.

We are often blinded by accidents of anachronistic language, or language whose referents have become blurred, from seeing essential similarities of approach. Even Sullivan fell into this trap. He invented the term "interpersonal relations" to cover an extremely important and original concept, that (1) what was central for psychopathology, if not human development in general, was the nature of the formative relationships in a person's life, and (2) that these "interpersonal relationships" become internalized as relationships among eidetic personifications, so that what is commonly thought of as intrapsychic phenomena is in fact only another aspect of interpersonal relations. Having invented the word to cover such a broad and bold concept he then, unfortunately in my view, went on to use it ambiguously to refer both to its specialized and radically new meaning, and at other times to its everyday meaning of what was going on in the here and now between people. This latter usage of the term was coopted by mainstream analysts with the result that the essential significance of the concept was overlooked. Alas, this usage has at times prevailed among interpersonalists themselves with the result of bearing out the charges of superficiality by those who are concerned with the intrapsychic, or as I would prefer it, with the structuralization of experience and meaning. It was this watering down of the interpersonal approach, the failure to develop fully the implications of the new and radical idea, that has led to an embracing by some of us, of the British school of object-relations theory.

Sullivan's eschewal of structure in favor of relation had some far-reaching consequences. It certainly made it difficult to diagram psychic phenomena in a manner analogous to what was possible with classical metapsychology, so difficult in fact that it led to the belief among classical analysts that there was no theory (i.e., metapsychology) in Sullivan's system. More importantly it was a stringent effort at ridding the field of the fetishistic structures that had come to be the shibboleths of psychoanalysis. Although Sullivan was anything but a Marxist, I believe it is fair to say that he was trying to build a non-fetishistic psychology (Ghent, 1962). Let me explain what I mean by this. Marx (1867/1906) put it this way: "[In commodity production, and this includes the production of ideas], the social relation between men assumes ... the fantastic form of a relation between things" (p. 83). Things like money or rent, are fetishes in that they obscure the relations between people, even though those relations may not be at all visible. We almost never think of money as an interpersonal or relational concept, at root an expression of claims on the labor of others. When with cash we buy food at the supermarket we are not aware that we are redeeming claims, sometimes highly exploitative claims, on the labor of many people all along the food chain, often on a global scale.[5]

In classical analysis such concepts as instinct, id, ego, superego likewise obscure and mystify the underlying relation between people. They are fetishes. One might say that the id is the fetishistic formalization of early experience. It is seen as inhering in "nature," so that the result (the id) of a process (human interactive experience) is, instead seen as its cause (Benjamin, 1977) ; cf. also (Loewald, 1978).

The disentangling of the fetish character of the commodity is a vital cornerstone of Marx' theory. Likewise the disentangling of personal relations as gelled in the character structure, is the fundamental contribution of Sullivan. By his lights all the part processes of psychic life—at least all those that are relevant to therapy, and this is an important rider—are conceived of in terms of their relational quality. The term interpersonal relations, in its deeper meaning, refers then to the non-fetishistic analysis of character, and only in a superficial sense to the coloquial "what goes on between people." Sullivan and Marx hold in common the concept that consciously or unconsciously everything of value and importance in human life has meaning only in terms of man's relation to man. I believe it would be fair to say that Fairbairn and Guntrip, and to a lesser degree Winnicott and even Kohut would share this belief. Recently, others such as Gill (1983) and Stern (1986) have begun building new systems with this view as a basic premise.

In his telegraphic *Synopsis*, Fairbairn (1963) summarized the basic principles of his object relations theory. Among them were "Libido is a function of the ego [today we would say self]. ... Since libido is a function of the ego and aggression is a reaction to frustration or deprivation, there is no such thing as an 'id.' ...The ego, and therefore libido, is fundamentally object-seeking [rather than pleasure seeking]" (p. 224). In this formulation it is unambiguous that at bottom what is central in the development of the personality is the relationship between people. While his condensed statements could be misinterpreted to mean that the infant seeks objects in lieu of seeking pleasure, it is clear from many contexts that what he means is that normally it is object-seeking as an end in itself that gives pleasure (See Guntrip, 1961, p. 305).

For Fairbairn the consequence of these basic principles is that to the extent that the infant meets with frustrating, rejecting or inappropriately stimulating caretaking, he in self-defense creates an inner world of internal part-objects and part-selves. Although Fairbairn added a vast richness of detail, it is my belief that Sullivan was moving in the same direction. Despite his allegiance to operationalism[6] his concepts kept pointing in the direction of the internal structuring of experience. Perhaps because of his ambivalence about mental structure, Sullivan contradicted himself repeatedly, as I see it, in the meaning he attached to the term interpersonal relations. Often he points to the self-system, itself by definition a structure that powerfully resists change, as the institutionalization of the eidetic personifications related to past significant others. These very personifications at times rise to an almost structural reality for Sullivan, as for example in the "bad mother" and "good mother." Also his conception of good-me, bad-me and not-me likewise began to take on the quality of internal entities. On the other hand at times he spoke of interpersonal processes in a narrowly operational sense—that which is manifest and can be observed. Unfortunately the term intrapsychic has been so long associated with drive theory, and with the implicit notion that the contents of the unconscious are largely innate in their origins, that it seems like a contradiction in terms to speak of interpersonal relations as being the very stuff of the intrapsychic. Yet if we disengage ourselves from two sets of prior assumptions, one being the essentially innately organized nature of the intrapsychic and the second one, Sullivan's over-reliance on an operationalist meaning of interpersonal processes, I see no difficulty in thinking of the intrapsychic in basically interpersonal terms. All the "structures of mind" then are viewed as the resultants of interpersonal experience within the constraints imposed by biologically organized templates and delimiters. I see no difficulty then for an interpersonalist to be as interested in the patient's "inner world" as in his externally observable interactional world. They complement one another.

In my view it is this intrapsychic aspect of interpersonal relations that offers the new vista for psychoanalytic therapy towards character change. It is basically by engaging and empathically experiencing this inner reality of eidetic personifications, or the world of internal selves and objects, or the "representational" world, and the ways it is being externalized in the external world, that we are afforded the opportunity to engage the person in the discovery of, and thereby the nourishing of undeveloped aspects of the self, and in the undoing of maladaptive motivational systems—ultimately permitting the gradual integration of self-fragments into a coherent self.

A controversy that frequently erupts in discussions of theory is the issue of the primacy of fantasy versus reality. Drive theorists and interpersonalists line up on opposite sides, but both agree, as Levenson (1983) points out that there exists "an irrevocable schism … between psychological reality as fantasy and psychological reality as mystified experience" (p. 10).

I look upon this bifurcation as a direct descendant of Freud's view of two mutually exclusive alternatives: (1) reality in the form of actual seduction, versus (2) innately generated sexual fantasies. Just as it was difficult to see why Freud would not allow the symbolic alternative, so too is it difficult to see why interpersonalists need to polarize this choice, and eschew the obvious alternative. If we allow that early interpersonal experience becomes patterned in ways that are resistant to change—structured—then the irrevocable schism vanishes: mystified or other harmful experience is the reality experience, which under the influence of a multiplicity of real experiences becomes intrapsychically structured or patterned. Once symbolic activity becomes a feature of the infant's life this pattern may now be expressed in the form of fantasy, a symbolic expression of a motivational thrust, whether that thrust be wishful or defending against a wish, or still more likely, some compromise formation. I believe this view has been ruled out by interpersonalists because of the argument that "intrapsychic" spells drive theory: drives create fantasies which then define the intrapsychic. This closed system leaves no room for another conception of the intrapsychic or the importance of fantasy.

It is unfortunate that interpersonalists cling to the inseparability of "the intrapsychic or inner world, and drive theory" as if they were a hyphenated unit, as for example in Levenson's (1983) description of object-relations theory as a "loosely affiliated group of theories, [which] to varying degrees, holds a commitment both to intrapsychic drive theory and to the significance of human relations" (p. 10). Even in the classical Freudian world the movement is away from this view of the intrapsychic. Loewald (1978) ten years ago stated "intrapsychic structure formation is brought about not by unilateral activities on the part of the infant organism, but by interactions taking place first within the infant–mother unitary field. ... If id, ego and superego have their origins in interactions with the environment that are internalized, interactions that are transposed to a new arena, thus becoming intrapsychic interactions, then psychic structure formation and individuation are dependent on object relations" (p. 494). I believe it is a radical formulation like this that prompted Gill (1983, p. 537) to imply that Loewald came to the brink of a major reformulation of psychoanalytic theory, but drew back from taking the step that his formulation required. The advantages in viewing reality and fantasy as interactive and complementary are two-fold. Not only does it account for the subjective experience of inner and outer worlds, but also allows for a two-way process in which fantasy can also create reality. The phenomena of transference and projective identification all hang upon the interaction of inner and outer worlds.

Clearly some of us have found ourselves undernourished on a diet restricted to Sullivan's interpersonal thinking. From my own teaching experience I resonate with Mitchell's (1983) observations about teaching Sullivan:

> It enhances rather than detracts from an appreciation of Sullivan's contributions to develop comparisons between his work and that of others struggling with the same issues: with Fairbairn's construction of an essentially interpersonal theory in a language based on fantasy, identifications and structural metaphors; with Winnicott's depiction of the infant/mother matrix and the earliest impact of the mother on the personality of the child; with Schafer's critique of the misuse of structural language; with Sandler's depiction of self/other configurations within a "representational world." Sullivan's work by no means forms an identity with these various efforts, but, taken together, they represent approaches to similar issues from different angles. Different angles yield different vistas. Attempts to teach Sullivan in isolation by granting him exclusive domain over psychoanalytic knowledge and

> innovation eventually subverts enthusiasm for Sullivan's work among candidates attempting to position themselves within the psychoanalytic tradition and current community of theorists and practitioners.
>
> (p. 139)

I believe the time is long since with us to let go of the battles that were being fought thirty and forty years ago, to let go of insularity and parochialism, to enjoy the ways interpersonalism has added to the field of psychoanalysis while receiving virtually no credit for it, to let go of the need for holding vanity above the expanding scope of understanding, to take stock of the advances in psychoanalysis and related areas over the years, to make friends with those whose views, while different in emphasis and dialect, are not totally foreign, and to learn by engagement with the views of others so as to expand our own horizons, not to mention those of our associates.

What follows is a non-exhaustive listing of overlapping items. Some involve alternative approaches; other are not mutually exclusive but reflect expansions of outlook to include alternatives in one's available ways of seeing, thinking and being. Each merits much fuller treatment, but in the interest of space I will only touch upon them at this point.

1. Attentiveness to the internal world of object relations, the intrapsychic world, in contrast to Sullivan's primary emphasis on external object relations.
2. The place of unique individuality; the self as active agent and psychic center, in contrast to the limited concept of Sullivan's self-system. True self in relation to false self. The role of the innate in human development as being discovered in recent studies on infants. Goals beyond the drive for human affiliation: ambitions, skills, talents, creativity.
3. A focus on the irrational as the secret avenue to the self, in contrast to an approach that is essentially socially adaptive. This transcends the issue to undoing childhood mystification. May we think of locating a hidden buried self, mystical but tangible and the center of vitality? Is this what Lacan is seeking when he blasphemously says, "Where ego was there id shall be?"
4. The role of providing a holding environment, the conception of a new beginning; the place of regression and surrender within the purview of revisiting the painful experiences of early life so as to be able to

integrate them (Ghent, 1983) ; (see also Bromberg, 1979 regarding the place of regression in interpersonal analysis).

5. The issue of empathic immersion in the patient's subjective world; the role of empathic failure in creating iatrogenic resistance.
6. The question of truth-seeking as the primary means towards cure, in contrast to the patient's need for mirroring, validation, being understood in one's subjectivity. The possibility of an atmosphere of play and creativity in lieu of one of confrontation and cross-examination. Is it true, as Sullivan implied (Chapman and Chapman, 1980), that all the garden needs is to pull out the weeds? From another point of view there is evidence that selective caring for the flower (after all it is not a garden, it's a single flower that we're concerned with)—the weeds will spontaneously recede; they were there more or less to fill a vacuum left by the weakened self. A sub-heading to this item might be the separation of interactionism from interpersonalism, especially that species of interpersonalism that regards confrontation of the patient with "the truth" as what is curative.
7. The use of *free-association*, that way of listening that hears the patient's productions on several levels: (1) the "objective" content, (2) as an ongoing "dream," (3) with reference to the state of the self. Sullivan was so much concerned with ongoing personal phenomena as a basis for understanding that this avenue as well as the full-scale application of transference and countertransference analysis was left undeveloped as an opportunity for a new experience in the here and now (cf. Gill, 1982) ; (Searles, 1979); (Racker, 1968; among others).
8. The role of the body and the essentially innately determined, drive if you will, yet distinguishing this from the drive of classical metapsychology. Many of what Sullivan refers to as tensions of need are innately derived motivational thrusts, as for example the need for human connectedness or attachment (cf. Bowlby), or the lust dynamism. Infant research is revealing a host of "hard-wired" infant capacities whose patterning can be greatly affected by the environing caretakers.
9. The role of sexuality. George Klein's (1969/1976) clinical theory totally eschews classical metapsychology, yet encompasses the phenomena relating to early sexuality or what he calls sensuality. Gill (1983) reflects: "Psychoanalysis must not only integrate the intrapsychic with the interpersonal, but it must also reach a synthesis between bodily and interpersonal interaction" (p. 541). We must recognize that

interpersonal interaction can symbolize bodily interaction, just as bodily interaction may symbolize interpersonal interaction. Many substitutive phenomena, sexual or aggressive—the so-called disintegration products of drive in Kohut's vocabulary, or disembodied drive phenomena, where pleasure-seeking has pathologically become an end in itself (Fairbairn)—may come to have the quality of what might be called "autonomous id functions" and that these "id functions" may have to be dealt with at least for a period of time in the form and language in which they present themselves. Perhaps this is another way of saying that I believe interpersonalists have made the same error as classical Freudians with regard to equating sexuality with drive theory (Klein, 1969). In one case the dirty bath water is retained with the baby; in the other the bath water has been discarded, and along with it, the baby.

10. This brings up another issue. Analysts of all schools have had successes with the failures of others. Does this mean there are more routes to Rome than one? Will we be able to transcend the phenomenon of each analyst having a procrustean couch, leaving the hapless patient to try one after the other until he or she happens to find one that fits?

It seems clear to me that a deep affinity exists with English object relations theory. Their language is such that it requires no great feats of translation to understand what usually turns out to be a rather congenial set of conceptions. Both, in contrast to classical Freudian theory, take as axiomatic that there is a natural growth force, that what lies buried in the unconscious are often derivatives of the healthiest, most vital and creative aspects of the person, that essential to successful analysis is an atmosphere of affirmation and acceptance, and that the human relationship between analyst and patient plays a significant role, along with interpretation, in the curative process. Many of the same things could be said about Kohutian self-psychology and indeed we can sense large areas of overlap, as well as significant differences.

The Self in Relation to a One-person and Two-Person Psychology

Before examining more deeply our relation to self-psychology, I believe there is a prior question to address, the self. The problem that I have yet to sort out fully is the relation between the self in a two-person psychology and the self in a one-person psychology. My meaning will become clear as the discussion unfolds.

We have already noted the shift from the two-person early Freudian psychology to the one-person instinct theory. With the advent of ego psychology, particularly in its later forms (Jacobson, Mahler, Kernberg) the "other", the second person, played an increasingly important role although still forced into the mold of the basically one-person drive theory. Sullivan, on the other hand, in a radical departure, developed a thorough-going two-person theory. In England, Melanie Klein developed a remarkable theory; at one and the same time it was an extreme version of a one-person psychology, and yet contained within it the seeds of a two-person psychology. It was those seeds which led the British "middle group" to fashion a loosely knit body of theory, all of it grounded in two-person psychology, and in the case of Fairbairn, exclusively so. Friedland (1978) at a symposium on the self said, "In abandoning instinct Fairbairn did not abandon the intra-psychic. In moving away from Freudian metapsychology, he, in fact, was developing a psychology of the self, interpersonal and intra-psychic" (p. 560).

The tide has been shifting to include a one-person perspective, not because of a return to an id psychology, not because it is anti-relational, but rather because of the increasing recognition of the self as the center of activity of the psyche, a focus that had largely been overlooked in the past, often dismissed because it smacked of free will, morality, even religion and other psychoanalytically taboo subjects.

Now, reinforced by the work of infant researchers it is becoming increasingly clear that there is a one-person self, distinct from the self-system of Sullivan, but less distinct from the ego/self of Winnicott and Fairbairn. The object relations theorists were moving in this direction with concepts like true self, and, in Fairbairn, the original or pristine ego. Sullivan eschewed the self as operationally unknowable, and irrelevant for the psychiatry of interpersonal relations. This view dovetails with his oft-quoted insistence on the illusion of personal individuality. In the framework of the self-system, personal uniqueness is indeed an illusion; it is by definition created out of compliance with significant others. The part of the psyche for which it is not an illusion, but a central, though difficult to realize, reality was ruled out of bounds by Sullivan on an a priori basis. The ego psychologists tried to deal with the self by defining it as a mental representation outside of the structural system, and by invoking such concepts as autonomous ego functions. In a critique of Kernberg's efforts to incorporate Fairbairn's ideas into classical ego-psychology Rubens (1984) emphasized that one of the most brilliant of Fairbairn's insights lay precisely in his recognition that the self, and not some ideational representation thereof (for who, in that case, would be the one doing the representing?), has as its primary and innate function, active relationship with the object world. In Fairbairn's view it was only the intervention of some pathological process, that led to ideational representations in the form of split-off selves. To alter this conception is to eschew the most essential thrust of Fairbairn's theory (p. 432). My own efforts back in the mid-1950's to extend Sullivan's "self," led to concepts such as the *integral system* as a counterpoise to the self-system (see Pearce and Newton, 1963, pp. 9, 21). The view was put forth that experience was organized according to two distinctly different but parallel sets of criteria: one system integrates experience with exquisite reference to the significant others (i.e. the self-system), such that those others acted as "filters" for what could be included in the self-system. The other system, the integral system, was seen as integrating the totality of experience, both external as well as internal (by which I mean those motivational thrusts that have their origin in bodily functions), regardless of whether or not these were "acceptable" to the parenting others. In retrospect I realize that my goal was (1) to account for an autonomous self, in contrast with the self-system, however inaccessible to consciousness it may be, and (2) to account for it on the basis of a thoroughgoing experiential interpersonal two-person psychology. The concept of integral system also bears a certain resemblance to Winnicott's true self, with the difference that the former is conceived of as largely experiential in origin, where the origin of the latter is left ambiguous, somewhat mystical.

Now Kohut has come along and embraced the self as the central issue for psychoanalysis, rather than a tangential adjunct to the tripartite structural system. So too Wolstein (1987) has advanced the view that psychoanalysis in the 70's and 80's has evolved beyond what he refers to as the ego-interpersona that characterized the major developments of the 40's and 50's. As I see it, this focus on the self, was already well under way in England over 30 years ago, not only in the work of Fairbairn, but also, less explicitly, in Winnicott's writings. His unfortunate reluctance to use this word consistently, often using "ego" when what we would today call "self" was intended, has obscured his central role in resurrecting the self as the active center of psychic organization.

In Kohut's hands, despite the repudiation of classical metapsychology, the treatment of the self has the quality of a one-person psychology. In spite of the great importance, indeed centrality, given to early human experience, the emerging self is nonetheless seen as the active center of being; the essential role that other humans play in infancy is a functional one, as the selfobject, to facilitate the maturation of the growing self. At first this does not sound very different than Winnicott's facilitating environment. The difference, however, is real. Winnicott and the other object-relations theorists are referring to real objects, where Kohut makes a sharp distinction between a real object and a selfobject, the latter being closer to a verb than a noun: for Kohut a selfobject is not a person, but a function that a person is performing, a function whose essential meaning lies in the provision and maintenance of a coherent and developing self. It is this same function that in the analytic situation, the analyst, by empathic immersion in the patient's experience, provides for the patient. Viewed in this light, the emphasis is again, or still, on a one-person psychology. As Arnold Goldberg (1986b) put it in responding to a critique of his paper by Philip Bromberg, "Self psychology struggles hard not to be an interpersonal psychology not only because it wishes to avoid the social psychological connotations of the phrase but also because it wishes to minimize the input of the analyst into the mix ... [so] as to allow a thwarted development to unfold. Since self-psychology is preeminently a developmental psychology it is based on the idea of a developmental program (one that may be innate or pre-wired if you wish) that will reconstitute itself under certain conditions" (p. 387). In another context, Goldberg (1986c), implies that Kohut was at great pains to not be an environmentalist like Winnicott. "[Kohut's perception] is simply not a 2-party theory, nor one of interaction *between* the self and the external world" (p. 481).

For Kohut the focus on a one-person theory has the advantage over two-person object relations theory in that it maintains a continuity with the traditionally one-person classical Freudian approach, even though the focus is radically different than the original one-person instinctivistic conception. For Wolstein as a post-Sullivan theorist the gain in pursuing this one-person approach comes from the opposite direction: redressing the two-person emphasis of traditional interpersonal theory, which has eschewed attention to the uniquely unfolding self.

Reflecting on the psychoanalytic scene briefly I believe it is possible to see other signs of restlessness heralding a swing of the pendulum towards a one-person psychology of the self, and here I am not only referring to Kohut's work. Lacan's fierce opposition to ego-psychology is rooted (apart from his political motives) in his repudiation of what he saw as the adaptivistic orientation in America, a sell-out in contrast with what he regarded as the central aim of psychoanalysis, the realization of the inner Other. In Stanley Leavy's (1983a) paraphrase of Lacan we can clearly hear the battle cry that wishes to bring down the banner of "where id was there ego shall be" and replace it with what at first blush looks like "where ego was there id shall be;" but I believe that is not it either. I hear him saying, "where ego was there self shall be."

Erich Fromm (1955), although at the center of the interpersonal relational movement, preserved a core of one-person psychology. He always stressed that there were non-negotiable basic needs of man, some of which, but not all, directly involve other humans. In this regard he was not strictly interpersonal, but was focussed as well on what I am referring to as a one-person psychology. It is probably not accidental that this point of view also attracted him to oriental philosophy, Zen Buddhism in particular.

Is it possible that many branches of psychoanalysis have been sensing, less or more consciously, a neglected organ of the body psychoanalytic—the self? Is it this common search that is making former enemies into, if not friends, at least colleagues, once again?

To further illuminate the conflict (or the complementarity) between a one-person and two-person psychology I turn to a closer look at the relation between self psychology and British object relations theory. Brandchaft (1986) noted that

> Balint (1968) was clearly observing the same phenomenology as Kohut described 3 years later, similarly following the rules of non-interfering facilitation (Kohut, 1971). However, Kohut in response developed his core concept of selfobject when he recognized the central pathology here as a defect in the cohesiveness of the self, and the "peculiar" relationship as one in which the patient was attempting to revive with the analyst a period of development of the self at the point

> at which it had been arrested. In this experience the analyst was not perceived subjectively as separate but rather as a part of the patient. the object relationship was characterized not by the analyst gratifying or frustrating desires and needs of the patient, according to Kohut, but by being looked to for his unquestioned and unquestionable provision of essential functions that the patient could not provide for himself.
>
> (p. 258)

How is this different from the holding environment? Is this the essential point of divergence of Kohut from object relations theory? Balint and others were concerned with the real object and its central importance in providing a new beginning. This was a severe challenge to classical theory on several grounds: It put primary importance on the real object in the therapeutic situation. Secondly, while eschewing gratification in any of the usual senses of that term, it did supply what the patient needed at that time—a new beginning, a sense of deep recognition, a healing or repair of the self at the point of its developmental arrest. And thirdly, if the real object was to be of central importance in reviving the arrested development in the patient then this is suggestive of the idea that a real object was responsible for the arrest in the first place. This line of thinking would clearly point in the highly unacceptable direction of a return to the traumatic or seduction theory of neurosis.

Kohut's problem, I believe, was how to deal with the same clinical data, and yet preserve some degree of acceptability in the world of American ego psychology. I suggest that he hit upon a brilliant strategy: the invention of the notion of selfobject. This at once dramatically played down the focus on the real object, and did away with the notion of the need for a new beginning with a real object, which smacked of the "corrective emotional experience" heresy. It removed from direct view the problem of gratification. It retained under the name of empathy what Balint and Winnicott were referring to as a special type of object relationship; empathy did not carry with it the opprobrium of a "real relationship with the patient." It retained the focus of psychoanalysis as a one-person psychology in contrast to what the object relations theorists were proposing—the centrality of a two-person psychology.[7] Further, by focussing on the realization of ambitions and talents rather than human relatedness as the primary concern, the one-person psychology was reinforced. And finally it avoided the taint of in any way being associated with interpersonal theory, any suggestion of which, in the atmosphere of the 1970's, would have sounded the death knell on self psychology in America.

The object relations theorists were very concerned with healing deficits in the self (see Winnicott, 1960/1965). However, by not being constrained to a one-person psychology they were free to account for the variety of roles or functions the analyst as object plays in relation to the patient (cf. transitional object, use of the object, etc., in Winnicott, 1971). Ironically it is this very issue that more recently is being addressed by Stolorow (1986a), (1986b); (Stolorow, Brandchaft and Atwood, 1987) where he tries to demystify and de-reify the notion of selfobject by referring to it as one of many functions served by the object. He expressed distress with Kohut's dualism regarding selfobjects and true objects, speaking instead of the function of objects. This then would seem to bring us back to what the object-relations theorists had been saying, but in more refined and explicit language.

Why is it that self psychology has taken hold in the United States where British object relations theory has had relatively small impact? I believe that Kohut (1977) was able to take what the British "middle group" were saying and translate it into a form that was more acceptable in America. In so doing he changed the focus. Nevertheless it did have the enormous advantage of opening up North America to the new views that neither the British object relations theorists nor Sullivan had had much luck in doing as they were viewed as too radical.

Ironically Kernberg, around the same time, was trying to do something rather similar: translating the work of Fairbairn into a form that would permit continuity with, and accommodation to, the mainstream world of classical psychoanalysis. Kernberg chose a more conservative path in that he tried to retain drive theory in the mix. Despite his acceptance by a sizable group of analysts, he like Kohut, has come under attack from both sides. Traditional analysts (Klein and Tribich, 1981, among others) see him as having abandoned drive theory, and relational theorists see him as having performed a trompe l'oeil feat in changing the system while keeping it the same. Arnold Cooper (1979) in discussing a presentation by Kernberg said,[8]

> I believe that Fairbairn was correct in resisting—in advance—the future attempt to make his object relations view compatible with the dual instinct theory. While Dr. Kernberg has, with great sophistication,

> demonstrated the interrelationships of many of the findings and views of Fairbairn, Bowlby, Mahler and Jacobson, I believe that Bowlby has demonstrated with irrefutable logic that an energic motivating system is superfluous to a biologically sophisticated instinct theory; and this is equally true of the object-relations theories of Kernberg, in which all psychic structure and consequent behaviors are understood in terms of the internalization of object relations and their affective dispositions. The point is not whether a libido economic point of view can be made compatible with object relations theory. It is sufficient to demonstrate that libido economics are not a *necessary* explanatory tool for it to have lost any scientific validity whatever. The rules of theory don't permit us to cling to a theory which is no longer essential.

Kohut's approach was more radical in that it did away with drive theory. However, even there Kohut kept a close eye on "not going too far." He tried at first to maintain a bipartite theory of the self, speaking on the one hand of the self in the broad sense and relevant to narcissistic character disorders, and on the other, of the self in the narrow sense in relation to neurotic disorders. In this way he was able to convey the impression that the new ideas, the outlook that rejected drive theory, only applied to narcissistic disorders. Even the diagnosis "narcissistic disorder" seeming to create a sharp distinction with both neurotic disorders and borderline disorders, has the ring of political expedience. So often in the history of psychoanalysis the starting point for a new departure in theory has been the application of psychoanalysis to a diagnostic category hitherto refractory to the standard procedure. This was true in the case of Sullivan as it was with Fairbairn and Winnicott. As self psychology became more accepted on the American scene self psychologists began to acknowledge that it really is intended to cover all psychopathology.

In one sense one could say that two of the most seminal figures in mainline American psychoanalysis, Kohut and Kernberg, may both be viewed as having directed their life work to bringing the centrality of object relations theory to North America. Incidentally, and certainly without any direct intent, they have also contributed to introducing interpersonal theory into the flux of contending theories on the American scene. In the past half-dozen years there has been an unprecedented flow of respectful discussions by interpersonalists at meetings sponsored by the American Psychoanalytic Association, and by classical analysts and self psychologists at the White Institute.

It is not surprising that Kohut has had rather little impact in Europe where, by and large, the underlying principles that gave root to his approach have long been part of the scene (Bollas, 1986). For example, it is difficult to see what Kohut, in his focus on shoring up the self to prevent fragmentation of the self, added to Winnicott's conception of annihilation anxiety. Likewise, the concept of maternal mirroring and the mirroring transference seems very similar to what was subsumed in Winnicott's holding environment.

Among the criticisms from the classical analysts that the self psychologists are at pains to refute are such issues as: Isn't empathy doing more than simply 'experience with' the patient? Isn't it also doing something, gratifying in some way, the patient? (see Friedman, 1986). Despite Kohut's efforts the awful specter of a two-person psychology, a psychology of participant observation, that is a psychology that embraces both a stance of empathic immersion and of participant observation, keeps reappearing like the proverbial skeleton in the closet. As Modell (1986) put it, it is rather difficult to distinguish Kohut's notion of transmuting internalizations from "corrective emotional experience." Ironically, at the end of his life Kohut seemed no longer distressed about the allusion to corrective emotional experience (Friedman, 1986, p. 333).

The Philosophy of Cure: Empathy, Truth Ethic, Developmental Deficit

One might gain the impression from my discussion so far that Kohut and self psychology have performed useful political functions, but that nothing essentially new has been contributed. This would be far from my view. Kohut also added the dimension of talents, ideals and ambitions, and in doing so tended to shift the emphasis in the direction of a one-person psychology, in contrast with the object relations and interpersonal theorists whose emphasis rests solidly on goals of human interaction. In fact a weakness of these latter theories is that they hardly dealt with issues that were not directly interhuman.

His philosophy of cure reveals a quite different, though not incompatible, viewpoint than Sullivan's focus on the undoing of "parataxic distortions." As Friedman (1986) puts it:

> The general plan of cure is to reinspire those efforts at growth by appreciating the environmental failure and by providing a new substitute to

> grow with. The patient stretches over the therapist's failures, because those failures are transitory and because their relation to growth needs is made visible. Kohut has always placed the greatest emphasis on the analyst's pointing out the results of his failure to be what the patient needs. He has described new psychic structure as the relative self-sufficiency a patient achieves when a sensitive therapist fails less grossly, persistently, and heedlessly than the parents did[9] … Kohut held that the fundamental human transaction is appreciating what something means to a person, and he identified that as empathy.
>
> (p. 322)

"Explanations" or interpretations are secondary in Kohut's view. They help by evoking in the patient a feeling of being cognitively understood as well as being understood empathically. They help insofar as the explanation can be recalled at will and can sustain the empathic bond when the analyst is either clumsy or absent. Also they help to consolidate gradually a different kind of relation with the analyst, one that is more distant and objective (Friedman, 1986).

What Kohut emphasizes over and again is that interpretations are of use only after the patient has come to feel deeply understood in the empathic mode, else what inevitably happens is that the patient becomes "resistant," and the therapist having failed empathically now fails again by not recognizing the source of the resistance, thereby compounding the resistance. This can even lead to a negative therapeutic reaction in which the therapist is stymied in large measure by his own counter-resistance, his difficulty in entering empathically into the inner subjective experience of the patient.

Kohut (1984) offers a moving example of this:

> I ... persisted in my efforts to understand my patient, tolerated his attacks on me as best I could—even including a temporary phase in which he bad-mouthed me openly to a colleague of mine with whom he became briefly acquainted at a reception. That my own reactions were imperfect, that I often became defensive under the barrage of attacks, is understandable since the patient always reproached me for real flaws in my emotional responses and intellectual performance. And I learned—again, of course, imperfectly—not even to respond by telling the patient that however germane his criticisms might be, they were exaggerated and disproportionate. The patient, as I finally

> grasped, insisted—and had a right to insist—that I learn to see things exclusively in *his* way and not at all in *my* way. And as we finally came to see—or rather as I finally come to see, since the patient had seen it all along—the content of *all* my various interpretations had been cognitively correct but incomplete in a decisive direction. The patient had indeed reacted to my having been away; he had indeed felt overwhelmed by the traumatizations to which he was now exposed by virtue of his expanding activities, and he continued to react with prolonged, intense suffering as a result of remaining broadly engaged with the world. What I had not seen, however, was that the patient had felt additionally traumatized by feeling that all these explanations on my part came only from the outside: that I did not fully feel what he felt, that I gave him words but not real understanding, and that I thereby repeated the essential trauma of his early life. The task that the analyst faces at such moments—the crucial moment in which a "borderline" condition either will or will not become an analyzable narcissistic personality disorder—is largely one of self scrutiny. To hammer away at the analysand's transference distortions brings no results; it only confirms the analysand's conviction that the analyst is as dogmatic, as utterly sure of himself, as walled off in the self-righteousness of a distorted view as the pathogenic parents (or other selfobject) had been. Only the analyst's continuing sincere acceptance of the patient's reproaches as (psychologically) realistic, followed by a prolonged (and ultimately successful) attempt to look into himself and remove the inner barriers that stand in the way of his empathic grasp of the patient, ultimately have a chance to turn the tide.
>
> (p. 182)

Speaking both from my own experience as well as much experience with supervisees both of interpersonal and Freudian persuasion, I do believe that we have much to learn from this illustration. So often I have witnessed the development of iatrogenic resistance at the hands of a therapist who is trying to convince the patient, however subtly, with his or her view of a situation, meanwhile failing utterly at comprehending the patient's subjective experience of the situation. At the same time, as Bromberg (1986) suggests, in responding to a vignette presented by Goldberg (1986a), the counterbalancing interpersonal view has much to contribute. "The patient's interpretation of the dream is that the problem is all her own (which at one level—the structural level—it of course is). But to have the deepest impact upon that structural level, the fact that the patient may be denying what is in front of her eyes with regard to the analyst, and denying the analyst's own role in this denial, are central pieces of data. As an interpersonal analyst I would see it as a powerful and empathic intervention to bring this possible meaning out into the open for scrutiny" (p. 385). As I see it, Bromberg's intervention lies in the area of overlap in the two approaches; it is at once interpersonal and self-psychological, perhaps more meaningfully empathic with the patient than the position espoused by Goldberg himself.

In Kohut there is a reciprocal relation between the focus on empathy as curative, as against truth as curative. My own impression is that this need not be quite so polarized. It is no accident that Kohut discovered self-psychology and the extreme importance of empathic immersion in his work with narcissistic patients, since it is they who are exquisitely sensitive to humiliation and tend to experience any interpretation as humiliating. But is this true of all people who come for psychoanalysis? Just as Kohut became extremely attuned to the patient's need for empathic response, so too was Sullivan extremely attuned to his patient's opposing needs: on the one hand not to be humiliated, or made more anxious than was needed for the dismantling of a tiny piece of the self-system, and on the other hand the need for expansion of the self-system, with the knowledge that growth rarely occurs without anxiety so that growth of the personality (Sullivan's word for self) could only happen at the expense of the intactness of the self-system (or what Winnicott would call false self). By Kohut's lights if the self is nourished by empathic understanding the second step will happen by itself. My own view is that there is more than one way to help a flower grow. Sometimes selectively nourishing or watering it is what is required, sometimes clearing some weeds will be helpful.

Kohut has railed at length against the truth ethic of classical Freudianism and criticizes Freud as having been neurotically insistent on confronting truth for its own sake. I believe that to some degree Kohut's emphasis on the healing aspects of empathy reflects an overcorrection of his view of classical Freudian psychoanalysis as being "censorious, authoritarian, argumentative, insistent and disciplinarian" (Friedman, 1986, p. 336). At the same time I believe the "truth ethic" is deeply implicated in interpersonal analysis as well, where so often as supervisor I find the therapist assuming he or she knows the truth as "objectively observed" and hence deeply distressed and mystified that the patient is not responding to the cognitive formulation. The suggestion at these moments that the therapist enter into the patient's subjective experience, his or her way of thinking and being, may come as a shock to the therapist, or it may come as a relief, a sudden recognition of what had been missing in the therapeutic situation. Roberto Assagioli (personal communication), once said that there need be four different approaches to patients, depending on the personality style of the patient: cognitive, affective, aesthetic, spiritual. For some people the cognitive truth ethic may be the only meaningful route to the patient's self. If Freud were the patient I am not sure that self-psychology would be the ideal psychoanalytic approach! In summary of this issue I believe Kohut's emphasis on empathic immersion has been extremely valuable for analysts of all persuasions. It is becoming a part of the body psychoanalytic. I hope that this does not auger its suffering the same fate as the word interpersonal, that is becoming trivialized.

What about the notion of developmental deficit, a theme that appears recurringly in controversies between self psychologists and classical analysts? I believe the notion of developmental defect or arrest can be misleading as it suggests a sharp distinction between defect versus conflict as the basis for a particular area of psychopathology. My own sense is that in general these two facets of experience are interwoven in the developmental sequence of a given person's life. I believe that the focus on developmental defect as something to be sharply contrasted with "conflict and defense" is a carry-over from drive theory. The notion of defect is a way of getting around the primacy of drive and the defense against it as the singular explanatory paradigm in classical Freudian analysis. If we sidestep drive theory in the first place we are left with a conception of a fabric of interweaving motivational systems, derived from the interaction of the child's experience with in-built and evolving and maturational needs. In this view there will be an interaction between motivational structures that derive primarily from environmental failure with other motivational systems that collide (i.e. are in conflict) with one another.

For example, in the case of an infant with an intrusive, overstimulating impinging mother, there will be a failure of self-formation—a defect—which in turn may cause withdrawal behavior (motivated), which in turn may collide with other motivated impulses (e.g. the need for tenderness, relatedness), the result of which may induce in the mothering one her own withdrawal or other behavior that then results in further deficit in the child's exerience, and with it, further defect in the structuring of the self.

It is interesting that although the notion of deficit has been presented as something rather new and revolutionary, Sullivan (1953) over forty years ago made it a central feature of his system. He spelled out its sequelae, and stressed the importance therapeutically of recognizing and addressing the point of developmental deficit or arrest.

Stern's Contribution

No discussion of the self, or the issue of a one- or a two-person psychology would be meaningful without reference to the landmark book by Dan Stern (1986), *The Interpersonal World of the Infant.* Taken in its broadest perspective the book has two separate but complementary thrusts. One is the central importance of the interpersonal environment in the infant's development. The other is the significance of the incredible array of more or less hardwired givens that presage an emergent self at or shortly after birth. Stern's book represents to me a highly original and fruitful approach in which the organizing principle of development is the evolution of the subjective senses of self. The account of development is unique in psychoanalytic theorizing; it is quite different than that of psychoanalytic theory in either its classical or its relational versions (although closer to the latter), and, because of its focus on the subjective, different than attachment theory. "As new behaviors and capacities emerge they are reorganized to form organizing subjective perspectives on self and other and the result is the emergence, in quantum leaps, of [four] different senses of the self" (p. 26).

In contrast to most psychoanalytic theories, Stern sees the self as present from birth. Fairbairn (1963), incidentally, is the only analytic theorist who considered the "ego" as present at birth. The earliest sense of subjective self, termed by Stern the *sense of an emergent self*, appears somewhere between birth and two months. The infant's "social capacities are operating with vigorous goal-directedness to assure social interactions. These interactions produce affects, perceptions, sensorimotor events, memories and other cognitions. Some integration between diverse happenings is made innately" (p. 28). Notice the phrase, "operating with vigorous goal-directedness to assure social interaction." Clearly we are dealing with a psychology rooted in autonomous goal-directed activity, that while it needs interpersonal experience for its development, it does not owe its existence to interpersonal activity. We are now in the realm of a mixture of a one-person and a two-person psychology.

The *sense of core self* begins somewhere between the second and the third month, when infants sense they and their mother are quite separate physically, are different agents, have distinct affective experiences, and have separate histories.

The *sense of subjective self*, a quite new organizing subjective perspective, begins somewhere between seventh and eighth month. This new perspective defines a qualitatively different self and other who can "hold in mind" unseen but inferable mental states such as intentions or affects that can guide overt behavior. It opens up the possibility of intersubjectivity and operates in a new domain of relatedness, the *domain of intersubjective relatedness*. "Mental states between people can now be 'read', matched, aligned with or attuned to (or misread, mismatched, misaligned, or misattuned)" (p. 27). With this new development comes the

> momentous realization that inner subjective experiences, the "subject matter" of the mind are potentially shareable with someone else. The subject matter at this point in development can be as simple and important as an intention to act ("I want that cookie"), a feeling state ("This is exciting"), or a focus of attention ("Look at that toy"). This discovery amounts to the acquisition of a theory of separate minds. ... It is not, of course, a fullblown theory. It is rather a working notion that says something like, what is going on in my mind may be similar enough to what is going on in your mind that we can somehow communicate this (without words) and thereby experience intersubjectivity.
>
> (p. 124)

I found myself wondering whether, perhaps, the roots of clinical narcissism lie in some failure to integrate adequately the mode of intersubjective relatedness, a wholly two-person psychological experience, either because the significant others were misattuned, underattuned or unpredictably attuned to this mode of relating. Could it be that people we encounter as patients may, despite being highly experienced in intellectual intercourse or sexual conjunction, nonetheless feel like frightened virgins when it comes to encountering this area of deeply longed for, yet warded off, intersubjectivity? Is it perhaps the deficit in this type of two-person experience that has even led to naming the phenomenon *narcissism*, an infelicitous term which carries the implication that a one-person psychology is at work? I believe, rather, that the phenomena of narcissism are largely rooted in a two-person psychology, derived in part from earlier senses of self, and in part from defensive operations designed to compensate for deficits in a coherent sense of self.

Another set of questions is forced upon us by the advent of this sense of subjective self, questions which have bearing on the issue of a one-person and/or a two-person psychology. Stern asks,

> Is this quantum leap simply the result of a newly emergent, specific capacity or skill? Or does it result from the experience of social interactions? Or is it the maturational unfolding of a major human need and motive state?
>
> (p. 132)

There is evidence for all three viewpoints and Stern concludes they all seem necessary for an adequate explanation of intersubjectivity. The second alternative, the approach of interpersonal meanings regards the achievement of intersubjectivity as the result of mother's entrance into "meaningful exchanges with the infant." This view has been carried farther in France and Switzerland where it is thought that "mother's 'meanings' reflect not only what she observes but also her fantasies about who the infant is and is to become. Intersubjectivity, for them, ultimately involves interfantasy" (p. 134). Incidentally, here again we see how fantasy may both be a product of reality and nonetheless itself have far-reaching consequences for what will become reality.

Finally there emerges the "*sense of verbal self* operating in the *domain of verbal relatedness*. This is a qualitatively new domain with expanding, almost limitless possibilities for interpersonal happenings. ... [It] rests on the new set of capacities: to objectify the self, to be self-reflective, to comprehend and produce language" (p. 28). It is not difficult to imagine types of pathological character development where there has been some failure in the domain of intersubjective relatedness along with relative success in the domain of verbal relatedness.

A matter of some importance regarding psychoanalytic theory is whether one believes the original or essential state of human existence to be one of aloneness or togetherness (p. 240 ff). Mahler chose togetherness and then went on to provide a theory of separation and individuation to account for the infant's development. "Attachment theory does the opposite. It makes the achievement of a basic sense of human connectedness the end point, not the starting point, of a long, active developmental course involving the interplay of predesigned and acquired behaviors. ... The British object relations school [and the interpersonalists] also postulate an early undifferentiated phase, but with emphasis on initial relatedness. ... Unlike Mahler however, they do not see the primary state of relatedness as something one grows out of during a separation/individuation-like phase. They see separateness and relatedness as concomitant and equal developmental lines."

Here again the issue of a one-person versus a two-person theory is fairly clearly drawn, with Mahler rooted in the former, the interpersonalists and object relations school in the latter. Stern, self psychologists and some post-Sullivan interpersonalists occupy a place that again lays stress on the one-person position but from a totally different perspective than Mahler. It rests more on an intrinsic self that exists from the start and, as the center of and originator of activity, is the focus of human activity. In a manner close to attachment theory, this self reaches out *to* the world and is hopefully met *by* the external world both human and non-human.

Another Kind of One-Person Self?

This brings us to a most interesting question. Are there perhaps, impulses, longings, needs which are more deeply rooted in the search for emotional contact with this self, the one-person self, although now a very different entity than the one-person ego/id of structural theory?

Francesco Alberoni (1981/1983), a well-known Italian sociologist, in his book *Falling in Love*, has developed a thesis that carries us beyond the primacy of object relations or the strictly interpersonal. He looks upon falling in love as a special case (since it involves only two individuals) of great collective movements, such as the Reformation, the student movement, feminism or the Islamic movement of Khomeini. Every such movement has the characteristics, as Durkheim (1953, quoted by Alberoni) pointed out, of great intensity, passion and renewal.

> "[These forces] lead to overthrow for the sake of overthrowing, as in play without any specific opbjective. ... At such moments, this higher form of life is lived with such intensity and exclusiveness that it monopolizes all minds to the more or less complete exclusion of egoism and the commonplace. ..." [Max] Weber attributes all these things to the leader, to his traits. In essence, he makes the same error that each of us makes when we fall in love: we attribute the extraordinary experience we are having to the traits of the person we love.
>
> (pp. 5–6)

Alberoni, and perhaps one can detect the influence of Lacan, is suggesting that in falling in love, what is longed for is that state of feeling intensely alive, nascent, transcendent, in contact with one's core, one's very center of being, and the object is secondary, a necessary medium through which the transcendental can happen. In fact the object may not only be the "lover," but may be God, a great cause or leader, a guru, or in true meditation, there may be no object at all.

In the case of the guru, he is a means for experiencing the transcendental, for bringing about the inner revolution. In ordinary everyday life we have few opportunities to experience this transcendental (surrendered) state. Sex is by far the most readily available. It is sufficiently "acceptable" to be available to large numbers of people, and sufficiently forbidden to permit partaking in a "revolutionary," transcendent, surrendered state of being.

An important corollary follows from this. The thrust of object relations theory has been to supercede Freud's objectless desire (libido as pleasure-seeking) with the formulation that libido is object-seeking. Object-seeking is seen as primary and pleasure is secondary and its detailed configuration is largely the result of experience with objects. Now, if we allow that there is some very deep-rooted need for transcendent experience which in some way uses objects for its fulfillment, are we perhaps returning to a new version of the Freudian view of there being a need for a state of being that allows oneself to feel alive, real, changing, intense, and that usually, for this to happen an object is needed? Instead of sex as a basic drive are we not positing this need for the feeling of transcendence, or heightened aliveness as central, and that very often it is realized only in a sexual context. For some people this revolutionary, transformative experience is not the one of falling in love, nor something sexual, but an intense creative drive, a mystical experience or drive, a passionate "need for power," a longing for submergence in some larger unit—all of which may be derivatives, at least in part, of this longing, and all of which make use of the various potential activities with which humans are endowed and are capable of: sexual, aggressive, mystical. Some of these are closer to the underlying need and are therefore potentially more fulfilling of that need. Others, for example violence and destructiveness, are much farther removed from the need, derivatives which cannot really fulfill the underlying quest, except in some form of perversion. How does this fit with object relations theory? In the first place under normal conditions the object is essential for the realization of this un-named longing for this nascent transcendent state. And, secondly, in infancy it is the mother as enabling agent for the child that permits him or her to realize one of the earliest forms of this state—transitional experiencing, the precursor to so much of what later is to be found in the area of creative and cultural experience (Winnicott, 1971).

Could it be said then that *love* is indeed rooted in a two-person psychology, perhaps its peak development, whereas *falling-in-love*, quite another matter is in a certain sense closer to a one-person psychology, with the proviso that these two psychologies are themselves complementary and interactive? Viewed in this light the significance of early object relations, or of interpersonal experience is re-instated. In fact I do not regard the psychology of self and the psychology of object relations as alternatives. The hard-wired object-seeking emergent capacities exist as potentials to be realized, shaped, integrated and structured by experience.

Drives and Motives

In concluding a paper that sets out to explore, on the one hand, a personal psychoanalytic belief system, and on the other, the relations between a one-person and two-person psychology, it seems to me that an important question remains: What about drives? Although the language of drive theory continues to hold sway in classical Freudian thinking, and has its roots in classical one-person psychology, the momentum toward abandonment of the metapsychology is picking up. The findings of infant research have borne out Rapoport's (1960) predictions of thirty years ago that concepts such as id, ego and superego were not likely to survive. Stern (1986) asks:

> Has classical libido theory, in assuming one or two basic drives that shift developmentally from one erotogenic zone to another and have a variety of vicissitudes during development, been helpful in viewing an actual infant? The consensus is no. The classical view of instinct has proven unoperationalizable and has not been of great heuristic value for the observed infant. Also, while there is no question that we need a concept of motivation, it clearly will have to be reconceptualized in terms of many discrete, but interrelated, motivational systems such as attachment, competence-mastery, curiosity and others.
>
> (p. 238)

The relationships among concepts such as drive in the metapsychological sense, "drive" in the sense of hard-wired organismic thrust, wish, need and motive is fascinating but beyond the present scope. Suffice it to note here that while concepts such as wish, need and motive, unlike drive, lend themselves to a two-person psychology, they are intrinsically neutral on this issue. Freud used "wish" before he elaborated the first instinct theory, when protopsychoanalysis was still a two-person psychology. Sandler (1981, p. 182) returns to this usage: "From a psychological point of view it is sufficient for us to take as a basic unit, the *wish*" (See also Holt, 1976).

If not rooted in drive, where then do we locate motive? In my perspective on psychoanalytic theory, a human being is seen as an active agent rather than passive reagent or robot (Chein, 1972); motivation is purposive and goal-oriented (vis-à-fronte), rather than driven by instincts or drives (vis-à-tergo) pressing for tension reduction. By stressing the psychological theory I wish in no way to diminish the biologically determined underpinnings and the importance of biologically determined differences in individual infants. Likewise by saying that motivation is purposive I am neither eschewing determinism, nor advocating teleology; I am suggesting that man's motivations operate as a fully-open system tending in the direction of increasing complexity, rather than as a closed-loop system with homeostatic mechanisms to maintain itself as it is. Regarding the biological as against psychological aspects of sexuality there are two special issues which, however parenthetical in this context, are important to mention: (1) the younger the infant the more inseparable is the psychological meaning of an event from the biological underpinning. Symbolization of the experience is usually in body language (breast, penis, etc.), and it is often only through re-awakening of this body language that the unique and vivid quality of the original (psychological) experience can be fully felt. (2) Often enough we see people in whom a large part of life seems to be occupied by a biological drive. This represents a breakdown in, or defective development of the ordinarily highly complex motivational derivatives of the biological drive; the drive then is co-opted to serve some other motivation system such as the need for power, the need to avoid the terror of self-fragmentation, etc.

If we detach drive from drive theory we open up the very important question of a general theory of motivation with regard both to its origins and to its increasingly complex interweavings. Fundamental, in my view, is the notion that virtually all human activity, even the most singularly biological is, at the human level, so vitally predicated on interhuman experience—(even feeding in a neonate is an activity that has to be integrated, and that leaves plenty of room for faulty integration)—that the most significant variable for psychology is the human envelope of the activity that matters, rather than the activity itself. Meaning, then, derives from what happens between people from earliest infancy on.

Arising out of the matrix of the earliest interhuman connections, increasingly complex motivations emerge, largely derived from the interactions among (1) already organized motivational needs (in response, say, to the primitive biologically organized thrusts of the infant), (2) maturational thrusts—external experience is required at every level of maturation, in order to adequately integrate the function; this is true even for something as physiological as vision—active "seeing," learning to "see" is required for the integration of the visual function, and (3) the environment, facilitating or otherwise. The most primitive motives, arising in response to biological tensions of need or discomfort, soon become organized into more and more complex motives, usually highly interwoven, and often colliding with one another.

As these motivational interactions begin to gel, motivational thrusts seem to end up in two broad categories, with opposing goals: (1) to maintain coherence and stability (cf. security needs, Sullivan; self-cohesion, Kohut) even when the system is poorly adapted to a new and better environment, and (2) to press for new experience that results in growth and expansion of the self (cf. the needs for satisfaction, Sullivan; the sexual and aggressive drives in classical theory, and here there is confusion between activity and assertion on the one hand, and destructiveness on the other). In important measure, it is the conflict between these broadly defined motivational systems that results in still more complex motivational systems which ultimately we recognize as character, and as symptoms, neurosis, and psychopathology in general. These two broad categories are characteristic of all structured open systems. There are always substructures aimed at maintaining the system as is and designed to resist change, and other substructures designed for the expansion of function, growth and development. This is evident in all manner of social systems, and is equally clear regarding such matters as theory, say psychoanalytic theory for example. Any given theory provides a more or less secure scaffolding on which to register one's perceptions, and build one's conceptions; at the same time, the theory by its very nature is limiting and constrictive, so that other forces in the form of new observations, new ideas, new techniques, new influences from other disciplines are constantly impinging on the theory and aiming at its expansion, or ultimately, at its replacement by a better theory.

By virtue of the biologically prepared neonate, and its being cared for in a human environment, the human infant soon acquires the beginnings of motivational systems which conveniently we refer to as psychological needs. Such a one is the need for connectedness or attachment to another. This may begin with a need for body contact, and proceed through relating to the other, to "using" the other (Winnicott, 1969) and ultimately, to loving and being loved by the other. Another such psychological need is the need for autonomy. Andras Angyal (1965/1982) wrote of these as dual tendencies: (1) autonomy, the drive to act, to make things happen for the sheer joy of action and experiencing oneself as the cause of changes: play, curiosity, creativity, mastery, competence, self-assertion. And (2) the trend towards homonomy:

> Human behavior cannot be solely understood as a manifestation of the trend towards increased autonomy. Seen from another angle human life reveals a basic pattern very different from self-assertiveness, from striving for freedom and mastery. The person behaves as if he were seeking a place for himself in a larger unit of which he strives to become a part. In the first orientation [the trend toward autonomy] he is struggling for centrality in his world, trying to mold and organize

> objects and events, to bring them under his own control. In the second orientation he seems rather to strive to surrender himself and to become an organic part of something that he conceives as greater than himself. Processes concerned with procreation are evidence that even at the physiological level the individual is integrated into supra-individual units. ... The superordinate whole may be represented for him by a social unit—family, clan, nation—by an ideology—or by a meaningfully ordered universe. ... I am certain that the second trend [homonomy] is as basic as the first. ... What we call love is a manifestation of the homonomous trend. ... In a more general sense the whole concept of homonomy could be equated with love.
>
> (p. 15)

Buber (1947, pp. 85–88), in *Between Man and Man*, interestingly refers to similar dual trends when he refers to the "originator instinct"—man's need to make things, and "the instinct for communion"—the need to enter into mutuality, and to share in a common undertaking. It is not difficult to see how the vistas offered by Angyal or Buber, although foreign to the language of psychoanalysis, nonetheless can be located in the two broad categories of motivation.

Here I will offer another non-exhaustive list, this time of what might be called motivational systems or psychological needs (depending on one's level of discourse) that seem to be part of being human, even though what is often encountered is evidence of interference with these functions:

- A need for protection of the self as well as all that is meaningful to it, including one's own body and the integrity of meaningful others.
- A need for a feeling of self-worth, dignity, self-esteem.
- A need for the expansion of awareness (and "aliveness"); for "knowing" as distinct from knowledge, the absence of which leads to feelings of "deadness."
- A need for inner integration of the self; the yearning to surrender "false self"; the quest for wholeness and unity, "centeredness." (see Ghent, 1983)
- A need for meaning, significance and coherence.
- A need for growth, that is, the integration of new function, in distinction to the execution of already integrated function.

It seems clear that there is much overlapping and intertwining as well as the potential for conflict among these various needs or motivational systems. I view the capacity to have these "needs" as part of the human equipment. Their actualization as needs, and the specific forms these needs take, derives from the quality of experience one has in one's personal evolution in the mostly human world. The specific patterning of these interacting needs (motivational systems or constellations), how they are expressed or stunted and distorted, constitute the unique individuality of each human being.

In closing let me remind the reader that this paper is about two subjects: one man's psychoanalytic belief system, and secondly, a study of the question of the role of one-person and two-person psychologies in psychoanalytic theory. I hope it is clear that both are actively in flux. Casement (1986) ended a recent paper called "Interpretation: Fresh Insight or Cliché?" with some lines from T. S. Eliot (1930, p. 141). I cannot think of a more fitting way to sum up my thoughts about theories, beliefs and practice in psychoanalysis.

> Last season's fruit is eaten
> And the fullfed beast shall kick the empty pail.
> For last year's words belong to last year's language
> And next year's words await another voice.
> (Little Gidding)

Notes

1. Presented in abbreviated form at New York University Postdoctoral Program in Psychoanalysis, December 5, 1986.
2. Rickman (1957), Balint (1950), Modell (1984) and more recently Lachmann and Beebe (1988) and Beebe and Lachmann (1988) have discussed the issue of one- and two-person psychologies from differing points of view.
3. The word "choose" also comes from the affective sphere, deriving from words denoting taste, e.g. gusto, gustatory.
4. In retrospect we might see another datum as supporting the notion of Freud's preference for sex rather than destructiveness as the root of man's irrational (id) forces: After the various shifts in the placement of destructive impulses, Freud ended up with their being a function of the death instinct. Not only was the fault found to be innate, but destructiveness was now seen as a necessary protection against an entropic impulse toward self-destruction. This was about as far as one could get from the idea that infants and children developed destructive impulses as a result of having been treated traumatically. Yet Melanie Klein did carry it further, to such an extreme in fact, that it probably

set in motion the revolution that led to the 2-person psychology of the British "Middle Group"—Winnicott, Balint, Fairbairn and others.

5. This raises a fascinating question, but one that is not directly related to our topic: Are our socioeconomic arrangements, as mediated through complex personal relations, represented in our unconscious? Are these invisible relations relegated to something one might call the socially sanctioned unconscious (Ghent, 1962)?
6. See Moore (1984) for an extensive discussion of the limitations of operationalism, and Sullivan's misapplication of Bridgman's ideas.
7. Stolorow (1986a, p. 398) spells out the misleading dichotomy between selfobjects and true objects that "originated historically in the embeddedness of [Kohut's] early ideas in classical drive theory," and offers a solution: "The theoretical pitfalls can be avoided if we use the term selfobject always and only to refer to a class of psychological *functions*, a dimension of experiencing the object" (see pp. 398–399).
8. The first part of this quotation reads as follows: "First, it is clear that the term libido as used by Fairbairn is so divergent from Freud's intent, that they share little other than superficial descriptive qualities—both refer to something pleasurable. However, Fairbairn clearly is not referring to a primary drive related to the sexual instincts. He states in his synopsis that the ego is present from birth, libido is a function of the ego, and the ego, and therefore libido, is fundamentally object-seeking. Here he is clearly closer to Bowlby in describing the child's tie to the mother, and in this version of instinct theory, there is absolutely no room for the energic concepts that Dr. Kernberg wishes to preserve. The infant does not pursue pleasure, he pursues specific interactions with objects in the environment, and the system functions by informational feedback loops, not by energy systems. Similarly, to be able to describe the hierarchical organization of aggressive behavior is a far cry from confirming the notion of an aggressive drive."
9. Stolorow (1986a, pp. 397–398) has amended this. To him, "structure formation ... occurs primarily when the [empathic] bond is *intact*, or in the process of becoming restored." In fact Stolorow regards the idea of structure formation based on optimal frustration as a remnant of drive theory, a direct descendant of Freud's (1923) proposal that the "ego is that part of the id which has been modified by the direct [frustrating] influence of the external world."

References

Alberoni, F. (1983). *Falling in love* (L. Venuti, Trans.). New York, NY: Random House. (Original work published as *Innamoramento e amore*, 1981)

Angyal, A. (1982). *Neurosis and treatment: A holistic theory.* New York, NY: Wiley. (Original work published 1965, New York, NY: Da Capo Press)

Balint, M. (1950). Changing therapeutic aims and techniques in psychoanalysis. *International Journal of Psycho-Analysis*, *31*, 117–124.

Balint, M. (1968). *The basic fault: Therapeutic aspects of regression*. London, UK: Tavistock.

Beebe, B. & Lachmann, F. M. (1988, November). *On the formation of psychic structure: A study based on empirical infant research*. Presented at a meeting of the Southern California Psychoanalytic Association.

Benjamin, J. (1977). The end of internalization: Adorno's social psychology. *Telos*, *32*, 42–64.

Bollas, C. (1986). Who does psychoanalysis cure? *Psychoanalytic Inquiry*, *6*, 429–435.

Brandchaft, B. (1986). British object relations theory and self psychology. In A. Goldberg (Ed.), *Progress in self psychology* (Vol. *2*, pp. 245–272). New York, NY: Guilford Press.

Bromberg, P. M. (1979). Interpersonal psychoanalysis and regression. *Contemporary Psychoanalysis*, *15*, 647–655.

Bromberg, P. M. (1986). [Discussion of the paper, "The wishy-washy personality" by A. Goldberg]. *Contemporary Psychoanalysis*, *22*, 374–386.

Buber, M. (1947). *Between man and man*. London, UK: Routledge & Kegan Paul.

Casement, P. (1986). Interpretation: Fresh insight or cliché? *Free Associations*, *1*, 90–104.

Chapman, A. H. & Chapman, M. C. M. S. (1980). *Harry Stack Sullivan's concepts of personality development and psychiatric illness*. New York, NY: Brunner/Mazel.

Chein, I. (1972). *The science of behavior and the image of man*. New York, NY: Basic Books.

Cooper, A. M. (1979, December). *Discussion of "The object relations theory of W. Ronald D. Fairbairn" by Otto F. Kernberg, M.D.* The Association for Psychoanalytic Medicine.

Cooper, A. M. (1985). Will neurobiology influence psychoanalysis? *American Journal of Psychiatry*, *142*(12), 1395–1402.

Cooper, A. M. (1986). Some limitations on therapeutic effectiveness: The "burn-out syndrome" in psychoanalysts. *The Psychoanalytic Quarterly*, *55*, 576–598.

Durkheim, E. (1953). Value judgments and judgments of reality. In *Sociology and philosophy* (D.F. Pocock, Trans.). Chicago, IL: Chicago Free Press.

Eliot, T. S. (1930). *The complete poems and plays*. New York, NY: Harcourt Brace.

Fairbairn, W. R. D. (1963). Synopsis of an object-relations theory of the personality. *International Journal of Psycho-Analysis*, *44*, 224–225.

Ferenczi, S. (1955). A confusion of tongues between adults and the child. In *Final contributions to the problems and methods of psychoanalysis* (pp. 156–167). London, UK: Hogarth Press. (Original work published 1933)

Freud, S. (1923). The ego and the id. *Standard Edition*, *19*, 3–68.

Friedland, B. (1978). Toward a psychology of the self. *Contemporary Psychoanalysis*, *14*, 553–570.

Friedman, L. (1986). Kohut's testament. *Psychoanalytic Inquiry*, *6*, 321–347.

Fromm, E. (1941). *Escape from freedom*. New York, NY: Rinehart.
Fromm, E. (1955). *The sane society*. New York, NY: Rinehart.
Ghent, E. (1962, September). *Scarcity: A governing principle in man's functioning.* New York University Postdoctoral Program in Psychoanalysis: Colloquium, New York, NY.
Ghent, E. (1983, December). Masochism, submission, surrender. New York University Postdoctoral Program in Psychoanalysis: Colloquium, New York, NY.
Gill, M. M. (1982). *Analysis of transference*. New York, NY: International Universities Press.
Gill, M. M. (1983). The point of view of psychoanalysis: Energy discharge or person? *Psychoanalysis and Contemporary Thought*, *6*, 523–551.
Goldberg, A. (1986a). The wishy-washy personality. *Contemporary Psychoanalysis*, *22*, 357–374.
Goldberg, A. (1986b). [Reply to the discussion of "The wishy-washy personality."] *Contemporary Psychoanalysis*, *22*, 387–388.
Goldberg, A. (1986c). Non omnis moriar. *Psychoanalytic Inquiry*, *6*, 479–491.
Guntrip, H. (1961). *Personality structure and human interaction*. New York, NY: International Universities Press.
Holt, R. R. (1976). Drive or wish? A reconsideration of the psychoanalytic theory of motivation. In M. M. Gill & P. S. Holzman (Eds.), *Psychology versus metapsychology*. New York, NY: International Universities Press.
Klein, G. (1976). Freud's two theories of sexuality. In M. M. Gill and P. S. Holzman (Eds.), *Psychology versus metapsychology*. New York, NY: International Universities Press. (Original work published 1969)
Klein, M. & Tribich, D. (1981). Kernberg's object-relations theory: A critical evaluation *International Journal of Psycho-Analysis*, *62*, 27–43.
Kohut, H. (1971). *The analysis of the self.* New York, NY: International Universities Press.
Kohut, H. (1977). *The restoration of the self.* New York, NY: International Universities Press.
Kohut, H. (1984). *How does analysis cure?* Chicago, IL: University of Chicago Press.
Lachmann, F. M. and Beebe, B. (1988, November). *On the formation of psychic structure in the transference*. Presented at a meeting of the Southern California Psychoanalytic Association.
Leavy, S. A. (1983). The image and the word: Further reflections on Jacques Lacan. In J.H. Smith and W.K. Kerrigan (Eds.), *Interpreting Lacan* (Psychiatry and the Humanities, Vol. 6). New Haven, CT: Yale University Press.
Levenson, E. (1983). *The ambiguity of change*. New York, NY: Basic Books.
Loewald, H. (1978). Instinct theory, object relations and psychic structure formation. *Journal of the American Psychoanalytic Association*, *26*, 493–506.
Marx, K. (1906). *Capital: A critique of political economy*. New York, NY: Modern Library. (Original work published 1867)

Mitchell, S. A. (1983). Reflections on the difficulties of teaching interpersonal psychoanalysis. *Contemporary Psychoanalysis*, *19*, 133–140.

Modell, A. H. (1984). *Psychoanalysis in a new context.* New York, NY: International Universities Press.

Modell, A. H. (1986). The missing elements in Kohut's cure. *Psychoanalytic Inquiry*, *6*, 367–385.

Moore, A. T. (1984). Unique individuality redeemed. *Contemporary Psychoanal*ysis, *20*, 1–33.

Pearce, J. and Newton, S. (1963). *The conditions of human growth.* New York, NY: Citadel Press.

Racker, H. (1968). *Transference and countertransference.* New York, NY: International Universities Press.

Rapoport, D. (1960). Structure of psychoanalytic theory. *Psychological Issues*, *2*, 1–158.

Rickman, J. (1957). *Selected contributions to psychoanalysis.* New York, NY: Basic Books.

Rubens, R. L. (1984). The meaning of structure in Fairbairn. *International Journal of Psycho-Analysis*, *11*, 429–440.

Sandler, J. (1981). Unconscious wishes and human relationships. *Contemporary Psychoanalysis*, *17*, 180–196.

Silone, I. (1955, Winter). On the choice of comrades. *Dissent*, *2*, 7–19.

Searles, H. F. (1979). *Countertransference and related subjects.* New York, NY: International Universities Press.

Stern, D. N. (1986). *The interpersonal world of the infant.* New York, NY: Basic Books.

Stolorow, R. D. (1986a). Clinical reflections on the theory of self psychology: An inside view. *Psychoanalytic Inquiry*, *6*, 387–402.

Stolorow, R. D. (1986b). On experiencing an object: A multidimensional perspective. In A. Goldberg (Ed.), *Progress in self psychology* (Vol. II). New York, NY: International Universities Press.

Stolorow, R. D., Brandchaft, B., & Atwood, G. E. (1987). *Psychoanalytic treatment: An intersubjective approach.* Hillsdale, NJ: Analytic Press.

Sullivan, H. S. (1938). Editoria. *Psychiatry*, *1*, 135–143

Sullivan, H. S. (1953). *Conceptions of modern psychiatry.* New York, NY: Norton. (Original work published 1940)

Sullivan, H. S. (1953). *Interpersonal theory of psychiatry.* New York, NY: Norton.

Winnicott, D. W. (1965). Ego distortion in terms of true and false self. In *The maturational processes and the facilitating environment.* New York, NY: International Universities Press. (Original work published 1960)

Winnicott, D. W. (1969). The use of an object. *International Journal of Psycho-Analysis*, *50*, 711–716.

Winnicott, D. W. (1971). *Playing and Reality.* London, UK: Tavistock.

Wolstein, B. (1987). Anxiety and the psychic center of the psychoanalytic self. *Contemporary Psychoanalysis*, *23*, 631–658.

Chapter 2

Surrender and self-discovery

Ghent's reflections on the "force for growth" and what impedes it

Jessica Benjamin

This essay contains many of Mannie Ghent's most original and radical insights, but it also expresses the unique form of his thought process: a blend of his own far-reaching aesthetics and passionate convictions with the more recognizable clinical thinking of other psychoanalysts. To begin with, I should note that I was in analysis with Mannie during the period when he conceived this essay and first presented it at the New York University Postdoctoral Psychology Program, where I was also a candidate. I read the paper in a copy of its typescript version, and remember the elegantly penned (with real ink) cursive comments written on its margins. At that time, Mannie was practically alone among the institute faculty in his interest in Winnicott, and the paper represented as much his integration of Winnicott's theory of false self as it did his other passionate interest in Buddhism and Eastern philosophy. The idea of regression we now associate with Winnicott's version of psychoanalysis was not well accepted, and most interpersonalists and Freudians alike (the two orientations in our analytic program) were inclined to see it as destructive rather than healing. The notion of regression that seemed to be in play here was one that would allow in Balint's (1969/1979) sense a "new beginning," and at the same time correspond to surrender in its Eastern sense as liberation or transcendence.

The signature idea, which I absorbed from what Mannie said as well as how he wrote about it, was that of the ever-ready look-alike, something that both represents and conceals a suppressed longing by producing a facsimile version of it. Or, as he expressed it so evocatively, the "defensive mutant" (p. 111). This idea, as in the statement that we often see need masked by neediness, appeared in different form in his paper on Paradox and Process. The equally powerful conviction Mannie articulated was that the analyst needs to *recognize* this longing in its disguised form, and find a way to enable the patient to bear the pain of this realization of what was hidden yet pressing to be known. In this sense, surrender was of the essence in clinical work, because surrender meant giving over to this realization and the dread it aroused in the presence of the analyst—not out of any form of acquiescence or compliance with the analyst's idea of what lies within, but out of one's own sense of truth. Although Mannie is careful to not say exactly what it is we surrender to but to admonish that it is certainly not a giving over to the other person, the analyst, both experientially and in my reading of the text I have the impression that what I am describing as "one's own truth" may approximate what he had in mind. This idea was expressed by reference to Winnicott's idea of the true self experience which the false self, a protector caretaker self, conceals through a way of living that involves adaptation and compliance to one's external or inner object world. Rather than living authentically through a sense of one's own agency or desire, the self has been in the course of development discouraged and despairing of such authentic life. Hence the yearning to be known might first be made manifest in its very opposite, in a renewed effort to engage in submission or masochistic fantasies or actions, in relation to the analyst himself (or herself).

The task Mannie set himself in this work, one which has resonated with new generations of clinicians who themselves perhaps identified with this struggle to liberate themselves from forms of compliance that denied their own truth, was to show how we psychoanalysts could find our way through this paradox, through the defenses or resistance, that we might contact the "'force' of growth." This entailed being able to anticipate and identify how the impulse toward growth might hide behind a renewed exercise of compliance, that is to say, masochism. It was in this sense that masochism represented a perversion or distortion of something else, something truer. And at the same time, to underscore along with Winnicott the idea that a certain form of regression would make it possible for the caretaker to be "handed over" to the analyst (Winnicott, 1954/1975). To use a metaphor from one patient's dream, if the patient's concern was to get the message through the enemy lines, the analyst had to be alert and able to spot the messenger snaking his way in the dark through the barbed wire without being outlined by the enemy spotlights, if not actually to serve as a guide. It seems to me that Mannie was, following Milner (1969), implying that we analysts had to become more deeply in touch ourselves with how the force of growth would *drive* a person to break through false adaptations but also create chaos, indeed breakdown.

Here we come to the next important move in this remarkable thought process, one that loops back to tie in Winnicott's (1974) now well-known "Fear of Breakdown" and grant the fact that the masochism of some patients not only expresses an aborted need to hand over the caretaker self but also an annihilation anxiety that veritably cries out for containing and holding. In other words, thinking in terms of the wish to give over to a powerful other who can hold tightly to the person who feels she is fragmenting or breaking into bits bears an important resemblance to the self-psychological formulation that masochism represents an effort to restore self-cohesion. Mannie, however, wanted to stress in addition that, paradoxically, the dissolution of self may be sought and not only feared as a way to heal and make whole a nascent self. He thought that not only do early trauma and deprivation lead to a lack of a stable, cohesive self, but they also lead to the development of a false compliant self, which becomes a kind of iron mask, hard to get out of in order to start again. In this sense, he thought that there was a difficult and complex question of whether a person might be seeking an opportunity to re-experience breakdown in order to heal from it, and how would we be able to distinguish that dread of surrender from the actually intolerable feeling of fragmentation.

Some of the more useful understanding Mannie contributes here is transmitted through his illustrations of how patients may cast the analyst in the complementary role of sadist, seeing his power as the real occasion for activating the patient's dread. Here, to my way of thinking, we confront the patient's propensity to experience everything in the mode of complementarity, and so the patient's feeling that the analyst must be inspiring this dread of submission becomes only a specific case of the analyst being the "doer" in the complementarity of "doer and done to" (Benjamin, 2004). The reversible nature of this complementarity is something Mannie seeks to explore by turning the coin over and looking at the way in which not only masochism but sadism represents the alienation of the wish for a true experience of the self—in this case, in terms of what Winnicott called object usage. In other words, it is necessary to look at the equally significant theme of fearing destructiveness as the only alternative to the false life of compliance. Mannie, following the logic of Winnicott's thought, goes on to show how living a false or unreal life is not merely the result of defending against the possibility of breakdown or self-dissolution, which, we might say, is only one side of the coin. The other side is the failure to develop faith, because life has only been experienced in the mode of reactivity—passive responses to impingement. The patient has not ever successfully experienced the action of destroying the object and having the object survive—in other words, finding the externality of the other as more than a bundle of projections by virtue of the other surviving. This means that the patient has come "to feel that he or she is destructive" (p. 124) and therefore is fearful of any assertion. Or, as Mannie suggests, the patient her or himself, feeling destructive, becomes involved in a "perversion of object usage" (p. 124) that involves controlling the other, much as masochism involved a perversion of surrender. Strikingly, Mannie takes this idea of the complement of surrender as the "desire to deeply know, penetrate, discover the other … to dive deeply into the other" (p. 125). This radical formulation of the reciprocity of the desire to know and be known is, to my mind, an extremely important outcome of this investigation of surrender, pointing to the mutuality of knowing and the necessity of being both able to use the object to overcome fear of the other and surrender, "in which both survive the use" (p. 126) and have gone beyond fear to love. What is suggested here seems to be that both partners engage in the mutuality of surrender.

It is not clear to me how much Mannie meant to say here about how the analyst him or herself surrenders. It seems implicit in what he writes at the end of this essay about Milner coming to accept and recognize the patient who was denying her analyst's right to protect her properly, wanting to create a mess. This "good-enough" analyst, who Mannie says carried the young girl "over the tortuous path from object relating to object usage," in fact seems to be able, in her perspicacity, to surrender in the sense that she "treads softly" on the patient's dreams or, in other cases, the masochism and submission through which longings are disguised (pp. 130–131). In his closing lines Mannie speaks of the transition from object relating to object usage as involving a risk for the infant or patient, and in this sense "a degree of surrender on the part of the facilitating caretaker, or later analyst" (p. 134).

It is not unusual nowadays to hear relational authors citing this essay when they wish to talk about the surrender not of the patient but the analyst. In fact, if I can judge by my own readings, there are many more discussions of the latter than the former. I, having also been moved in this direction, wrote an essay for Mannie's seventy-fifth birthday celebration, which became a longer essay (Benjamin, 2004), developing speculations about what it is we surrender to, and suggesting the idea of surrendering to the Third. In a sense, I was then experimenting with taking the idea of surrender as a jumping off point to get to an idea of the space of thirdness, which serves—like ideas of God, or love, or truth, or being true to the self—as a way to let go of the oppositional/compliant form of relating that Mannie saw as the result of impingement. The idea was that if both persons surrender, or are able to find themselves in the space of thirdness, then the impasses and struggles that arise from defensive "false" relating can be transcended. This bi-directional idea of surrender seemed to me to solve the problem that is left open in this work, that is, the problem of how the relationship with the analyst can create the safety and holding that will allow the patient to feel contained without being controlled by him or her, to thus let go with less fear of falling into bits. The question associated with this pertains to the idealization of the analyst, and how this can become a source of safety rather than submission. I don't know if dealing with this question felt like a can of worms best left unopened, but I do know that there is one interesting omission in the text. When citing Rilke's (1912/1939) poem, Mannie left out the lines of the stanza right before "For Beauty is nothing but beginning of terror that we are just able to bear, and why we adore it is because it serenely disdains to destroy us …" (p. 21). The lines are, "Who if I cried would hear me among the order of angels? And even if one of them suddenly pressed me against his heart I should dissolve in his mightier being." What happens when the analyst is felt to be this angel, wonderful and terrible, liberating and frightening, is something Mannie hints at but does not fully "embrace" in this essay, leaving us with questions about submission, love and adoration in the transference.

In light of this omission, I will take the liberty of suggesting that, in one sense only, we might read this essay with a bit of skepticism. This relates to my suspicion that Mannie himself might have held back because of his own discouragement by the psychoanalytic climate in that era. Even as he describes Eigen's powerful sense that some patients need to withdraw to a place deep inside the self, to contact something true, silent and inviolable (Winnicott, 1954), something "intensely alive and active" (Eigen, 1973, p. 497), "many therapists would be frightened by this ..." (Ghent, 1990, p. 115). I wonder if Mannie's sense of the powerful force of growth in the patient was more radical than many of his colleagues because he felt this vital force needed to be present in the analyst, as it was in him, as well. So I am tempted to question Mannie's statement that the analyst, like the guru, is only "an excuse, an ally for true self to come forth" (Ghent, 1990, p. 112). We know that gurus are often adored, as are analysts. But at the very least, a patient might well want and need a guide, the term he also used, more than an excuse or even an ally— a guide is supposed to have some familiarity with the terrain, and know where many of the pitfalls lie, even to encourage us when the going gets rough. Now, I suspect that most of those analysts who were in analysis with Mannie would attest that, at least at certain moments, he strongly conveyed that his third ear, the ear of an accomplished musician, could distinguish the hollow or flat notes of the false self, so the player might wish to take that again and see if she or he could get a little more in tune with her or himself. In plain language, but in a voice mellifluous and calming, he might have gently asked, what did the little boy or girl feel or want to say right then? Mannie's own prescient knowledge of affect regulation, attuning to sound and gesture, certainly made surrender seem more possible. We relational analysts who think more explicitly in terms of both patient's and analyst's surrender are enormously indebted to the path he cleared for us.

References

Balint, M. (1979). *The basic fault: Therapeutic aspects of regression*. London, UK: Tavistock (original work published 1969).

Benjamin, J. (2004). Beyond doer and done to: An intersubjective view of thirdness. *Psychoanalytic Quarterly*, *73*(1), 5–46.

Eigen, M. (1973). Abstinence and the schizoid ego. *International Journal of Psychoanalysis*, *54*(4), 493–498.

Ghent, E. (1990). Masochism, submission, surrender: Masochism as a perversion of surrender. *Contemporary Psychoanalysis*, *26*(1), 108-136

Milner, M. (1969). *The hands of the living God*. New York, NY: International Universities Press.

Rilke, R. M. (1939). *Duino elegies* (J. B. Leishman & S. Spender, Transl.). New York, NY: Norton (original work published 1912–1922).

Winnicott, D. W. (1974). Fear of breakdown. *International Review of Psychoanalysis*, *1*, 103–107.

Winnicott, D. W. (1975). Metapsychological and clinical aspects of regression within the psycho-analytical set-up. In *Through paediatrics to psycho-analysis* (pp. 278–294). New York, NY: Basic Books (original work published 1954).

Masochism, submission, surrender: Masochism as a perversion of surrender[1]

Emmanuel Ghent

Surrender, in striking contrast to masochism, is a word that is seldom encountered in the psychoanalytic literature, and even then it often bears an ambiguous meaning. My goal in this paper is to give the term a certain clarity of definition and to study its relation to submission and masochism, which I regard as antitheses to surrender. In order to span the full compass of the meaning I give to surrender, my plan is to broaden the scope implied by the title and touch on some other issues that are related to surrender: object usage (Winnicott, 1969/1971) and its perversion in the form of sadism, creativity, and the apperception of threatening meaning.

Let me say at the outset that by masochism I mean all that is customarily intended by the term including both its sexual and characterological meanings. By perversion I mean something akin to distortion, corruption, diversion, misconstruction. The meaning I will give to the term "surrender" has nothing to do with hoisting a white flag; in fact, rather than carrying a connotation of defeat, the term will convey a quality of liberation and expansion of the self as a corollary to the letting down of defensive barriers. I hope the meaning of surrender, in its most inclusive sense, will gradually reveal itself as we encounter it in a variety of contexts. Nor am I convinced that "surrender" is the right word for what I would like to convey. Alternative words will crop up from time to time and perhaps help give form to the conception.

The thrust of this paper is not to challenge or discredit the vast literature on masochism and the ever sharpening insight into its psychic functions and meanings, but to attempt to illumine the shroud of mystery that still hangs over this curious human phenomenon—the seeking out of submission, pain or adversity—by drawing attention to another dimension that in my view plays a major and often deeply buried role in its varied expressions.

By way of circling around the meaning of surrender I would like first to draw upon a paper by Michael Eigen (1981), a remarkable analysis of the work of Winnicott, Lacan and Bion in which he locates a dimension of faith that underlies some of their most basic conceptions. "By the *area of faith*," Eigen says, "I mean to point to a way of experiencing which is undertaken with one's whole being, all out, 'with one's heart, with one's soul, and with all one's might.'" Faith, surrender, the beginnings of creativity and symbol formation all intersect in the world of transitional experiencing "when the infant lives through a faith that is prior to a clear realization of self and other differences."

Later, with object usage, there comes a new awakening in which "the core sense of creativeness that permeates transitional experiencing is reborn on a new level, insofar as genuine not-me nutriment becomes available for personal use" (Eigan, 1981). One might imagine the subject saying to the object, "I went all out, completely vulnerable, in the faith [or surrender] that someone was out there—and it turned out to be true, as I could only have known by destroying you with all my might, and yet here you are. I love you."

Throughout this paper I imply that there is, however deeply buried or frozen, a longing for something in the environment to make possible the surrender, in the sense of yielding, of false self. "For this to occur," Winnicott (1954/1975) says, there must be "a belief in the possibility of a correction of the original failure represented by a latent capacity for regression." Here, regression and surrender are close relatives.

In describing the course of an analysis, Winnicott (1954/1975) wrote, "The false self gradually became a 'caretaker self,' and only after years could a caretaker self become handed over to the analyst, the self surrender to the ego. ... The theory is being put forward of regression as part of the healing[2] process" (p. 281). The yearning for surrender of this false self is emphasized by Winnicott: "The organization that makes regression useful has this quality distinct from the other defense organizations in that it carries with it *the hope of a new opportunity* (italics mine) for an unfreezing ..." (Winnicott, 1954/1975). My point here has been to highlight the centrality, despite its buried secrecy, of a *longing* for the birth, or perhaps re-birth, of true self.

As tags of meaning begin to attach to our notion of surrender, it seems to take on the sense of being in some way the obverse of resistance. Resistance is the name given to motivational forces operating against growth or change and in the direction of maintenance of the status quo. Surrender might be thought of as reflective of some “force” towards growth, for which, interestingly, no satisfactory English word exists. Submission, on the other hand, either operates in the service of resistance, or is at best adaptive as an expedient. The superstructure of defensiveness, the protections against anxiety, shame, guilt, anger are, in a way, all deceptions, whether they take the form of denial, splitting, repression, rationalizations, evasions. Is it possible that deep down we long to give this up, to “come clean,” as part of an even more general longing to be known, recognized? Might this longing also be joined by a corresponding wish to know and recognize the other? As to the developmental origins of such longings I would locate them as being rooted in the primacy of object-seeking as a central motivational thrust in humans.

To develop further the meaning of surrender, some features that characterize it may be enumerated:

1. It does not necessarily require another person’s presence, except possibly as a guide. One may surrender “in the presence of another,” not “to another” as in the case of submission.
2. Surrender is not a voluntary activity. One cannot choose to surrender, though one can choose to submit. One can provide facilitative conditions for surrender but cannot make it happen.
3. It may be accompanied by a feeling of dread and death, and/or clarity, relief, even ecstasy.
4. It is an experience of being “in the moment,” totally in the present, where past and future, the two tenses that require “mind” in the sense of secondary processes, have receded from consciousness.
5. Its ultimate direction is the discovery of one’s identity, one’s sense of self, one’s sense of wholeness, even one’s sense of unity with other living beings. This is quite unlike submission in which the reverse happens: one feels one’s self as a puppet in the power of another; one’s sense of identity atrophies.
6. In surrender there is an absence of domination and control; the reverse is true in the case of submission.
7. It is easily confused with submission and often confounded with it for exploitative purposes. Certainly in life they are often found together. Considering the central thesis of this paper, that submission be viewed

as a defensive mutant of surrender, this juxtaposition should not be surprising. (Nonetheless they are intrinsically very different.)

8. The distinction I am making between surrender and submission helps clarify another pair that are often confused. Resignation accompanies submission; it is heavy and lugubrious. Acceptance can only happen with surrender. It transcends the conditions that evoked it. It is joyous in spirit and, like surrender, it happens; it cannot be made to happen.

In the West surrender has meant "defeat." In the East it has meant transcendence, liberation. In the West "ego," as used in the vernacular, has meant one's strength, rationality, a very close relative, until recently, of one's self. In the East "ego" has meant maya, (dream, the illusion of one's self), a concept close to Lacan's "the Imaginary" or Winnicott's "unit self" world of identifications and projections, or Fairbairn's closed inner world. The goal in all of these systems is the awakening from the "dream world." In the East, to quote Heinrich Zimmer (1954), "the primary concern—in striking contrast to the interest of modern philosophers of the West—has always been, not information but transformation, a radical changing of man's nature and ... a renovation of his understanding both of the outer world and of his own existence." Perhaps we see vestiges of this distinction in the schism between analysts whose emphasis is informational (insight is what cures) as against those for whom the focus is transformational (with cure comes insight). Seen in this light the controversial "short hour" of Lacan acquires new meaning, its intent and sometimes effect being to at least momentarily awaken the analysand from the world of the Imaginary, the dream ... and perhaps provide a glimpse of something closer to the Real.

It has been said that there are no gurus, only disciples. The guru an illusion—an illusion which permits the disciple to yield, surrender false self, and therein have a chance at finding himself. The process may be thought of as allowing the disciple to re-enter the exhilarating world of transitional experiencing—wherein the guru is the transitional object. The "ego," false self, and "mind" want to argue; the guru won't argue. He knows that all engagement at this level reinforces the strength of the "ego" (false self). Surrender in this sense does not need a guru. The indirect object of the surrender could as well be a tree, the sun, God ... anything or anyone that will not impinge with its own "ego." The process is what is important; the object to whom one surrenders is irrelevant. However, because we are so impressed by our "ego," we need to find something or someone who so totally transcends our experience, whose presence is so total and affirming that we will take a chance on surrendering. Hence the guru, and in a different world, the analyst. He is an excuse, an ally for true self to come forth.

For most of us in the West this notion of surrender is something so foreign as to be barely comprehensible. Perhaps a detour into the world of art or creativity in general will serve as a bridge to grope into the meaning of surrender as distinguished from submission. Marion Milner (1957), in paraphrasing Jacques Maritain (1953), says that "any 'explanation' of art which is only in terms of the context of repressed wishes ... leaves out what is essential ... to art. It leaves out this deliberately fostered getting in touch with, not just hidden wishes but *a different way of functioning* (italics added); and a way of functioning which is essential if something new is to be created."

In her book, *On Not Being Able to Paint*, Milner (1950/1957) drew attention to another phenomenon that I would include under the umbrella of meaning provided by the word surrender. She speaks of "the blanking out of ordinary consciousness when one is able to break free from the familiar and allow a new unexpected entity to appear." One's ordinary sense of self seems temporarily to have disappeared. Composers often have the feeling that the musical idea comes from some source external to themselves; Mozart said he was not a composer, merely an amanuensis to God. This subjective "blanking out" as in the so-called oceanic feeling, or as "emptiness," the beneficent state of being that is at the center of the *Tao*, have been likened by analysts to the state of blissful satisfaction at mother's breast. Milner goes on to ask if these may not also reflect an essential part of the creative process, not just of painting, but of living: "May they not be moments in which there is a plunge into no-differentiation which results (if all goes well) in a re-emerging into a new division of the me-not-me ...?"

I have already hinted at the notion that these phenomena that I am encompassing as surrender are not mere descriptions of a particular way of functioning, but are as well characterized by a quality of need, mostly operating out of awareness, yet seemingly with a relentlessness that is not easy to account for in traditional psychoanalytic terms. By "need" I am not implying that there is something like an inborn instinct for the integration of self. My view rather is that in normal development the most primitive functions and needs of the infant, when adequately responded to and interacted with by the environing others, give rise to ever more sophisticated and complex conative structures, which later we recognize as having the valence or motivational quality of need. Milner (1969), too, seems to imply something akin to a need, when towards the end of her deeply compelling book, *The Hands of the Living God*, she concludes, "Certainly, some patients seemed to be aware, dimly or increasingly, of a *force* in them to do with growth, growth towards their own shape, also as something that seemed to be sensed as *driving them* to break down false inner organizations which do not really belong to them; something which can also be deeply feared, as a kind of creative fury that will not let them rest content with a merely compliant adaptation; and also feared because of the temporary chaos it must cause when the integrations on a false basis are in process of being broken down in order that a better one may emerge" (italics added) (pp. 384–385).

We are left with many questions: Is this phenomenon a different kind of integrative force? If so, what is its nature, and what are its antecedents in the developing human? My hunch is that there is something like a universal need, wish or longing for what I am calling surrender and that it assumes many forms. In some societies there are culturally sanctioned occasions for its realization in the form of ecstatic rituals and healing trances. In other societies, perhaps most notably in Japan where the psychology of *amae*[3] is so central to one's way of being, something akin to surrender is experienced as almost universally desired and desirable. In many people in our own culture the wish for surrender remains buried; in some it is expressed in creative and productive ways, and in others its derivatives appear in pathological form, deflected away from normal channels by that most unwelcome price-tag: dread. I suspect further that this dread is something that we have encountered in other contexts and have conceptualized as annihilation anxiety, dread of dissolution, ego fragmentation and so on. Perhaps what I am saying is that just as in so many other aspects of living, where there is a dread, so, too, there is a wish, a longing, however disguised its expression may be. Poets have captured in a line or two what takes the rest of us pages of gropings to contact. Rilke (1912/1939, p. 21) confides in us about his experience of surrender when he writes

> ... For Beauty's nothing
> but beginning of Terror we're still just able to bear,
> and why we adore it so is because it serenely disdains to destroy us.

The intimate relation between dread and wish is as old as psychoanalysis. Guntrip (1969) spoke of ego dissolution in two seemingly opposite ways; it reflected the deepest dread and at the same time was inseparable from the ultimate longing of the frozen-in true self to be discovered. Eigen (1973) noticed with surprise how a number of patients had spontaneously undertaken periods of profound abstinence for the sake of their personal development.

> It was as though a reaction to the over-stimulating pleasure orientation had begun to set in. ... The practical-social milieu was viewed increasingly as lacking in crucial respects and discounted as a place one could want to take root in. Neither people nor things seemed any longer to offer the promise, pleasure or satisfaction 'similar' patients just some years before had compulsively sought. ... The process took place "blindly" and was often frightening. Most generally, patients felt they were being drawn down out of the world as though by a magnet towards a sense of self they knew they had at bottom. ... Often a state of seemingly endless, painful emptiness preceded the clear experiencing of this I-kernel.
>
> (pp. 493–494)

Many therapists would be frightened by this, viewing it as either depression or withdrawal or even a heralding of psychosis. As I understand it, however, what Eigen is describing is a phase in successful analysis when the patient begins to get in touch with what Winnicott (1965) referred to as that "true, silent, inviolable self, beyond all usual communication with the outside world." The self structure described by Eigen (1973), unlike the regressed ego of Guntrip, is "intensely alive and active. ... It is experienced in an aura of power. ... The respite here is not passivity in the womb, not a sleep, but an active seeing stillness, compact and electrifying."

The main hypothesis of this paper is that it is this passionate longing to surrender that comes into play in at least some instances of masochism. Submission, losing oneself in the power of the other, becoming enslaved in one or other way to the master, is the ever available lookalike to surrender. It holds out the promise, seduces, excites, enslaves, and in the end, cheats the seeker-turned-victim out of his[4] cherished goal, offering in its place only the security of bondage and an ever amplified sense of futility. By substituting the appearance and trappings of surrender for the authentic experience, an agonizing, though at times temporarily exciting, masquerade of surrender occurs: a self-negating submissive experience in which the person is enthralled by the other. The intensity of the masochism is a living testimonial of the urgency with which some buried part of the personality is screaming to be exhumed. This is not to be minimized as an expression of the longing to be healed, although so often we bear witness to its recurring miscarriage.

Having put forth a substantial portion of my thesis, it now feels essential to place it in perspective. The literature on masochism is vast and this is clearly not the place for a critical review. In the early years of psychoanalysis masochism was seen essentially as an expression of drive derivatives, or as a superego phenomenon (Freud, 1924). Later, based on the work of Reich (1933/1949), Horney (1935), Berliner (1947), Menaker (1953) among others, it was seen as a defensive reaction of the ego. Brenman (1952) showed how masochism served a multiplicity of functions at the same time. Stolorow and Lachmann (1980) add yet another function: that "masochistic activities may ... represent abortive (and sometimes primitively sexualized) efforts to restore and maintain the structural cohesion, temporal stability, and positive affective coloring of a precarious or crumbling self representation" (p. 30). The formulation I am suggesting is not intended to replace others but to add a depth of focus to them. It has a paradoxical relation to the self-psychology formulation in that it implies in the long run a strengthening, a wholling of the self; on the other hand, it implies that a surrender, a controlled dissolution of self-boundaries is at times *sought*, not only feared; that the masochistic phenomena are symptoms of the derailment or distortion of a wish, not just the defense against a fear. As in Eigen's (1981) formulation about *The Area of Faith in Winnicott, Lacan and Bion*, there is a tone of sought-after vitality and joy, rather than escape from doom.

Masochistic phenomena have often been traced to deprivation, traumata and developmental interferences suffered in the early preoedipal years. Stolorow and Lachmann (1980, pp. 30–31) suggest that these early traumata would also leave their mark by interfering with the development of a cohesive and stable self-representation. The masochistic tendency then would serve to shore up the lack of cohesion of the self. An alternative view might be that in response to these early traumata a false self based on compliance is built up. This eventuates in a continuing longing to surrender this false self in the hope of a "new beginning" (Balint, 1968). Any movement in this direction would likely lead to the re-experience of the mortification and annihilation anxiety that first led to the development of the false self. One might expect a certain "invitation" of masochism and a submissive attitude, "mistaking" submission for surrender, since submission, as in the perversion of surrender, is the closest the person has likely come to knowing about surrender. Winnicott (1974), in *The Fear of Breakdown*, threw further light on what I am generically calling the longing to surrender. In effect, he identified the fear of breakdown as really being the fear of re-experiencing, and the wish to re-experience, the breakdown that has already occurred so early in life that it cannot be remembered. I will deal with this more fully in connection with the role of surrender in the apperception of meaning.

An appropriate question arises from this mélange of masochism and surrender. What are the roots in experience that eventuate in this clinical picture? Perhaps a partial answer is to be found in an earlier paper by Winnicott (1950–55/1975, pp. 211 ff.) a study on what he called motility and what we might now call activity, or assertiveness. He described three patterns. In one, the healthy pattern, through motility the world outside the baby is constantly being discovered and re-discovered so that contact with the environment is an experience of the individual. Only under these conditions may the individual start to exist. In the second pattern the environment impinges on the baby and instead of a series of individual experiences there is a series of reactions to impingement. Under these circumstances, only withdrawal allows an individual existence.

> In a third pattern, which is extreme, this is exaggerated to such a degree that there is not even a resting place for individual experience, and the result is a failure in the primary narcissistic state to evolve an individual. The "individual" then develops as an extension of the shell rather than of the core, and as an extension of the impinging environment. … The individual then exists by not being found.

> In the second and third patterns it is only through environmental impingement that the motility potential becomes a matter or experience. Here is ill health. To a lesser or greater degree the individual must be opposed and only if opposed [I would add: or imposed upon] does the individual tap the important motility source. This is satisfactory while environment consistently impinges, but environmental impingement must continue … and must have a pattern of its own, else chaos reigns, since the individual cannot develop a personal pattern.

For our purposes, what bears emphasis is that in the second and third pattern the individual or "non-individual" that has developed in an atmosphere of impingement has a continuing need for environmental impingement. I believe Winnicott is identifying here at least one source of the masochistic syndrome, pointing to the need for patterned impingement. Is this a euphemism suggestive of a need to be the object of sadistic experience? "Impingement" is not far from "penetration." The deeper yearning, which remains invisible behind compulsive masochistic activity (in itself needed to forestall chaos or disintegration), is the longing to be reached and known, in an accepting and safe environment. The individual then becomes free to use his or her own motility to discover and be discovered in such a way that contact with the environment can become an "experience of the individual."

Fantasies of being raped can have all manner of meanings, often superimposed. Among them, in my clinical experience, one will almost always find, sometimes deeply buried, a yearning for what I am calling surrender. Erotic fantasies in relation to the analyst (usually, but by no means only, in the case of a female patient with male analyst) or the wish to make love with the analyst so very often turns out to have as its root the intense longing to surrender in the sense of giving over, yielding the defensive superstructure, being known, found, penetrated, recognized. The closest most of us come to the experience of surrender is in the moment of orgasm with a loved one. Little surprise it should be then for the sexual scene to be the desired focus for such letting-go. It is not primarily the sex that is longed for except as the vehicle for the glimpse of surrendered bliss that we are speaking of. Sometimes the roles are reversed and the fantasy is of the analyst's total surrender with the patient. This turns out ultimately to be a half-way house on the way to the ultimate longed-for goal of self-surrender and being known in one's nakedness. Often the erotic fantasies have a distinctly masochistic flavor, as, for example, in being forced, tricked, seduced into lovemaking, or being overpowered by the sheer masterfulness of the other. The masochistic expression here is the disguise, or what I am calling the perversion of the wish for surrender. If by mischance the analyst should enter into the patient's real world in sexual response, the masochism of the patient soon flourishes, and all hope of what the patient had really longed for, genuine surrender, is lost. The fantasy of rape is a foil for the disguised expression of the longing for surrender. Real rape, be it by the penis, or the "ego" (psychological rape, no matter how subtle), violently forecloses and, by not recognizing or not caring about the genuine longing, has deeply betrayed it. It is important to emphasize that I am not trying to reduce the entirety of an erotic transference to this dynamic; many other layers are often involved and have to be dealt with.

The sexual arena is not the only area where passionate, even ecstatic intensity lends itself to being a masochistic substitute for surrender. The excitement of recklessness or dangerous, near-death activities is another, as is the pull to manifest infantilism and helpless demandingness. Both of these quasi-masochistic configurations—and there are others—can be very intense and can function as disguised expression of the longing for surrender.

In the analytic situation this longing for, dread of, and pain in, surrender is most frequently first encountered in the defensive reactions that are designed to contain the impulse, a kind of compromise where the impulse is deflected and only appears in some disguised, distorted form. Sometimes the patient, experiencing the beginnings of the dread we are speaking of, attributes it to the dangerousness of the analyst, his or her intrusiveness, malevolence, empathic unresponsiveness, seductiveness. Often enough, some expressions of these features may well appear and even be fanned by an intensifying transference-countertransference interaction. An erotic transference may develop, or a paranoid transference, or masochistic or sadistic acting out, even a variety of negative therapeutic reaction. But what is common to all of these manifestations of the impulse towards, and dread of, surrender is some aspect of masochism.

Perhaps a few vignettes will illustrate what I mean by masochism as a perversion of surrender. A borderline young woman, exceedingly demanding, whiny, and manipulative, left the session with an involuntary smile saying, "That was a good session," implying that this time, in contrast to all others, I had not failed her. During the session I had remained firm but gentle against a barrage of demands and complaints. At one point I had said "You know, I somehow think that if you had your way you would feel deeply disappointed." She smiled involuntarily and after a long, very unwonted silence, said, "You mean if I win, I lose?" I said, "The part of you that's hiding, and we're trying to find, she's the loser." Another long silence. Next day her first words were, "You really got through to me" and then reported with much embarrassment, that after the session she had gone home, beat herself, forced a stick into her anus and masturbated with fantasies of being tortured. My understanding of the sequence was that she had felt her defensive barrier come down, there had been a glimpse into the possible existence of an undefended lovable self and with it the nascent excitement of a beginning surrender. Quickly the impulse to surrender had to be redefined in terms of false self, as its masochistic counterpart. Feeling reached, known, "gotten through to" was translated into 'penetrated' (in its ambiguous meaning) and beaten. A momentary new reality was translated back into the old familiar inner reality; the impulse to surrender (she had often said, "Please do not let me fool you") had to be experienced as its perversion, masochism.

A professional woman of 30 dreamed, "I am hiding under the table from what seems to be the forces of repression, Franco men. There is a man with a gun there. He had a black beard. I had to get a secret message, a very important message that concerned the secret location of our forces, to an older man. I was extremely nervous and did not think I would be able to do it; yet actually I did. Still I felt I had not done well enough." Among the various meanings reflected in the dream is the one that concerns us here: that the very impulse to be known, to get the vital message through to the analyst about her secret inner strength—this impulse had to be experienced in the context of pain and the dread of being killed or raped. It is as if this woman (as the masochist) needs the powerful force of violence, the fascist with the gun (that is, the image of the analyst as sadist), because only under his presence and force is she able to get the secret to the old man. In other words, "I have to invite danger and perhaps sex with the analyst, that is, be the masochist, in order to provide the cover for getting the secret message to the analyst, the wish to surrender and be known."

Masud Khan (1973/1979) makes the convincing point that "all perversions accrue from a symbiotic complicity between two persons, which is both unconscious and empathic." He then goes on to describe in his characteristically vivid style a young woman who had for years been in a state of inertia and depression. Slowly but surely she was won over by a man who tantalized, excited her to intense passion, and degraded her; in his power she felt totally helpless. Khan notes, however, how the relationship with the lover helped her exteriorize her psychic pain and her rage, and furthermore, initiated experience for her. He reflects on how the pervert has a great advantage over a therapist in being able to mobilize the "passive will" in a person inasmuch as he can initiate and execute experiences through his "active will." Nonetheless, the therapist is not without the exercise of his will and power, as manifested for example by the various demands made by the analytic setup, which, if not adhered to, the analyst treats as resistance.

During the course of therapy, this same patient began asking him frequent questions as to how she should behave in various social situations. When these went unanswered, the patient would withdraw into a state not unlike the original depressed, apathetic state that preceded the love affair. "Once I had decided to answer her questions," Khan observes, "what followed was very revealing. She would instantly accept and agree to what I said. But then she would *play around* (original italics) with what I had said: question and correct it until she would find the right solution for herself. I was very struck by her capacity to play with different possibilities of conduct, once I had suggested a course. If I abstained she would invariably go inert and become resourceless. This use of the analyst's will and power with which she could identify and internalize, proved extremely helpful to her." My reading of the situation is that the patient had identified with the analyst's power in the sense that she became the "active will," and he yielded (surrendered) to her initiative in such a way that there developed, to use Winnicott's words, "an area of play in the analytic situation" (Winnicott, 1968/1971).

Khan asks, "How was playing in the 'analytic contract' different for this patient from participating in 'games' that her lover had made her an accomplice to during her 'perverted contract?'" He then answers: "The crucial difference seemed to [lie] in the different *use* of the patient by her lover and by her analyst. … Her lover compelled her into the role of his 'subjective object.'" That is, he forced her to play a passive part in his inner drama.

> He had to devalue and disrupt all functions in her that gave her a separate identity and existence. ... What she had experienced was merely an intensely excited and passive surrender to his will. ... In the analytic contract, per contrast, she sought help to be enabled to find her own will and power in her life situation. The empathy she required was in the service of the actualization of her own capacities and functions towards personal autonomy.
>
> (p. 208)

To return to the theme of this presentation, I would describe her relation to her lover not at all as surrender but as that of submission, a pseudo-surrender, a masochistic object of the sadist. Anna Freud (1952) has diagnosed the emotional predicament in perversion formation as the dread of emotional surrender. It is surrender, in the sense I have defined, that the patient was longing for, the wish to be found, recognized, penetrated to the core, so as to become real, or as Winnicott put it in another context "to come into being."

In this case with the lover we witness the perversion of the process, where instead of the patient's autonomy being freed and her identity found, she becomes a captive puppet. With the analyst, on the other hand, a mild kind of surrender, again in the sense that I mean it, has occurred, incidentally on the part of the analyst as well as the patient, with the result that the patient feels found, enriched and more whole.

Sadism as a Perversion of Object Usage

It is difficult to do justice in a few paragraphs to Winnicott's concept of object usage (Winnicott, 1969/1971) as against object relating. Yet, as a preamble to the question whether there is a formulation for sadism analogous to the one I am proposing for masochism, it merits review. In transitional experiencing the mother allows, encourages, the infant to bathe in the illusion that she or some part of her is part of baby. With the evolution of creative play and the very gradual disillusion by the mother, the baby discovers and in effect, creates, bit by bit, both self and external reality. In object *relating* both self and other are perceived largely through projections and identifications. The self at this stage may be thought of as a "unit self" in that relating can be described in terms of an "isolate," the individual subject; the object then is the subjectively perceived object. The *use* of an object, object-usage, however takes object-relating for granted. New features enter that involve the nature and behavior of the object in external reality. "The object, if it is to be used, must necessarily be real in the sense of being part of shared reality, not a bundle of projections" (p. 88). Winnicott (p. 89) gives an almost diagrammatic example:

> Two babies are feeding at the breast; one is feeding on the self in the form of projections, and the other is feeding on (using) milk from a woman's breast. … The change does not come about automatically, by maturational process alone. … Mothers, like analysts, can be good or not good enough; some can and some cannot carry the baby over from relating to usage. [This transition] is the most difficult thing, perhaps, in human development … [and] the most irksome of all the early failures that come for mending. … The change [from relating to use] means that the subject destroys the object [as subjective object] and the object, if it survives destruction, is now real. … 'Hullo object!' 'I destroyed you.' 'I love you.' 'You have value for me because of your survival of my destruction of you.'

In effect, destruction has created the reality, placed the object outside the self. The word 'destruction' may seem out of place here in what might naively appear to be a piece of straightforward development. Yet it is needed "not because of the baby's impulse to destroy, but because of the object's liability not to survive" (Winnicott, 1969/1971). The varieties of non-survival include retaliation, withdrawal, defensiveness in any of its forms, as overall change in attitude in the direction of suspiciousness or diminished receptivity, and finally, a kind of crumbling, in the sense of its losing one's capacity to function adequately as mother, or in the analytic setting, as analyst.

This conception of development involving the difficult passage from object relating to object use implies a radical departure from the usual analytic notion that aggression is reactive to the encounter with external reality (the reality principle). Here it is destructiveness that creates the very quality of externality.

But the main reason for this discussion of the development of the capacity for object usage is to explore its relation to surrender, masochism, and now, sadism. The essence of both transitional experiencing and the transition into object usage is the heady and wonderful world of creative experiencing wherein self and other have the opportunity to become real. Failures in either or both of these developmental currents lead to the development of one or other variety of false self; from the baby's point of view they might well be called failures of faith.

A principal cause of failure in transitional experiencing is what has already been referred to as impingement by the caretaker. We have seen how this intrusiveness interferes with true experiencing or "coming into being," with the distressing result that for the infant to "exist," continuing impingement is required. Here we saw the beginnings of masochism. I have suggested also that in many people there is an impulse to surrender, perhaps in order to reengage that area of transitional experiencing, the miscarriage of which impulse or longing appears as masochism or submission.

I now suggest the possibility that failure of the transition from object relating to object usage would result from a different (but probably related) failure of the caretaker: retaliation, defensiveness, negativity on the part of the caretaker or crumbling of her or his effectiveness. In either case the triple misfortune is that the subjective object never becomes real but remains a bundle of projections, and externality is not discovered; as a corollary the subject is now made to feel that he or she *is* destructive; and finally, fear and hatred of the other develops, and with them, characterological destructiveness comes into being. In short we have the setting for the development of sadism (in what remains a unit self, a self as isolate), the need to aggressively control the other as a perversion of object usage, much as we have seen in masochism as a perversion of surrender. An excerpt from a session will perhaps add a little flesh and blood:

> I desperately want you to stay in control no matter how hard "the mouth with teeth" tries to destroy you—not destroy you as a person, but as a competent analyst. I need you to be strong, to never "explain" anything. If you explain, I feel it as defensive and, therefore I am back in control and I have forced you to defend yourself. The mouth that babbles on vindictively and vengefully needs to be allowed out and to be here. Don't tell him to give up control. He also wants to give up control but will do so only if he feels your strength not to be afraid of him in his full presence.

There is a reciprocity here—a wish for surrender (which in this excerpt reveals only hints at masochism), a plea for what we have been calling object usage, and an awareness that what now exists as biting sadism is a derivative of the wish to discover the reality of the other, and thereby truly experience the self.

Here we see an outreaching, penetrative version of surrender. Earlier we saw how a defensive mutation of the longing to be recognized, deeply known, penetrated, a desire for what might be called "receptive" surrender, becomes transformed into a seeming quest for submission, submergence of self. Now we come upon another version of surrender, the complement of the earlier variety. We see it here in the desire to deeply know, penetrate, discover the other. One might say that the longing is to dive deeply into the other, or in Winnicott's terms, "use" the other, and discover what might be called "true other" in contrast to the false other. False other corresponds either to the false image of the other or the false self of the other. If the other has not been destroyed in the process, false other turns out to be (or to have been) the false image or representation of the other. On the other hand, if the other was destroyed, rendered useless, then the false other corresponds in all probability to the false self of the other.

Use of an object is not a very felicitous expression, because it too closely resembles the vernacular "using the other as a sexual object," as well as "objectification." Perhaps better words to express Winnicott's meaning would be un-cover, dis-cover, penetrate. Unfortunately, except for "penetrate," these do not easily permit the ambiguity that "use" affords wherein attack may be the effect, although not at all the intended goal, which by contrast is to discover, or to un-cover the real other in lieu of the subjective other. We seem to need a word as a container of the meaning that resides in both aspects of the phenomenon under discussion, what might be called the autoplastic and the alloplastic versions of surrender. The lack of such a word points up the foreignness of these conceptions to our ordinary way of thinking. Perhaps this is an expression of the awkwardness in our own language of expressing the opposite of intentionality, a state of being that is not marked by active conscious goal seeking. Even in expressing this thought I seem to require locutions that frame it in terms of what it is not. Yet the frequency with which reference is made in the psychoanalytic literature to Keats' famous lines "on negative capability"

(Rosen, 1960), Green (1973), Hutter (1982), attests to its being a focus of some importance.

The sexual experience can be, for example, an instance where the meaning of surrender and object usage almost lose their distinctive meaning, and blend. On the surface it appears as though the woman is surrendered, and the man "using the object," that is, active. But in the kind of interaction we are speaking of, each is surrendered and one might say, involved in object usage, in the sense of un-covering, dis-covering the reality of the other.

In my view love and hate are not opposites. The real polarity is between love and fear. Only when there is no fear, love flourishes. When fear or anxiety is present, it often becomes manifest in a reactive and compensatory form as hatred (or indifference), with the result that love and hate (or love and indifference) appear to be the polarities. The successful use of the object, or being used by the object in the form of surrender, is one's bid at overcoming the fear of the other. Hence, the successful use and surrender, in which both survive the use and have therefore transcended fear of the other, are necessary precursors in the development of love. In fact, a deep sense of love is what is actually felt in either of these experiences.

The Apperception of Disorganizing Meaning

I would like now to shift focus and explore the relevance of our notion of surrender to another group of phenomena. The area I am looking at has to do with what might be called the apperception of disorganizing meaning, and has bearing on the so-called repetition compulsion and the question of identification. We encounter, daily, in our practice the phenomenon of a patient who can say, "my mother was sadistic," and describe events to nail down the assertion, and yet one has the impression that the patient ends up with the feeling of "but somehow I can't believe it's true." The patient seems not to have been able to "take in" the perception of what he or she has witnessed. It is as if the perception would shatter the prevailing belief system and induce chaos were a complete perceptual letting-go to occur, a surrender to the experience. A total revision of one's perception of, in this case, mother, would have to happen in which the image of mother being sadistic would reside alongside and integrated with other images of mother.

A brief illustration. Many years ago, while vacationing in the country, my 3-year-old niece noticed that my knee was scratched and bleeding slightly. She immediately said, "Oh! Blood! You have a cut. (slight pause). I'll go get you a band-aid. (slight pause). How did it happen?" I, jokingly: "We were playing in the sand and your mom pushed me!" She: "There's no cut. I don't see any blood." I: "That was just a joke; your mom didn't push me; I fell." She (greatly relieved): "That blood needs a band-aid." She immediately went off to fetch a band-aid. The story well illustrates that if a perception is threatening to a belief, either the belief or the perception has to go. In this case the idea that good mommy could cause harm to someone was so unacceptable that the perception, as long as it carried significance that would be disorganizing, had to be denied. In other words it could not be "taken in." In older children and adults a perception may be registered but its significance denied; we refer to this as the mechanism of isolation.

Another way of looking at this process is that the child's developing perceptual and cognitive skills probably outgrow the meanings he or she can safely take in. Surrender to "what is" would, in some instances, lead to a disorganizing, threatening state of being. A compromise develops, driven by the wish to surrender to the perception, and opposed by the threat it implies. The result is the masochistic solution; recurring situations are created in which each fresh opportunity for clarity is subverted by the dread, which by now is so shrouded in history as to feel nameless and "existential." Again, as we have seen earlier in our discussion of surrender, the dread and the wish are two sides of the same coin. The wish is to return to the scene of the dread and expresses not so much the wish "to master the experience" as to integrate the experience.

In effect, I am suggesting that some instances of masochism may be rooted in a deep quest for understanding, for undoing the isolation. It is as if with one mind the person is setting up situations in which he is "done in" or caused pain by the other, an authority, friend, lover, and with the other, is struggling with the inner question that remains tantalizingly unanswered: What happened? How did it happen? A loved one could not have done that to me! That is inconceivable. Then how did it happen? He did it! … but somehow I cannot "take it in." It just cannot be. Maybe next time I can create a situation that's more clear. … Then I will be able to "take it in, perceive, conceive it."

Masochism, rather than being an expression of some "aggressive drive turned inward" may, at least in some circumstances, be a distorted representation of what I have called the wish to surrender, or as in this context, to confront and "take in" the inner truth, to perceive self and other as they really are, that is, without regard to the false selves erected out of compliance to early authorities. This compulsion to repeat, masochistically, self-destructive behavior may turn out to be another form of trying to "take in" some reality, in this case the unthinkable destructiveness of a significant other. The act of "taking in" may involve a considerable degree of disorganization in order for this to be possible and, by analogy to the creative moment in art, it may mean that one has to give up, surrender the conventionalized "surface mind" view of an object, a tree or whatever, and allow the gestalt free "depth mind" (Ehrenzweig, 1953) to take over. This may mean a transition to a period of chaos in the "depth mind" before the new reality can be taken in and comprehended or expressed.

In discussing the negative therapeutic reaction, Esther Menaker (1969/1979, p. 90) touches on this very question even using the same expression, "take in." She writes, "the patient is faced with the single ultimate choice: will he choose growth or refuse it—can he *take in what is* (italics added), *permit the resultant disorganization of the status quo of the self … ?*" (original italics).

There is more yet to be said about this issue, the wish and dread of "taking in" experience. I am thinking of Winnicott's "axiom" (Davis and Wallbridge, 1981, p. 50) that "*The clinical fear of breakdown is the fear of breakdown that has already been experienced*" (Winnicott, 1974) (original italics). He asks,

> Why does the patient go on being worried by this that belongs to the past? The answer must be that the original experience of primitive agony cannot get into the past tense unless the ego can first gather it in [cf. "take it in"] to its own present time experience and into omnipotent control now (assuming the auxiliary ego-supporting function of the mother (analyst)). … In other words, the patient must go on looking for the past detail which is *not yet experienced*. This search takes the form of looking for this detail in the future.
>
> (p. 105)

Winnicott (1974) goes on to extend this fear of breakdown to related issues such as the fear of death (annihilation) and the feelings of emptiness and non-existence. He adds, "When Keats was 'half in love with easeful death' he was, according to the idea I am putting forward here, longing for the ease that would have come if he could 'remember' [or I would add, 'take in'] having died; but to remember he must experience death now."

"Beinglessness" was the word discovered recently by a patient as he was groping for the sensation that crept over him like death when no one was there to assuage the urgent needy feelings for someone to "fill him up," to continuously affirm his existence. "It looks like I need admiration," he said, "but that's not it; it's as if I need someone to keep telling me I'm alive—or else I sink into horror—just that horror that I could feel the beginnings of when the word 'beinglessness' came to me." As deep as the dread of that state, so too is the pull to revisit it, to dig around the edges of it. I am suggesting that by reaching into the is-ness of the circumstances that led to that horror, or the events that did not happen that might have otherwise brought him into being, he is unconsciously seeking a chance to come solidly into being. As the session in question came to a close the patient said, "I have to hold onto this place and never forget it. If I lose it would be like the most important page of a book torn out. The book would be meaningless." Although in this instance it did not happen, the search, the wishing for surrender to experience, may miscarry, and in its miscarried forms may well bear the marks of masochism.

I would like now to address a related issue, another outcome that may result from the incomplete "taking-in" of experiences whose full and meaningful apperception would be disorganizing. This outcome is usually thought of as "identification with the aggressor." But what does this phrase mean? How does it happen? I have found myself wondering if the wish to perceive, "take in," comprehend something may require a certain quality of activity. It has long been known that in order to perceive a triangle, the child first has to move his eyes from point to point, and, eventually, after many repetitions of this motoric act, he becomes able to perceive and, still later, to conceive, a triangle (Hebb, 1949). Schilder (1964) similarly ties motility with perception. "Primitive perception is a state of motion. ... Development is in the direction of the elimination of the inner motion of the perception." If what is being perceived would require inner disorganization to a degree greater than the child can handle, is it possible that a child does something analogous to what a painter does in trying to express an aspect of reality that is beyond formulation? The painter uses his available medium, paint, to represent "the unthinkable."

Could it be that the child or infant uses his available medium, his quite plastic self as his medium, separates part of it and makes a creative representation of what he has partially perceived in the external reality? Is this perhaps another example of how, under adverse environmental conditions, the impulse to surrender, in this case the let-go, the taking-in, of this isness of the "unthinkable" situation, goes awry, now resulting not simply in masochism, but in an identification with the aggressor in whatever style characterizes the aggressor.[5]

Many of us have had the experience of a spouse or good friend chiding us in irritation, "You are behaving just like your father!" If and when we recover from our injured innocence and reflect on the event in question, we, at times, with a little self-analysis, discover exactly what unique version of subtle hostility we were engaging in. At that moment, if we are lucky, another insight may break into consciousness with the thought, "Oh, I see! So that's what father was up to when he did such and such!" The identificatory process has finally paid off; it has at last revealed what one had not been able to see, "take in," recognize, or understand in the father.

In discussing Francis Bacon, "the skillful and challenging artist of our time who goes on and on painting the human face distorted significantly," Winnicott (1967/1971, p. 114) conjectures, "In looking at faces he seems to need to be painfully striving towards being seen, which is at the basis of creative looking." I would like to add to the conjecture that he is painfully striving to perceive something that he has not dared to see. If this be the case, it would be a kind of intermediate example between the painter who represents with paint what he cannot "take in" and the child who does the same with his self.

Surrender, Masochism and the Creative Process

I would like now to return to the notion shared by Ehrenzweig (1953) and Milner, that "this self-destruction is perhaps a distorted, because frustrated, form of self-surrender which is inherent in the creative process" (Milner, 1958/1959). Much of Milner's analytic work has been an exploration into the pathology of the creative process. In particular her paper, "The Role of Illusion in Symbol Formation" (Milner, 1952/1955) offers deeper insight into the meaning I have given to the word surrender. She describes a young girl of eleven who

> fervently and defiantly scribbled on every surface she could find. Although it looked as if it were done in anger, interpretation in terms of aggression only led to increase in the defiance. In fact, the apparent defiance did not change until I began to guess that the trouble was less to do with faeces given in anger and meant to express anger, than with faeces given in love and meant to express love.
>
> (p. 106)

Milner gradually came to look upon the scribbling in a fresh way:

> By refusing to discriminate, and claiming the right to scribble over everything, the young patient was trying to deny the discrepancy between the feeling [she experienced] and the expression if it; by denying completely my right to protect any of my property from defacement she was even trying to win me over to her original belief that when she gave her messes lovingly they were literally as lovely as the feelings she had in giving of them. … She was struggling [with the problem of the identity of the symbol with the thing symbolized …] with the very early problem of coming to discriminate … between the lovely feeling in giving [making, creating] the mess and the mess itself.
>
> (p. 107)

Although this was written long before Winnicott's paper on object usage, it provides a wonderful example of a "good-enough analyst" who was able to carry this girl over the tortuous path from object relating to object usage. Had this not occurred, the child's efforts to discover the real object and thereby real self—cleared of the debris of the identifications and projections that kept alive the con-fusion of symbol with thing symbolized—would have been defined as sadistic; the patient would likely have developed into what we think of as a sadistic, narcissistic woman.

Fortunately, Milner's perspicacity enabled her to recognize the child's struggle with the agony of disillusion in giving up the belief that everyone must see in her dirt what she sees in it. Another patient, a young boy said, "'My people' are to see these empty trucks and 'think it's gods.'" In fact, Milner muses, "he is saying what the poet Yeats said: 'Tread softly, because you tread on my dreams'" (p. 107).

We ought also to "tread softly" on patients' masochism and submissiveness. These too are often expressing in a disguised and a distorted way a deep yearning to be found and recognized. Unlike Milner's children they are not so much defacing her walls as their own walls. They too are "struggling with the problem of the identity of the symbol and the thing symbolized," in this case between the longing to yield control, to give up one's protective superstructure (as the thing symbolized) and inviting rape and other overpowering action (as the symbol).

We must note, of course, that acting out is no solution. It would not help Milner's patients if all she did was let the children scribble on the wall and celebrate the scribbles as their expressions of love. The same is true of submissive masochistic behavior. What is needed in both cases is that the patient get in touch with, and be validated in, the real longing to be recognized, known, perhaps penetrated with enough gentleness that the patient can feel safe enough to discover his or her own motility, while still having a symbolic foot in the need for continuing impingement, the absence of which would be so unfamiliar as to evoke panic or chaos.

Growth and Healing

In reviewing the territory covered by the term surrender, a subtext is revealed. The longing for surrender seems to emerge as a special detail in a more inclusive picture: growth and the restitution of impeded growth, healing. The literature abounds with papers and discussions of resistance; yet how little we study the vagaries of the force that is on the side of psychic healing, the impulse to grow, to surrender, to let-go. If this paper has said anything, it is that the pain and suffering of the masochist (and less obviously the sadist, at least in some instances) may well be the excuse the caretaker self has devised to get the true self to where it has a chance of being found, a signal that something deep inside is rent, a tear in the self, that unbeknown to its bearer, seeks healing, and that the masochistic patterns, especially if a certain satisfaction and pleasure accrues, are really expressions of the patient's efforts at self-cure. Masud Khan (1970/ 1974, p. 97) has said, "very few illnesses in a person are difficult to handle and cure. What however, is most difficult to resolve and cure is the patient's practice of self-cure." Chasseguet-Smirgel (1983) goes even further. In her explorations of the meaning of perversions she writes, "I consider that perversion is one of the essential ways and means [a person] applies in order to push forward the frontiers of what is possible and to unsettle reality. I see perversion not just as disorders of the sexual nature affecting a relatively small number of people [but] as a dimension of the human psyche in general, a temptation in the mind common to us all." The underlying theme, as Menaker (1969/1979) suggests, is about growth, the healing and expansion of the self. She asks: "Will the patient choose it or refuse it?" Will he or she let us into the living kernel from which true growth is possible—and are we up to the challenge?

Let us not overlook the role of masochism and surrender in being a member of our profession. What other occupation requires of its practitioners that they be the objects of people's excoriations, threats, and rejections, or be subjected to tantalizing offerings that plead "touch me," yet may not be touched? What other occupation has built into it the frustration of feeling helpless, stupid and lost as a necessary part of the work? And what other occupation puts its practitioners in the position of being an onlooker or midwife to the fulfillment of others' destinies. It is difficult to find a type of existence, other than that of the psychoanalyst, who fits this job description. In a sense it is the portrait of a masochist. Yet I suspect that a deep underlying motive in some analysts at least, is again that of surrender, and their own personal growth. It may be acceptably couched in masochistic garb or denied by narcissistic and/or sadistic exploitation. When the yearning for surrender is, or begins to be, realized by the analyst, the work is immensely fulfilling and the analyst grows with his patients.

Michael Polanyi (1958/1964), the physical-chemist who turned his brilliance to sweeping inquiries into how the scientist works and to the psychology of thought, wrote: "We owe our mental existence predominantly to works of art, morality, religious worship, scientific theory and other articulate systems which we accept as our dwelling place and as the soil of our mental development. Objectivism has totally falsified our conception of truth, by exalting what we can know and prove, while covering up with ambiguous utterances all that we know and *cannot* prove, even though the latter knowledge underlies, and must ultimately set its seal to, all that we *can* prove" (quoted in Brenman-Gibson, (1976)).

Some of the ideas addressed in this paper are at the level of hunches, and demand the follow-up of intellectual rigor as well as careful observation in our clinical work to see whether they stand the test of careful scrutiny. Also, in stressing the complexity of the matters at hand, it is important to remind ourselves that in the flush of putting forth one set of ideas, many other complicating considerations have been put aside and remain to be integrated.

Overview

As used in this paper, surrender, implies not defeat but a quality of liberation and "letting-go." I have explored the thesis that at least in some instances masochism is the result of a distortion or perversion of a deep longing for surrender, a yearning to be known, recognized, "penetrated," and often represents the miscarriage of a wish to dismantle false self. Similarly, some instances of sadism are traceable to the obverse of this phenomenon: a failure in the consummation of a more active "penetrative" type of surrender as in object usage. Successful transition from object relating to object usage involves an act of surrender and risk-taking on the part of the infant (or later, patient), as well as a degree of surrender on the part of the facilitating caretaker, or later, analyst. To round out the conception of surrender I have touched on related issues such as creativity and the apperception of disorganizing meaning.

Notes

1. First presented at New York University Postdoctoral Program in Psychoanalysis, December 2, 1983.
2. It is worth noting here the relation between *healing*, making *whole*, and *holy*, all of which are etymological cognates. In this connection note Winnicott's (1971, pp. 28–29) description of false self as "missing the boat," or at times simply as "missing," "being absent." In the old testament the Hebrew word designating *sin* has as its literal meaning *to miss* as in "missing the boat," "missing an opportunity to be present, alive" (Fromm, 1966, p. 132). The cure for *missing* is to become whole through surrender; the cure for sinning, in this sense, is to come alive, to be present in full awareness, authentic, centered in true self, holy. Rycroft (1966) has observed that "there would seem to be no necessary incompatibility between psychoanalysis and those religious formulations which locate God within the self. One could, indeed, argue that Freud's Id (and even more Groddeck's It), the impersonal force within which is both the core of oneself and yet not oneself, and from which in illness one becomes alienated, is a secular formulation of the insight which makes religious people believe in an immanent God ..."
3. I am grateful to Dr. Jean-Yves Roy of Montreal for having brought to my attention the work of Takeo Doi (1973), (1986) on the psychology of *amae* and its relation to the phenomenon of surrender. The word *amae* has variously been translated as dependence, a form of love, the play of indulgence. In some contexts, the verb *amaeru* conveys a meaning of surrender that resembles its usage in this paper. The *amae* psychology underpins a sense of oneness between

mother and child, and plays an indispensable role in the development of a healthy spiritual life (Doi, 1973, p. 75). Zen *satori* (enlightenment) might be looked upon as an affirmation of *amae* (p. 77). The person who seeks *amae* often experiences frustration with the result that some people turn to Zen and other religions, while others out of a similar motivation are driven to the pursuit of beauty (p. 79). In the West, freedom has usually meant freedom from dependence, and we see it in the celebration of autonomy at the expense of human connection. At the root of the *amae* psychology of the East is the reverse emphasis: the freedom to bond, rather than the Western focus on freedom from bondage (pp. 84ff).

4. For purposes of expressive clarity I will at times use the masculine pronoun generically; it is not intended to convey any gender significance.
5. I recently came across a paper by Minna Emch (1944) in which she describes a phenomenon in children that adds weight to this hypothesis. "When the … experience is one which *cannot yet* be assimilated by the child, the "next best" tool at its command is the *attempt* to know through an attenuated repetition of the disturbing stimulus-experience, especially as it relates to the mediator of that experience." She adds that both observations of children and clinical material from adults indicate that this attempt at knowing, by acting out the likeness of a situation, takes place very early, and may result in patterns of astonishing mimicry and even the "most caustic of caricatures" (p. 14).

References

Balint, M. (1968). *The basic fault: therapeutic aspects of regression.* London, UK: Tavistock.

Berliner, B. (1947). On some psychodynamics of masochism. *Psychoanalytic Quarterly, 16,* 459–471.

Brenman, M. (1952). On teasing and being teased: and the problem of "moral masochism". *The Psychoanalytic Study of the Child, 7,* 264–285. New York, NY: International Universities Press

Brenman-Gibson, M. (1976). Notes on the study of the creative process. *Psychological Issues, 9* (4), 326–357.

Chasseguet-Smirgel, J. (1983). Perversion and the universal law. *International Review of Psycho-Analysis, 10,* 293–301.

Davis, M. and Wallbridge, D. (1980). *Boundary and space, an introduction to the work of D. W. Winnicott.* New York, NY: Brunner/Mazel.

Doy, T. (1973). *The anatomy of dependence.* Tokyo, Japan: Kodansha International.

Doy, T. (1986). *The anatomy of self.* Tokyo, Japan: Kodansha International.

Eigen, M. (1973). Abstinence and the schizoid ego. *International Journal of Psychoanalysis, 54* (4), 493–498.

Eigen, M. (1981). The area of faith in Winnicott, Lacan and Bion. *International Journal of Psychoanalysis, 62* (4), 413–433.

Ehrenzweig, A. (1953). *The psycho-analysis of artistic vision and hearing.* London, UK: Routledge & Kegan Paul.

Emch, M. (1944). On the "need to know" as related to identification and acting out. *International Journal of Psychoanalysis, 25*, 13–19.

Freud, A. (1952). A connection between the states of negativism and emotional surrender. In *Indications for child analysis and other papers*. New York, NY: International Universities Press.

Freud, S. (1924) The economic problem of masochism. *Standard Edition, 19*, 159–170 London, UK: Hogarth.

Fromm, E. (1966). *You shall be as gods: A radical interpretation of the old testament and its tradition*. New York, NY: Holt, Rinehart and Winston.

Green, A. (1973). On negative capability. *International Journal of Psycho-Analysis, 54*, 115–119.

Guntrip, H. (1969). *Schizoid phenomena, object relations and the self.* New York, NY: International Universities Press.

Hebb, D. O. (1949). *The organization of behavior*. New York, NY: Wiley.

Horney, K. (1935). The problem of feminine masochism. *Psychoanalytic Review, 22*, 241–257.

Hutter, A. D. (1982). Poetry in psychoanalysis: Hopkins, Rosetti, Winnicott. *International Review of Psycho-Analysis, 9*, 303–316.

Khan, M. M. R. (1974). Towards an epistemology of cure. In *The privacy of the self* (pp. 93–98). New York, NY: International Universities Press. (Original work published 1970)

Khan, M. M. R. (1979). Pornography and the politics of rage and subversion. In *Alienation and perversions* (pp. 219–226). New York, NY: International Universities Press. (Original work published 1972)

Khan, M. M. R. (1979). The role of will and power in perversions. In *Alienation and perversions* (pp. 197–209). New York, NY: International Universities Press. (Original work published 1973)

Maritain, J. (1953). *Creative intuition in art and poetry*. New York, NY: McClelland.

Menaker, E. (1953). Masochism—a defense reaction of the ego. *Psychoanalytic Quarterly, 22*, 205–220.

Menaker, E. (1979). Will and the problem of masochism. In L. Lerner (Ed.), *Masochism and the emergent ego:Selected papers of Esther Menaker*. New York, NY: Human Sciences Press. (Original work published 1969)

Milner, M. (1955). The role of illusion in symbol formation. In M. Klein, P. Heinemann, and R.E. Money-Kyrle (Eds.), *New directions in psycho-analysis* (pp. 82–108). London, UK: Tavistock. (Original work published 1952)

Milner, M. (1957). *On not being able to paint*. London, UK: Heinemann, and New York, NY: International Universities Press. (Original work published 1950)

Milner, M. (1959). Psychoanalysis and art. In J. D. Sutherland (Ed.), *Psychoanalysis and contemporary thought*. London, UK: Hogarth, and New York, NY: Grove. (Original work published 1958)

Milner, M. (1969). *The hands of the living God*. New York, NY: International Universities Press.

Nass, M. (1984). The development of creative imagination in composers. *International Review of Psycho-Analysis, 11*, 481–491.

Polanyi, M. (1964). *Personal knowledge: towards a post-critical philosophy*. Chicago, IL: University of Chicago Press. (Original work published 1958)

Reich, W. (1949). *Character analysis*. New York, NY: Orgone Institute Press. (Original work published 1933)

Rilke, R. M. (1939). *Duino elegies* (J.B. Leishman and S. Spender, Transl.). New York, NY: Norton. (Original work published 1912–1922)

Rosen, V. H. (1960). Imagination in the analytic process. *Journal of the American Psychoanalytic Association, 8*, 229–251.

Rycroft, C. (1966). Causes and meaning. In C. Rycroft (Ed.), *Psychoanalysis observed* (p. 22). New York, NY: Coward-McCann.

Schilder, P. (1964). *Contributions to developmental neuropsychiatry*. New York, NY: International Universities Press.

Stolorow, R. D., & Lachmann, F. M. (1980). *Psychoanalysis of developmental arrests*. New York, NY: International Universities Press.

Winnicott, D. W. (1965). *The maturational processes and the facilitating environment*. New York, NY: International Universities Press.

Winnicott, D. W. (1971). Mirror role of mother and family in child development. In *Playing and reality* (pp. 111–118). London, UK: Tavistock. (Original work published 1967)

Winnicott, D. W. (1971). Playing: a theoretical statement. In *Playing and reality* (pp. 38–52). London, UK: Tavistock. (Original work published 1968)

Winnicott, D. W. (1971). The use of an object and relating through identifications In *Playing and reality* (pp. 86–94). London, UK: Tavistock. (Original work published 1969)

Winnicott, D. W. (1971). *Playing and reality*. London, UK: Tavistock.

Winnicott, D. W. (1975). Aggression in relation to emotional development. In *Through paediatrics to psycho-analysis*. New York, NY: Basic Books. (Original work published 1950–1955)

Winnicott, D. W. (1974). Fear of breakdown. *International Review of Psychoanalysis, 1*, 103–107.

Winnicott, D. W. (1975). Metapsychological and clinical aspects of regression within the psycho-analytical set-up. In *Through paediatrics to psycho-analysis* (pp. 278–294). New York, NY: Basic Books. (Original work published 1954)

Zimmer, H. (1951). In J. Campbell (Ed.), *Philosophies of India* (Bollingen Series). Princeton, NJ: Princeton University Press.

Chapter 3

Medicine Man(nie)

Commentary on Emmanuel Ghent's "Paradox and Process"

Muriel Dimen

Collectively, Emmanuel Ghent's papers constitute a manifesto for the relational turn in psychoanalysis.[1] They are guides to the work. They provide crucial trail markers to the new paths being cut in the conduct and comprehension of clinical psychoanalytic process as reformulated in the last quarter of the twentieth century.

"Paradox and Process" conceptualizes a tension key to this new way of psychoanalytic working. One might call it a "central" tension, but I think "key" is a better metaphor, because Ghent's insight into how clinical psychoanalysis actually works unlocks the shackles of binary thinking all of us find so seductive and comforting. In a postmodern sort of way, Ghent is deconstructing dualities found throughout psychoanalysis, even if in the end he too succumbs to one particularly enticing specimen.

In this essay, Ghent aims to show the links between two apparently contradictory aspects of clinical work—the ongoing engagement between analyst and patient, and the naming and interpreting of problems. He notices them as contraries, and asks how we can understand their simultaneity. The tension he comes up with by way of answer is that between paradox and process.

His inspiration here is Winnicott, who introduced "paradox into the dry sobriety of psychoanalysis" (Ghent, 1992, p. 136). Redelivering Winnicott to us, Ghent then puts his own spin on the story. Paradox, yes, but process too. An ecstatic suspension of the need for closure, negative capability—these are what Winnicott asks of and wishes for us. To this, Ghent the scientist, the medical man, adds thinking, knowing, cognizing as well, the process from unknown to known, and back again.

It is vital, in doing psychoanalytic work, to inhabit the unknown, to be comfortable with the discomfort of uncertainty. Negative capability, in

John Keats' phrase of 1817—about which many analysts, most famously Bion (1970, p. 125), have written—is a reflective state in which one "is capable of being in uncertainties, mysteries, doubts without any irritable reaching after fact & reason" (http://en.wikipedia.org/wiki/negative_capability, accessed January 25, 2014). Negative capability makes it possible, desirable, and expectable to bear irresolution, or what you might call "unknowing."

Still, analysts have to deliver. Not only that—Ghent argues that, as thinkers and as helpers, we want to deliver. It is our habit of mind to move from the state of unknowing to knowledge. We do that because we are human, and we do that because, as analysts, we have expertise in systems of meaning, in how people go about making meaning, creating narrative, and knowing the limits of these. Ghent does not invoke Bion's K, although one might well include that sort of knowledge-in-the-bones as a moment in the process Ghent elucidates. Harry Stack Sullivan, a founder of the school of thought in which Ghent trained, insisted in *The Psychiatric Interview* (1954) that the analyst has an obligation to offer the patient an opinion, an assessment, because the therapist is an expert, the benefit of whose knowledge the patient deserves.

The most important point is this: between the state in which paradox is accepted and the point at which an interpretation is made lies a path, a process. It is not predictable. Rules cannot be offered about when to engage in it. No manualization can capture the tension and flow between floating in unknowing and taking a crack at formulating what's going on.

But it's what analysts do. Ghent's contribution here is to show that this back-and-forth between acceptance of not-knowing and speech about what can—even for a moment—be known, is ubiquitous in clinical psychoanalysis. His essay demonstrates this ubiquity by taking us through the work of a range of clinician-scholars, all of whom have been influenced by Winnicott: Balint, Khan, Kohut, Bollas, Mitchell, Benjamin. His method is to find, in the work of each of these analysts, a binary that he then goes on to resolve, by first tolerating the contradiction it entails and then revealing how behind, underneath, inside of the opposition is a connective process between the dualities that reveals new meaning.

His choices evince the hot topics of the early 1990s, issues that, however, have been implicit in psychoanalysis since its inception: is there or is there not a baby inside the patient? How do one- and two-person psychologies relate? "In present-day psychoanalysis, a tension exists between those analysts whose focus is on internal conflict and the analysis of defense, as against those like Balint, Winnicott, Bollas, and, from a different point of view, the self psychologists, whose approach is also more centrally informed by developmental considerations" (Ghent, 1992, p. 137). Are benign and malignant regression the only opposites? What about need and neediness? Action and speech? Gratification and interpretation?

For example, Ghent (1992) recounts Mitchell's creative resolution of apparent contradictions. Does the analyst facing a patient who experiences her neediness as a hungry baby or clinging toddler interpret "the need for unfulfilled infantile dependence (Fairbairn) or symbiotic fusion (Mahler) or mirroring (Kohut)?" (p. 141). Mitchell proposes a conflict-relational solution: to view the adult's neediness as a manifestation of a need quite suitable to adults that anxiety dismisses as infantile. The analytic focus is then the anxiety.

To this, however, Ghent offers an alternative—one that, however, undermines his own paradox/processual "belief that no one has a lien on ultimate truth" (p. 139). Ghent's solution to the problem created by Mitchell's solution is to postulate what Ghent calls a "real" need: for example, an adult's neediness is a need to be heard, or to be able to count on the other's presence. This is not an infantile need. It is not the pseudo-need of neediness. It is a "real" need.

In "Paradox and Process," though, Ghent does not interrogate the implicit contradiction between a "real" need and a "non-real" need. Is a "real" need "objective"? Bedrock? If there is a real need, does it have an opposite number, a "false" need, an "untrue" need? Strangely, here his deconstructive process seems to stop, for he then, disconcertingly, begins to consider the possibility of "'bad need' and 'good need.'" Although he puts scare quotes around these polarities to tell us that he doesn't intend them literally, and although he goes on to discuss the importance of ambiguity in understanding such apparent contradictions, still he adheres to the idea of the "real."

This adherence is most naked when he adduces another seemingly "ultimate" truth, the "true self." On his way to introducing the sort of verity he's earlier disclaimed, Ghent offers what I have found to be an extremely useful insight for clinical work: "The likelihood is high that in the clinical process, particularly with some patients, both real need is expressed, and along with it, a curious species of camouflage, the blackwashing of need—neediness. The neediness, by being easily confounded with genuine need, is well designed to keep the real need from being known by the analyst, let alone the patient. It is often expressive of true self, whereas neediness, garbed in protective coloration, is the impersonator" (p. 142). Real need, he goes on to elaborate, consists in "genuine longings for human warmth, empathic responsiveness, trust, recognition, faith, playful creativity —all the ingredients we think of when we speak of love" (p.142).

It sounds so good. But I don't buy it. If I am to follow what I learned from Ghent, I am going to have to say that true self, love, goodness, empathy, warmth—these need to be paradox-ed and processed. We need to sit with them, not knowing whether they are bedrock, the end of the story, the telos of analysis, or only other stops in a process. Who is to say that their opposite numbers—chicanery, violence, the pleasures of cruelty, indifference to others—are not equally the bottom line, the alpha and omega of desire?

The Winnicottian story—which I like to think of as the West Side story—may not be the only truth here. Winnicott argues that badness comes from hurt, deprivation, and trauma, the idea being that if all went well, we would all be good. As one boy says to a judge in Stephen Sondheim's (1961/1992) "West Side Story": "I'm depraved on accounta I'm deprived!" Yes, this is an enigma still insufficiently plumbed. But it needs deconstruction, not silent acceptance. Here I think Ghent unconsciously followed the opposition to the Freudian metapsychology found in the interpersonalism in which he was educated, which was, like relational psychoanalysis, articulated against Freud. Instead of hanging in there with ambiguity—the classical tension between sex and aggression, say, or a newer one between true and false, or as we might say now, multiple selves—he let the paradox collapse into a single source, the truth of goodness and love, of true self over false self.

When I re-read "Paradox and Process" for this book, I was not surprised to find Ghent staking his money on the true self. What surprised me was that I'd never previously noticed that he'd left it undeconstructed. Yet why did my dissociation take me by surprise? Yes, idealization—Ghent was my supervisor and second analyst—paves a diamond path toward surprise when the unforeseen and even untoward dimensions of a revered figure shine in the light of day. But let's also remember that at the time of Ghent's writing, we were all passionately bent on creating a new psychoanalysis, and Winnicott was our leader. Even those of us whose first introduction to his insights was R. D. Laing's (1965) *The Divided Self* were caught in the (1960s) romance of the true self that would finally speak truth to power.

As I pondered my surprise, the irony of intellectual history caught up with me. It was only Ghent's teachings, his in effect postmodern deconstruction of Winnicott's notion of paradox, that, in the early 1990s, set the tone for those of us influenced directly by him and now writing our own manifestos deconstructing every binary we could find within psychoanalysis. In other words, I'd never have come to this critique of "Paradox and Process" without having taken in what he had to offer us, the importance of the ceaseless process of paradox and meaning that constitutes our work, that animates and guides my own work every day.

I also have a suspicion, or at least a hope, that he knew the opposition between true and false self was a bit more complicated than he stated. I say this because I was struck, on this re-reading, by a sentence I'd not noticed before: Of the patient's genuine longings for love, he cautions, "Parenthetically, I would want to make clear that I am by no means suggesting that all of the longings, as they appear in the adult, can be, or should be, directly responded to in the analytic setup" (p. 142). Now, this is the sort of thing that analysts often say when they fear their clinical pointers might be taken as advice or incitement to act rather than speak. Curiously, indeed, he says it not long after he tells of analysts who responded directly to longings—Winnicott to Margaret Little's need for holding; Khan's returning a stolen book on behalf of a patient who couldn't bring herself to make things right with the bookseller. We can't know what Ghent meant. I am going to wish, though, that he was of two minds about the ultimate truth of the good, loving self.

This disclaimer was also the sort of statement that, back in the 1990s when the relational position was cohering, was often being made. This epoch brought the well-documented understanding of the analyst's personal response to and effect on the patient, and the decision by many to disclose these affects and fantasies. It is no doubt out of anxiety about this radical departure from long-prescribed, even hallowed anonymity and abstinence that led many an analyst to assert that the voicing of affect—a speech act—was not accompanied by a physical act. And yet, read from the contemporary analytic scene, where such self-disclosure, if not mandatory, is also not uncommon, these disclaimers ring with a certain tone of guilt. Whether this was guilt toward the canon from which relational psychoanalysis had departed, or guilt over fantasies and wishes or even actions that individual superegos were rattled by, is not, of course, ascertainable. We are human, we are theoreticians, we are clinicians, we think, we do, we act, we act out and enact and try not to … can we hold this too muchness in paradox, and process it as well?

I own a Native American sculpture made by the Cheyenne artist E. Martin Reynolds. It reminded me of Mannie, and so I bought it. Cut from rusting iron, it's a figure that contains multitudes. You know it's bi-gender because it's got short hair on one side and long hair on another. Earrings drop from its ears. Its arms cradle its torso as though wrapped around a pregnant belly. From its torso's bottom protrudes a penis. Its left foot lifts in a dance step, a cut-out tear falls below its left eye. Its square mouth is moaning or laughing, singing or wailing. It knows, I like to imagine, that both good and evil, truth and falsity, dwell in us, and are equally fundamental.

"Paradox and Process" rustles with an elemental tension between the bohemian Buddhist composer and the hard-headed scientist who, as a medical student, once deemed psychoanalysis "moosh." Mannie Ghent, medicine man?

Note

1. Thanks to Velleda Ceccoli for a helpful reading of an early draft.

References

Bion, W. R. (1970). *Attention and interpretation*. London, UK: Tavistock.

Ghent, E. (1992). Paradox and process. *Psychoanalytic Dialogues*, *2* (2), 135–159.

Laing, R. D. (1965). *The divided self.* New York, NY: Penguin.

Sondheim, S. (1992). Gee, Officer Krupke. *West Side Story* [CD]. Los Angeles, CA: Sony (Recorded 1961).

Sullivan, H.S. (1954). *The psychiatric interview*. New York, NY: Norton.

Paradox and process

Emmanuel Ghent

> The endeavor of science is to resolve ambiguities by making … critical and decisive tests between alternatives. An experiment to this end is as beautiful as any line of poetry, but it puts its imagination to a different endeavor; unlike poetry, it does not seek to exploit its ambiguities, but to minimize them. This is the paradox of imagination in science, that it has for its aim the impoverishment of imagination. By that outrageous phrase, I mean that the highest flight of scientific imagination is to weed out the proliferation of new ideas. In science the grand view is the miserly view, and a rich model of the universe is as poor as possible in hypotheses.
>
> (Bronowski, 1971, p. 51)

By introducing paradox into the dry sobriety of psychoanalysis, Winnicott made room for spontaneity, ambiguity, illusion, and creativity as features that are essential to real living, despite the lack of a proper place for them in standard metapsychology.

"My contribution," he (Winnicott, 1971) wrote, "is to ask for a paradox to be accepted and tolerated and respected, and for it not to be resolved.[1] By flight to split-off intellectual functioning it is possible to resolve the paradox, but the price of this is the loss of the value of the paradox itself" (p. xii). Kumin (1978), in a paper celebrating this germinal contribution of Winnicott, adds that "in the adult, failure to perceive a paradoxical reality is a defensive operation of the ego" (p. 479).

In this paper, by juxtaposing paradox with process, I am suggesting that there is yet another level of paradox to be enjoyed: a paradox may (paradoxically) both be and not be; and, following Winnicott, I ask that this level of paradox also be respected and not resolved. Paradox lives in the world of the aesthetic; it points the way to insight without laying an interpretation upon us. Process, on the other hand, lives in the world of science; it clarifies and then waits for us to grasp at the next mystery, the next paradox. The scientist may say, "There is no such thing as a paradox; all paradoxes represent a confounding of different logical types (Bateson, 1979), or of different referents." It is precisely here that a study of process comes in; the goal is now to specify the nature of the relation between the contradictory statements, in effect to comprehend and thereby resolve the paradox. In the famous aphorism, "Plus ça change, plus c'est la même chose" (the more it changes, the more it is the same), what changes is different from what remains the same; one refers to phenotype, the other to genotype. The study of the process that connects contradictory elements will lead, ultimately, to a resolution. Paradox, by contrast, owes its value to going beyond the confines of what the mind can readily process with concepts that are already familiar and well integrated. It stretches us, inviting us to transcend the familiar. It expands the purview of awareness and poses a mystery. Its value is heuristic. Clearly, it is not a matter of choosing between paradox and process; both are of great value and bear a complementary and somewhat paradoxical relation to each other.

I will be dealing with a number of interrelated paradoxical issues, riddles, perhaps. Among the questions are: How can there both be and not be a baby inside? How can there be both need and no need at the same time? Or, touching on the question of object use, how can there be both destruction and transcendence in the same moment?

To prepare the way, I would like first to recount a story. It happened once that two gurus were discussing the question of how one becomes enlightened. The first said that it was like traversing a wall, leaving the enclosed room one has always been living in, and entering into another chamber, another domain, another atmosphere. There is a door, but it has no handle, no way of opening it; so one must knock and knock and knock, hour after hour, day after day, year after year until one day, perhaps, when one least expects it, suddenly it opens, and one finds oneself effortlessly translated into another world. The second guru demurred. "No," he declared, "the truth is there is no door; there never was one. All one need do is walk right through." Who, then, is right? Both are enlightened beings and in touch with truth. A third guru appears and says, "I've been listening with great interest to your discussion. We have here a paradox. You are both right. The higher truth is, of course, that there is no door. But how does one find out that there is no door? One must knock and knock and knock, hour after hour, day after day, year after year, until one day, perhaps, you look, and to your astonishment, you see that there is no door and realize that there never was one!"

In present-day psychoanalysis, a tension exists between those analysts whose focus is on internal conflict and the analysis of defense, as against those like Balint, Winnicott, Bollas, and, from a different point of view, the self psychologists, whose approach is also more centrally informed by developmental considerations. The "conflict analysts" tend to the position that there is no baby within; there is only the adult in whom one may certainly see ample indications of the residues from childhood. They question the wisdom of engaging a baby inside on the grounds that it could be infantilizing and disempowering of the patient.

An interesting case has been made by Mitchell (1988), in which he proposed a very engaging image, the "developmental tilt," to account for the dramatic appearance upon the psychoanalytic stage of the "modern baby," the preoedipal baby, the baby of object relations theory. It "postulates that Freud was correct in understanding the mind in terms of conflicts among drives *and* that object relations are also important, but *earlier*. … [In effect] the traditional model is jacked up and new relational concepts are slid underneath" (pp. 36–37). The thrust of the argument is that the use of the developmental tilt to position "the modern baby *beneath* Freud's baby" offers the great political advantage of affording theoretical innovation without challenging the basic structure of classical theory. I am in agreement that the focus in Freudian psychoanalysis on the preoedipal baby has contributed to the staying power of classical metapsychology; it has also led to a variety of conceptions like the need for a new beginning (Balint, 1968) and the theory of developmental arrest (Stolorow and Lachmann, 1980, and implied in Kohut, 1977), all of which were proposed as add-ons so as not unduly to perturb classical theory. Even Balint's distinction between benign and malignant regression—about which I will have more to say—is rooted in this effort.

Does, then, the focus on the baby of object relations theory have any intrinsic value, or is it essentially a theoretical makeshift in the interest of political expediency? Is there, then, a baby inside, a baby who is in need of being found?

Let me now return to the story. When the first guru says, "You have to knock and knock," he means you have to live through what may be a prolonged experience of devoting yourself to what seems to be a senseless, irrational, and illusory task. The second wise man says, "No need; rationality will prevail; use the fresh air of analytic understanding to clear away the underbrush of unconscious conflict and defense, and you will see there is no door, and you will walk through."

The third guru, knowing that many contradictory issues are not most usefully resolvable into "either/or" but are more fruitfully conjoined with "and," affirms the validity of both positions and adds, "There is a *process* involved in this paradox." However true it is that there is no baby living in the adult patient, and however true that there is continuous construction (Zeanah et al., 1989) of character and of psychopathology, so often it happens that the route to truth is through the intensity of illusion. Is not analysis a veritable playpen for transference and countertransference, and what are these if not vehicles for finding truth by knocking on the walls of illusion? Are not dreams the quintessential illusions, fictions? Are not most art forms—lines on a flat plane or ambiguous words in blank verse or people playing roles on stage—are not these all built on illusion? And do not all these lead us, through illusion, to encounter a level of truth and reality that is otherwise inaccessible? Yes, there is a baby dwelling inside, and the more authentically we can surrender ourselves to the experience of that baby, the more likely we will discover ultimately that, of course, there is no baby inside; nor are there internal objects and selves inside. These are all fictions, but we need the compelling intensity that accompanies surrender to our inner experience. Through immersing ourselves in the intensity of what we fear and desire, immersing ourselves by engaging the language and imagery that those fears and desires knew in the moments when they were alive with nascent intensity, we may ultimately discover, having found within ourselves our own authentic voice, that, indeed, there is no door, no obstacle after all. Freud created intensity by hewing to sex and aggression; Jung changed the venue but maintained the intensity through mythology and religious passion; and with the object relations theorists the content again changed, this time to the inner world of objects and selves, all of whom had at one time an intense connection with passionate realities.

I hope that the third guru conveys my belief that no one has a lien on ultimate truth. Even as I portray the difference in viewpoints in this paradoxical way, I am aware that further complexities abound. I speak only for myself when I say there is something missing when all is clearly articulable in rational terms. Hence the quest for surrender and for the mystical, so as to make possible a reencounter with the transitional world of semi-illusion, or of creative surrender. I believe that quest is related to the wish to encounter that state of altered consciousness, a self-state that is deeply rooted in a one-person psychology and that, in most of us as adults, is confined to the moment of orgasm. Encountering the infantile in oneself affords another avenue of experiencing this quality of mix between one- and two-person psychologies (see Ghent, 1989).

Beyond this, I believe the patient has a stake in experiencing forbidden needs as infantile, in part because intense longings that have long been suppressed began to take formative shape in infancy or early childhood, so that the symbols used in adulthood to express these longings are affectively connected to these early periods. Second, the very fact that such needs are experienced by the patient as somehow allowable to infants and children opens a bridge for their reintroduction and reintegration in adulthood, with the goal that they can ultimately find a place in adult living. Of course, we as adults can make the theoretical distinction that such needs and longings are by no means confined to infancy; but this does not mean that we should require this adult rationality of our patient, who needs the bridge of actual experience. And, finally, the focus on the infantile, the body language of breast and penis, and the worldlessness of affect memory all contribute to retaining a modicum of irrationality and the untranslatable, which tend to get lost in the purely interpersonal position. In this regard I was deeply struck by Stern's (1983) drawing attention to how our theory and practice may be quite limiting. He asks: "What happens to affect memories when a language-based code arrives on the scene? … Are they encoded in two parallel systems, a semantic system and an affect system? … [E]ven current affect memories are only roughly translatable into a language code." He suggests that "our inability to establish greater continuity between pre- and postverbal periods may stem largely from our failures to be imaginative in [psychotherapeutic] technique and from the presence of a discouraging [psychoanalytic] theory" (p. 17).

Perhaps the difference between the two relational positions regarding "the baby inside" resides in the relative emphasis on the view from inside as against the view from outside. From the conflict-relational perspective (Mitchell, 1988),

> viewing the *analysand as child* often helps us to organize the pieces and fragments of the analysand's experience into coherent, understandable

> patterns. … In employing infantilism as a basis for interpretation, we are using our image of the baby as a metaphor. The analysand is not really a baby, but if we think of him in these terms, as wishing, fearing, and experiencing like a baby—we find meaning and patterns in otherwise inchoate fragments of experience.
>
> (pp. 127–128)

The view here is from the outside; the patient is the object that is being understood. In the other, more developmental-relational approach, the emphasis is on the subjective, the (re)experiencing of fragments of childhood experience, much as experiencing a vivid dream is a most compelling avenue of self-integration. It is not a matter of choosing one over the other; both are important. There will always be differences of emphasis as functions of the personalities and psychopathology of the analysand and of the analyst and of the stage of the analysis, as well as of the conception of the healing factors in the psychoanalytic process.

An illustration may shed some further light on the question of the baby inside. How is one to deal with a patient's neediness, when the need is "subjectively experienced as identical to that of the hungry infant or that of the clinging toddler" (Mitchell, 1988)? If the analyst understands the problem in terms of the need for unfulfilled infantile dependence (Fairbairn) or symbiotic fusion (Mahler) or mirroring (Kohut), it "makes the analysand's neediness difficult to resolve or work through, because it leads to two equally unappealing options … an ultimate renunciation of 'infantile' wishes … or an immersion … in the gratification of those wishes in the analytic relationship" (Mitchell, 1988). The conflict-relational way out of this bind is to look upon the neediness in the adult as an expression not of the baby inside but of perfectly appropriate adult need that has, under the influence of a great deal of anxiety, come to be experienced as "infantile." The therapeutic thrust, then, would be addressed to understanding the source of the anxiety, with the ultimate goal of being able to integrate current desires and longings.

I believe there is room for an alternative, or at least complementary, relational perspective. In some clinical situations what appears to be neediness may, in fact, be an expression of real need, say an urgent, even desperate need to be "heard," a need, above all, for presence and reliability, the breach of which leads not to anxiety but to disintegrative panic. In these instances any effort at interpreting in the relational-conflict mode is out of the question.

How, then, to understand the relation between neediness and need, between "bad need" and "good need"? As with most paradoxical and ambiguous situations, our intellect and our scientific imagination wish to choose between alternatives, to come down on one or the other side. It is either this or that. But in real life we are often in an intermediate zone, where ambiguity occupies center stage and requires of the analyst a remarkable capacity for living in uncertainty.

The likelihood is high that in the clinical process, particularly with some patients, both real need is expressed, and along with it, a curious species of camouflage, the blackwashing of need—neediness. The neediness, by being easily confounded with genuine need, is well designed to keep the real need from being known by the analyst, let alone the patient. It is often expressive of true self, whereas neediness, garbed in protective coloration, is the impersonator. It is the expression of protector self, that aspect of false self that serves simultaneously as usurper of selfhood and protector of the integrity of true self. It is also hinting to us that behind the noisy fiction and the drama of neediness lives a true self whose genuine need is awaiting discovery and response. For those who feel Sullivan's idiom to be more congenial, I would describe the process in the following way: genuine need, however dissociated and relegated to the not-me, is always trying to break through the boundaries of the self-system with the aim of furthering its expansion and enrichment. The self-system, however, the structured residence of good-me and bad-me, has as an essential function, the warding off of the anxiety that this breach would entail. In its efforts to resist expansion, the self-system, being by definition a system with a powerful stake in self-perpetuation, brings into play a particular set of security operations, neediness and demandingness, which, by virtue of their imposturous verisimilitude to genuine need, constitute a remarkably effective and stable defense.

My reason for using the word "paradoxical" here is that two equally valid but contradictory statements apply: There is no need; what looks like need is a manipulative, at times vengeful demandingness, which is, in large measure, an expression of rage at lifelong deprivation of one form or another; far from aiming to secure an appropriate response to real need, it is directed either at obtaining some immediate satisfaction, which, contributing nothing nourishing to the inner feeling of emptiness, amplifies the feeling of deprivation, or at provoking the alienation or empathic remove of the other thereby adding another notch in the tally of deprivations. On the other hand, there is need—genuine longings for human warmth, empathic responsiveness, trust, recognition, faith, playful creativity—all the ingredients we think of when we speak of love. Parenthetically, I would want to make clear that I am by no means suggesting that all of the longings, as they appear in the adult, can be, or should be, directly responded to in the analytic setup.

What so often complicates matters further is that one can often sense both thrusts in operation, oscillating unpredictably in ambiguous and overlapping ways. At any given moment it can be most unclear which is in the foreground. To borrow from the great master of paradox, Heraclitus, "One can never step in the same analysis twice!" Everything is in endless flux.

In the course of analytic work we often find ourselves welcoming the beginning appearance of such dark forces as envy, greed, hatred, especially as they seem to be heralding the (re)vitalization of some genuine need. We may have to hold for a long period the paradoxical meaning of these intense feelings: in one moment, defensive and constrictive and, in the next, progressive and vital; in one moment, a surface gloss of positive feeling whitewashing unacceptable destructive feelings, and, in the next, storm clouds of aggression blackwashing frightening feelings of an awakening desire to take ownership of one's self or to reach out to another.

Rather than coming down on one side or the other, I believe one has no choice but to live with the paradox, often for long periods of time, and always run the risk that at any moment one may be out of sync with the analytic current. Depending on the personalities of both therapist and patient, there may be a tendency to err in one direction more than the other and so leave plenty of room for empathic failures.

It is difficult to maintain the tension of appropriate response to these opposing expressions of need. One attempts to respond to what one feels is genuine need, especially when one senses the need emerging in forms that the patient is unaware of. I think of this type of response as validation of real need, rather than as "gratification," which I look upon as belonging more to the area of demand.[2]

An excerpt from Little's (1985) personal record of her psychoanalytic treatment with Winnicott will convey a clear sense of responding to need where there is rather little indication of ambiguity, although I would not be at all surprised that many analysts would view it as an index of inappropriate countertransferential gratification.

> [Winnicott] used the word "holding" both *metaphorically and literally*. Metaphorically he was "holding the situation," giving support, keeping contact on every level with whatever was going on, in and around the patient and in the relationship to him.
>
> Literally, through many long hours he held my two hands clasped between his, almost like an umbilical cord, while I lay, often hidden beneath the blanket, silent, inert, withdrawn, in panic, rage or tears, asleep and sometimes dreaming. Sometimes he would become drowsy, fall asleep and wake with a jerk, to which I would react with anger, terrified and feeling as if I had been hit.
>
> (p. 21)

In another context:

> He was as honest as anyone could be, responding to observations and answering questions truthfully unless there was a need to protect another person, but it was essential to *know* when his answer was not wholly true, and why.
>

> He would answer questions directly, taking them at face value, and only then considering … why it was asked? Why then? And what was the unconscious anxiety behind it?
>
> (p. 23)

When Khan (1960), in describing a case of a woman in a state of regression to abject dependence, volunteered to return a book that the patient had stolen, I look upon his action as a response to a need that the patient was only dimly aware of, if at all. Indeed, it was his response that brought the full intensity of need for a caring, responsive, and knowing other into consciousness, an important step in the ultimate integration of the need into the self.

Benign and Malignant Regression

Closely related to the ambiguity surrounding need and neediness is the question of benign and malignant regression, as formulated in Balint's (1968) marvelous monograph, *The Basic Fault*. In the psychoanalytic atmosphere of the 1950s, need was looked upon as an expression of drive. It could be either gratified, a response that was antitherapeutic, or denied gratification. Balint found himself dealing with a paradox: he encountered an area of need that he knew required gratification if therapeutic result was to be obtained. How, then, to resolve this problem? Earlier I stated that in every paradox an underlying process is involved. In my view, Balint understandably, given the psychoanalytic atmosphere of the times, sidestepped an explicit examination of the process involved in this paradox and instead resolved the matter by postulating that two unrelated processes were at work. In one, malignant regression, the patient confronts the analyst with ever increasing demands for gratification. This spiraling of neediness he attributed to the patient's drives. In the other, benign regression, he made a very convincing case for an altogether different phenomenon, one that has no place in classical metapsychology, the patient's need to be recognized, to be found in his authenticity.

The many analysts (among them, Winnicott, E. Balint, Khan, Little, Milner, and Bollas) whose work reflects similar concerns in the treatment of schizoid disorders all find similar locations to describe what happens in the interaction with the patient under these circumstances of benign regression. All have stressed the attunement with the patient, the listening for the creative moment that spontaneously emerges from the patient, the quality of somewhat altered consciousness that prevails, the urgent importance of not intruding on the patient with interpretations.

With the advantage of 20 or 30 years, I think it is now possible to see the two forms of regression as related in a unifying process, one that has the additional benefit of accounting for why, in many patients, neither form of regression appears in pure culture, but, instead, both often make themselves known in subtle blends, so that in one moment there is malignant need and in the next we may glimpse the benign variety.

Insofar as malignant regression is seen as originating in the instinctual id impulses, it is not hard to see how the therapist can soon find himself helpless, at the mercy of the overpowering id impulses of the patient. If, on the other hand, one views the situation from a totally different perspective, that of a false self desperately trying to retain the status quo under the threat of the availability of a real object who is capable of recognizing and responding to his true self, the malignant regression takes on another cast entirely. It is now seen as a defensive mutant of benign regression, *a defense against benign regression*. One is no longer dealing with a Pandora's box bursting at the seams under the pressure of id impulses; one is dealing, in relational terms, with a desperate person who is trying to hold himself together with whatever angry demandingness he can muster. If he succeeds in threatening the analyst, he staves off the threat of his true self being reached.

Yet only if this happens—a meaningful encounter with the dissociated and exceedingly vulnerable true self—can a "new beginning" come into play.

The suggestion that benign need or regression and malignant need or regression are related by a type of paradoxical process causes me to wonder if this relationship may also be true in other areas. Indeed, I believe it is.

The main thesis of another paper (Ghent, 1990) is that submission and its variant as masochism, in at least some instances, represent a defensively organized perversion of the longing for surrender. By surrender, I mean not defeat, but a quality that encompasses the range of experience from "letting go" to the yearning that might be represented as a wish to dismantle false self.

> Submission, losing oneself in the power of the other, becoming enslaved in one or other way to the master, is the ever available lookalike to surrender. It holds out the promise, seduces, excites, enslaves, and in the end, cheats the seeker-turned-victim out of his[3] cherished goal, offering in its place only the security of bondage and an ever amplified sense of futility. By substituting the appearance and trappings of surrender for the authentic experience, an agonizing, though at times temporarily exciting, masquerade of surrender occurs: a self-negating submissive experience in which the person is enthralled by the other. The intensity of the masochism is a living testimonial of the urgency with which some buried part of the personality is screaming to be exhumed. This is not to be minimized as an expression of the longing to be healed, although so often we bear witness to its recurring miscarriage.
>
> (pp. 115–116)

Viewed in this light, one might consider renaming surrender "benign surrender." Submission, then, would be "malignant surrender," whose place in the scheme of things would be as usurper of the territory that, but for dread, belongs to surrender proper, or benign surrender. Here again semblance turns out to be the best cover for reality, the best disguise for truth.

Illusion

Another area in which this type of ambiguity can be traced is in relation to narcissistic illusion. Under the vivid metaphor "The Wings of Icarus,"

Mitchell (1988) spells out the two opposing views of narcissistic illusion: (1) illusion as defense, a position shared by Freud through Kernberg in classical thinking, as well as by Sullivan and Fromm, and (2) illusion as creativity, as reflected in Winnicott and Kohut, among others, each of whom in his own distinctive way "regards infantile narcissism and subsequent narcissistic illusions in later life as the core of the self and the deepest source of creativity ... the growing edge of the patient's aborted self" (pp. 187–189).

I reveal my own viewpoint by suggesting that here, too, one might look upon the paradoxical relation between illusion as "bad" and illusion as "good" by exploring the possibility of there being an underlying process at work. Indeed, I would suggest that there is a meaningful analogy with benign and malignant need, such that one could think of benign and malignant narcissistic illusion; the malignant form would be seen as the defensive derivative of benign narcissistic illusion, the result of failure of the process of benign narcissistic illusion. The implication here is that rather than the defensive variety representing a defense against something bad—like the loss of infantile omnipotence (Freud), persecutory anxiety and murderous rage (Klein), aggressive impulse and envy (Kernberg), feelings of insecurity (Sullivan), or alienation from the existential realities of life (Fromm)—it may often be a defensive lookalike of creative illusion, an intruder that has come to poach in the territory left vacant by the failure of the normal processes of creative illusion and play as, for example, the successful negotiation of transitional experience.[4]

Object Use

I would like now to explore another area that is replete with paradox and process—the concept of object use, one of Winnicott's (1969) most seminal contributions. The focus is on the transition from object relating, a more primitive mode of human connection, where the self as isolate relates to the object as subjectively perceived, to object usage where the other is encountered as a true object who can now be used for growth and self-expansion.

In object relating, both self and other are perceived largely through projections and identifications. The self at this stage may be thought of as a "unit self" in that relating can be described in terms of an "isolate," the individual subject; the object then is the subjectively perceived object. In the use of an object, however, object relating is taken for granted. New features enter that involve the nature and behavior of the object in external reality. "The object, if it is to be used, must necessarily be real in the sense of being part of shared reality, not a bundle of projections" (p. 712). Winnicott offers an almost diagrammatic illustration of the process:

> Two babies are feeding at the breast; one is feeding on the self in the form of projections, and the other is feeding on (using) milk from a woman's breast. … The change does not come about automatically, by maturational process alone. … Mothers, like analysts, can be good or not good enough; some can and some cannot carry the baby over from relating to usage. [This transition] is the most difficult thing, perhaps, in human development … [and] the most irksome of all the early failures that come for mending. … The change [from relating to use] means that the subject destroys the object [as subjective object] and the object, if it survives destruction, is now real. … "Hullo object!" "I destroyed you." "I love you." "You have value for me because of your survival of my destruction of you."
>
> (pp. 712–713)

In effect, destruction has created the reality and placed the object outside the self. The word "destruction" may seem out of place here in what might naively appear to be a piece of straightforward development. Yet it is needed, "not because of the baby's impulse to destroy, but because of the object's liability not to survive" (pp. 714–715). Nonsurvival can take many forms: retaliation, withdrawal, defensiveness in any of its forms, an overall change in attitude in the direction of suspiciousness or diminished receptivity, and finally, a kind of crumbling, in the sense of losing one's capacity to function adequately as mother or, in the analytic setting, as analyst.

One paradox lies in the subject's needing to destroy the object in order to discover the object that was always there. This paradox is reminiscent of the paradox of the gurus. You must keep knocking and knocking, trying and trying, working at penetrating to the other, and, if all goes well, one day you discover "there was no door"; the object was always there. You have "dis-covered," indeed, created a reality—the objective other who was always there. But was he always there? Not quite. The fantasy of the subjective other had first to be destroyed for the objective other to be realized. Besides, in this case, the metaphorical wall, the other, is a live human being and as such can be destroyed. It can fail to survive the destructive knocking, as, for example, by retaliating, by withdrawing, by being rendered impotent as facilitator.

While this destruction is, paradoxically, an act of discovery and creation, the very real liability of the object to failure caused Winnicott to emphasize the importance that destruction plays in the process. At the same time, he made it very clear that it had nothing to do with anger; the destruction is innocent; there is no expectation that the other will not survive, unless by now the other has already repeatedly not survived.

The next question is, What if the object does fail to survive? As I see it, the result is not only that the subject remains a self-as-isolate, but, perhaps more important, he or she has been implicitly defined and labeled as destructive by the very fact that the object has been destroyed. The triple misfortune is that the subjective object never becomes real but remains a bundle of projections, and externality is not discovered; second, the subject is now made to feel that he or she is, indeed, destructive; and, finally, fear and hatred of the other develop, and with them, characterological destructiveness may come into being. In short, we have a setting for development in the direction of sadism, the need to control the other aggressively. In other words, the stage is now set for the development of a tendency toward *"ab-use" of the object as a complication of, and defense against, object usage.* Object abuse is a state of affairs akin to Sullivan's (1953) malevolent transformation.

If object abuse has come into play, we are likely to witness in the adult the overlap of two processes analogous to those we encountered in benign and malignant need. The analyst will now both observe and become the target of a complex blend of what might be called (1) benign object use, the continuing effort to undo earlier failures in the transition from object relating to object use, and (2) malignant object use—or object abuse—the defensive overlay that bears testimony to all the prior failures. Just as with need, regression, and illusion, it may at times be difficult to disentangle the fluctuations from moment to moment as to which is ascendant. Here, too, one will find oneself living in ambiguity during much of the therapeutic work.

The fact that object usage has been referred to under the rubric of Winnicott's theory of destruction (Benjamin, 1988, p. 40) points to the necessity of distinguishing between process and goal in the matter of object use. The *process* refers to the transition from object relating to object use, the transition from the more primitive position where the self remains an isolate, relating to the object as subjectively perceived, to a more advanced position where the object has been "dis-covered" in external reality and can now be used. In this sense the use of an object is the *goal* of the process. The object is now objectively perceived and is, therefore, now available for use. The analysand, for example, can now make use of the analyst and be nourished by his interpretations.

Winnicott leaves ambiguous the relation between the process and the goal. He says the process involves destruction, in fantasy, of the subjective object. He implies that while the process is characterized by the impulse to destroy, the goal is the effort to create reality by probing, attacking, uncovering the subjective other, so as to be able, ultimately, to use him, to make use of him as a reality instead of living off illusion. At the same time, Winnicott seems to refer to the entire phenomenon as "use of the object." What, then, to call the process? Calling it "destruction" does not seem satisfactory on several counts, not the least of which is that it would lead to a logical conundrum wherein failure of the process of destruction leads to destruction!

As I see it, there is an evolving reciprocity between the process and the goal of object usage such that I tend to use the term "use of the object" both for the process, which involves destruction of the subjective object, and for the goal, namely, the capacity to use the object. A spiraling evolution in the capacity for object usage is probably never fully complete. If I were to seek a term that distinguishes between the process and the goal, I think I would employ the term *object probing* for the process and *object usage* for the capacity, the goal. Probing implies a degree of "penetration" and effort to reach and recognize, that "use" does not. It carries also the connotation that there is a possibility that what is being probed, or proved, could break and be destroyed by the process, hence fail the implied test.

Probing also carries the connotation that if successful, something new is discovered—in this case the objectively perceived object, which ironically turns out to be none other than a newly encountered other. Here we encounter another area of paradox. Is the newly discovered other an object or another subject or perhaps a transitional entity that is no longer merely an object, yet is not quite a subject; and if the other is a subject, is the process we have been describing actually a representation of the beginnings of intersubjectivity? Benjamin (1988) has focused on exactly this aspect of the process. She directs our attention to the lack, in all versions of psychoanalytic theory so far, of a psychology that views the relation between infant and mother not simply as subject and object, with mother being the object of the infant, but rather as two subjectivities. In effect, psychoanalytic theorists have until now taken for granted the culturally sanctioned role of mother as object, implicitly denying her own subjectivity and desire. Stern's (1985) work on the infant's capacity for intersubjective experience provides the underpinnings in infant research for a significant advance in this area of theory. It is precisely at the point of a successful transition to object usage that a new paradox comes into prominence. Is mother the objectively viewed object or is she now endowed with a subjectivity of her own, which the child is beginning to have the capacity to share? On a different plane one might ask, With successful negotiation of the transition into object usage in the analytic situation, does the analyst become the objectively viewed object, or is he becoming endowed with a subjectivity of his own, which the patient is beginning to have the capacity to share?

Other Polarities

I would like now to extend the motif of benign and malignant modes by touching on a few other areas that we encounter in the clinical situation. Let us look first at the problem of the so-called repetition compulsion. We have all witnessed innumerable examples in which the function of the seemingly endless iterations of an unchanging pattern is clearly defensive, in the sense that an ancient drama is being replayed without any appreciable learning from experience. What is visible is the tenacity with which the person holds to the status quo, so that little appears to change. Mystified by this behavior, we ask ourselves, What is the invisible force, the motor, that is driving the person to keep on trying?

Now and then, for example, we are able to catch a glimpse that what is being sought is a reenactment that is not simply in the spirit of a hurdy-gurdy grinding out the same old tune just because it is so familiar. Instead, we sense a hint that some other goal, perhaps an attempt at self-healing, is being perseverated, as, for example, in the creation of a piece of live theater where the secret goal is, at last, to be able to recognize, "take in" the meaning, the "what's going on here" of the scenario so as to demystify some earlier traumatic set of experiences that could never be integrated. Which of these impulses—the force that is pulling for the status quo or the force that is expressing the yearning—is the one that is responsible for the repetition? Clearly both are. Often, however, we are tempted to throw up

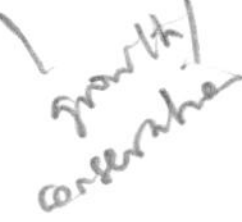

our hands in despair at the "malignity" of the repetition, the intrasigence that gives little visible indication of what might be called the benign repetition, the roots of which lie in the dissociated area of the personality or, in Winnicott's language, in true self. Yet, just as in the case of benign and malignant need, both are present.

Acting out is a closely related phenomenon where ambiguity again invites attention. Often enough what looks like acting out and would evoke opprobrium, if not outright condemnation, by many analysts is the first sign of the patient's finding his or her independent voice. Here, too, one could usefully think in terms of benign and malignant acting out.

Another such issue is the matter of hope. In this case, however, unlike acting out, hope is ordinarily regarded as "good" rather than "bad." Nonetheless, the same paradoxical relation prevails between what might be called false hope or malignant hope and benign or true hope. Someone once said I should hang a sign from my door on which would be inscribed, "Abandon hope, all ye who enter these portals." We had been working on the illusion-tinged, garden-variety version of hope that so often is a species of malignant hope. It tends to proliferate much like malignant need or malignant regression and occupy more and more of the space that one would wish to see filling up with the faith that stems from true self—benign hope. The distinction between benign and malignant hope (or true and false hope) was never as clearly recognized and expressed as when Winnicott's (1960) analysand, "who had had much futile analysis on the basis of False Self, cooperating vigorously with an analyst who thought this was his whole self, said to [Winnicott]: 'The only time I felt hope was when you told me that you could see no hope, and you continued with the analysis'" (p. 152). As I see it, malignant hope is the defense against the hopelessness of false self. In Bollas's language false hope is a prisoner of fate, in contrast to benign hope, which reflects the strength that inheres in a person's sense of destiny, as rooted in true self. There is an apocryphal story that, having traveled to India and studied with Buddha's disciples, Jesus knew about and believed in reincarnation. On his return, however, he kept it secret and never breathed a word about it in his preaching, because he felt it would simply encourage false hope in people—that in the next lifetime things would be better, so why bother knocking ceaselessly on the door in this lifetime?

All this talk about the benign and the malignant brings me to a metaphor that perhaps sums it all up. While "shit" is ordinarily looked upon with disgust as foul and contaminating—even the word is repugnant and shunned in respectable discourse—we often forget its key place in the cycle of nature, where it becomes the very fertilizer, the life-giver to us all. In the early stages of the new crop, the excrement and the growing nourishment are all mixed together and very difficult to tease apart. We even devise a new word, "manure," to ensure the split and hide the paradox.

There are other types of paradoxical processes in the psychoanalysis of every day that are of a different type from those we have been discussing. When, for example, is comprehending not understanding? The question sounds like some esoteric, paradoxical riddle. In actuality, the process at issue is quite straightforward, and yet it is often honored in the breach in psychoanalytic work. There are two distinctly different meanings to "understanding." One is cognitive comprehension; this is understanding from the outside. The other (as, for example, in "I wish you could understand me!") has to do with being empathized with, having the feeling that one's subjective experience is truly recognized—the view from the inside.

As Kohut (1977) emphasized repeatedly, there is probably no greater precipitant of resistance in analysis than this misunderstanding. If what he spoke of as the first step—empathic understanding—is not integrated, the second step—cognitive understanding, perhaps better known by its official name, interpretation—either falls on deaf ears or, more likely, evokes a storm of resistance or, even worse, elicits obeisant compliance in the form of intellectual assent. If the iatrogenic resistance is fierce and the patient complains in one or another way of not being empathically understood, the analyst is apt to enter into the counterresistance by thinking or, at times, protesting that he, in fact, is being the more deeply empathic—in touch with a level of the patient's experience that the patient is fiercely resisting knowledge of in himself.

Here again while, for descriptive purposes, I have separated the meanings of understanding, in practice they often blend. If the analyst keeps the two-step process in mind and thereby avoids the potential confusion in the meaning of understanding, I believe he is much more likely to sort out what is called for at any given moment. Unlike many of the processes discussed earlier, this process is, in the normal course of things, sequential in nature.

Then there is a quite different type of process, which, to those sophisticated in the vagaries of human development, is clearly not paradoxical. Nonetheless, as it is often encountered in child rearing and also, though more subtly, in the analytic setting, I would like to elaborate on it. I am referring to the confusion that is apt to result when a particular behavior comes into play that has quite different meanings at different developmental stations. Let me use possessiveness as an illustration. At one point in life, the fierce insistence, "It's mine! And you can't have it!" is a vital experience that reflects the child's struggle not only for autonomy but especially for a sense of self-identity. If, at this point, the parent punishes the child and thwarts any such expression of "It's mine!" on the grounds that being possessive is not nice and that "everything should be shared," we are asking for trouble not only in the child's acquisition of a healthy sense of self, but also by throwing a monkey wrench into the satisfactory integration of a subsequent piece of development, the capacity to share, the capacity to experience the other as another subject. Now the entire sharing experience has come under a cloud; it has become obligatory, a function of false self. In the analytic situation issues similar to this are always around and are usually dealt with under the guise of interpretation. What one chooses to interpret and the way it is interpreted are, in themselves, metacommunications; they inform the patient as to how the analyst is evaluating his behavior. If the analyst interprets a piece of self-involved, possessive behavior as some effort in the direction of discovering and owning a sense of self, a feeling of identity, a very different message will be conveyed than if the analyst interprets it as a piece of spoiled-brat behavior, an unwillingness to share. Both are likely to be true, but focus on the second half of a developmental process without a satisfactory integration of the first half can only compound the difficulties already besetting the patient.

In the early stages of development, the idea that the child splits the object into a loved and hated object seems by now to have almost achieved the status of fact. One way of looking at it is that the child cannot tolerate the paradox of living with both feelings at the same time. In this sense the arrival of the depressive position, signaling the acquisition of the capacity for ambivalence, is of extreme importance, not only as regards the integration of loving and hating impulses, but as regards the beginning of the integration of the function of being able to hold onto the tension of paradox in general, the capacity for multiple perspectives, without having to arrive at a resolution where no true resolution is possible.

Conclusion

Understanding process and paradox presupposes a high degree of maturity. It means that one has transcended in significant measure the need for splitting and other defensive operations; that one can tolerate, if not enjoy, uncertainty; that one can maintain the tension between the need for discovery and the need for closure; that one can live in the flux of subjectivity, one's own and the patient's, while at the same time residing in the externality that affords the perspective of distance. I believe this capacity for tolerating and living with paradox is closely related to what I think of as acceptance. Resignation, by contrast, is the impersonator of acceptance, where the maturity involved in accepting paradox is not well developed. Kumin (1978) notes how

> [e]ven in health, paradox is rigidly defended against. We see signs of this defence in our ubiquitous reliance upon secondary process modes of thought, [in our] ordinary obliviousness to the inevitability of death, and [in] the blind adherence to belief systems. Each individual has experienced sudden moments when certitude has vanished, only to be replaced by the simultaneous equal presence of an antithetical truth. It is a painful experience, dizzying. That it happens so infrequently suggests that even the healthy ego is suave in its successful repression of the nothingness which resides between the poles of paradoxical opposites. Such experience of nothingness is a benign and transient episode of depersonalization, and may be a preverbal memory of an infantile state which predated personalization.
>
> (p. 482)

I believe we are witnessing currently an important development in psychoanalysis. Almost since the beginning, our field has been marked by reductionistic dissension of one sort or another: "It's not this; it's that!" As a result there have been innumerable theoretical divergences, dialectical swings. Now, however, I believe there is a chance for a new outlook, one that is built on the capacity for entertaining paradox. I do not mean synthesis, which ultimately attempts to dispel paradox. Likewise, it is not simply a matter of a dialectical process,[5] nor is it a syncretistic effort to combine theories that are based on different premises and are therefore incompatible.

Earlier I referred to Mitchell's (1988) discussion of illusion. His conclusion is that it is not useful to choose and that for most analysts, a delicate balance, a necessary tension, prevails between the positions. His title, "The Wings of Icarus," elegantly captures this view.

Ogden (1988) conceives of human experience

> as the outcome of a dialectical relationship between three modes of experience [the autistic-contiguous, the paranoid-schizoid, and the depressive]. ... Experience is always generated between the poles represented by the ideal of the pure form of each of these modes. ... Psychopathology can be thought of as forms of collapse of the richness of experience generated between the poles.
>
> (p. 42)

It seems to me he, too, is speaking here about the necessity of maintaining a continuing tension among the three contestants for one's experience of any situation. I would refer to these modes of experience as paradoxically related rather than dialectical, as there is no synthesis; on the contrary, there is continual flux in health, and pathology is marked by any severe reduction in that flux.

Benjamin (1988), in a major contribution to psychoanalysis and feminism, concludes:

> In mutual recognition the subject accepts the premise that others are separate but nonetheless share like feelings and intentions. The subject is compensated for his loss of sovereignty by the pleasure of sharing, the communion with another subject. But for Hegel, as for Freud, the breakdown of essential tension is inevitable. The hypothetical self presented by Hegel and Freud does not *want* to recognize the other, does not perceive him as a person just like himself.
>
> (p. 53)

> The paradox is that the child not only needs to achieve independence but he must be recognized as independent—by the very people on whom he has been most dependent ... [pp. 52–53]. True independence means *sustaining the essential tension* of these contradictory impulses, that is, both asserting the self and recognizing the other. Dominance is the consequence of refusing this condition.
>
> (p. 53)

The issue of surrender as against submission has been of great interest to me; perhaps it has bearing here. Insofar as the need for recognition is enacted in the mode of submission rather than surrender and, conversely, the need for autonomy is enacted as domination in lieu of what I have also been calling surrender, another species of surrender, these two poles remain in opposition. But insofar as they are juxtaposed in the mode of surrender, the twin needs for autonomy and recognition not only are not in conflict but represent a vital complementarity as merely two different expressions of surrender. I find myself asking whether what Benjamin is referring to as "sustaining the essential tension" is what I have been calling the mode of surrender and whether, perhaps, an important ingredient in that mode is the capacity to live in paradox and not have to come down defensively on one side or the other.

Perhaps it is fitting to conclude here by echoing that in many areas of life, true independence or maturity likewise means sustaining the essential tension of contradictory pulls, the paradoxes that we need both to cherish as paradox and to cherish as process.

I close with a few words from Stephen Jay Gould (1989): "The beauty of nature lies in detail; the message in generality. Optimal appreciation demands both" (p. 13).

Notes

1. Khan (1972/1974) significantly emended Winnicott's meaning by adding an important modifier: "and not resolved precipitately" (p. 272).
2. I believe I am indebted to Harold Searles for this distinction but am unable to find a reference to this usage in his published works.
3. For purposes of expressive clarity I will at times use the masculine pronoun generically; it is not intended to convey any gender significance.
4. I believe Winnicott (1935) had something like this idea in mind when he said: "Omnipotent control of reality implies fantasy about reality. The individual gets to external reality through the omnipotent fantasies elaborated in the effort to get away from inner reality. … Omnipotent fantasies are not so much the inner reality itself as defense against the acceptance of it" (p. 130). Khan (1975) amplified this statement by adding that "Winnicott considered that fantasying can become an organized way of sustaining the False Self organization in a person" (p. xvi).
5. The argument has been made that my usage of paradox and process is really very close to the notion of the dialectic. Insofar as I see paradox pointing the way to a new level of understanding that is as yet unclear, it begs an understanding of the process that relates the apparent opposites. As this understanding comes about, the paradox gradually vanishes, and is often replaced by a new

paradox, a new pointer to the as yet not fully understood. From this perspective, the use of paradox is very much like dialectical thinking, where, indeed, there gradually evolves a synthesis between the opposing pulls. However, there is another perspective, one that is rooted in subjective experience. The value of holding on to paradox in the more static sense, the not precipitously seeking after resolution or synthesis, is exactly what Winnicott is emphasizing—that what is so vitally important is being able, subjectively, to hold on to the apparent contradiction, to live with and gradually integrate it, and not to flee it by rushing into a premature intellectual understanding of the process that underlies it.

References

Balint, M. (1968). *The basic fault: Therapeutic aspects of regression.* London, UK: Tavistock.

Bateson, G. (1979). *Mind and nature: A necessary unity.* New York, NY: Dutton.

Benjamin, J. (1988). *The bonds of love: Psychoanalysis, feminism, and the problem of domination.* New York, NY: Pantheon Books.

Bollas, C. (1989). *Forces of destiny: Psychoanalysis and human idiom.* London, UK: Free Association Books.

Bronowski, J. (1971). *The identity of man.* New York, NY: Natural History Press (American Museum of Natural History).

Ghent, E. (1989). Credo: The dialectics of one-person and two-person psychologies. *Contemporary Psychoanalysis, 25*, 169–211.

Ghent, E. (1990). Masochism, submission, surrender: Masochism as a perversion of surrender. *Contemporary Psychoanalysis, 26*, 108–136.

Gould, S. J. (1989). *Wonderful life: The Burgess Shale and the nature of history.* New York, NY: Norton.

Khan, M. M. R. (1960). Regression and integration in the analytic situation. *International Journal of Psycho-Analysis, 41*, 130–146.

Khan, M. M. R. (1974). Dread of surrender to resourceless dependence in the analytic situation. In *The privacy of the self.* New York, NY: International Universities Press. (Original work published 1972)

Khan, M. M. R. (1975). Introduction. In *Through paediatrics to psycho-analysis.* New York, NY: Basic Books.

Kohut, H. (1977). *The restoration of the self.* New York, NY: International Universities Press.

Kumin, I. M. (1978). Developmental aspects of opposites and paradox. *International Review of Psycho-Analysis, 5*, 477–484.

Little, M. I. (1985). Winnicott working in areas where psychotic anxieties predominate: A personal record. *Free Associations, 3*, 9–42.

Mitchell, S. A. (1988). *Relational concepts in psychoanalysis: An integration.* Cambridge, MA: Harvard University Press.

Ogden, T. H. (1988). On the dialectical structure of experience. *Contemporary Psychoanalysis, 24,* 17–45.

Stern, D. N. (1983). Implications of infancy research for psychoanalytic theory and practice. *Psychiatry Update, 2,* 7–21.

Stern, D. N. (1985). *The interpersonal world of the infant.* New York, NY: Basic Books.

Stolorow, R. D. and Lachmann, F. M. (1980). *Psychoanalysis of developmental arrests.* New York, NY: International Universities Press.

Sullivan, H. S. (1953), *The interpersonal theory of psychiatry.* New York, NY: Norton.

Winnicott, D. W. (1975). The manic defence. In *Through Paediatrics to Psycho-Analysis.* New York, NY: Basic Books. (Original work published in 1935)

Winnicott, D. W. (1965). Ego distortion in terms of true and false self. In *The Maturational Processes and the Facilitating Environment.* New York, NY: International Universities Press. (Original work published in 1960)

Winnicott, D. W. (1969). The use of an object and relating through identifications. *International Journal of Psycho-Analysis, 50,* 711–716.

Winnicott, D. W. (1971). *Playing and reality.* London, UK: Tavistock.

Zeanah, C. H., Anders, T. F., Seifer, R., and Stern, D. N. (1989). Implications of research on infant development for psychodynamic theory and practice. *American Academy of Child and Adolescent Psychiatry, 28*(5), 657–668.

Chapter 4

Introduction to E. Ghent, "Interaction in the Psychoanalytic Situation"

C. Seth Warren

It is a pleasure to introduce Emmanuel Ghent's paper "Interaction in the Psychoanalytic Situation." I was fortunate to take a number of seminars with Mannie during the middle 1990s, and it was during this time that I first heard the story of the Scottish throw (recounted in Ghent, 1995). It was for me, as I imagine it may have been for others, a powerful clinical vignette, and one that I often refer back to in my mind.

Like others of Ghent's papers, "Interaction in the Psychoanalytic Situation" is understated, and one might easily overlook the range and subtlety of the ideas put forth in this work. I have been rewarded by repeated readings of it, which have gently expanded my views about the nature of the therapeutic process. Ghent takes pains to ensure that the reader does not conclude that he is articulating a general theory of therapeutic change, but merely intends to highlight one particular facet of therapeutic interaction. But one senses that perhaps he is being modest. There is something important about the kinds of interactions he identifies, their place in psychoanalytic treatments, and what they reveal about the nature of the therapeutic process.

Like musical motifs in a complex score, this delightfully rich paper presents many of the central themes of relational psychoanalysis in novel and provocative ways: the role of enactment and dyadic features of repetition in the clinical situation; a revisiting of the notion of need outside the sway of drive theory; a reworking of the concept of "gratification" as a therapeutic response to an unformulated need quite separate from the "acting out" of drive theory; and the importance and place of dissociated emotional experience. But above all, Ghent advances the idea of an *interactive* psychoanalysis, one that is concerned with therapeutic transformation through new experience as much as it is with intellectual insight via interpretation.

Each of the clinical vignettes illustrates the central points Ghent wished to make in his paper. First, that there are unexpected moments in the clinical encounter. These moments cannot be planned or prepared for, but rather must be simply accepted and acknowledged by the two participants:

> Like a bell sounding in each of the illustrations, the phrase, "to my surprise" was a part of the therapist's reaction. It is as if the therapist's attention has been claimed by something unexpected, a loud hint that a new vista, a new *insight*, is brewing.
>
> (Ghent, 1995, p. 485)

Each of the examples involves contact between patient and therapist that was unexpected, unplanned for, unanticipated and decidedly "outside" of the usual frame of the therapy process. Each therapist in the examples identifies the event as significant—we can infer this from the fact that they have been selected out of the innumerable possible interactions.

But, fundamentally, each vignette emphasizes a therapeutic *experience* and *interaction*, as opposed to *insight*, as has been traditional in psychoanalytic therapy. In this way, Ghent advances a relational model of psychotherapy in continuity with a long tradition in psychoanalysis dating back to Sandor Ferenzci, Winnicott, Balint, Sullivan, Searles, and Kohut (among many others), in which cognitive understanding via interpretation is seen as playing a relatively diminished role, while the role of new experience through interaction in the therapeutic dyad is recognized as playing a greater part in the therapeutic process and outcome.

The clinical vignettes in this paper bring to mind another famous psychoanalytic anecdote that we also read and discussed in one of Ghent's seminars: the famous "somersault" reported by Michael Balint (1968) in *The Basic Fault*. Balint's story has the same quality of spontaneity as those in this paper: a story that is similarly both surprising and moving. In his idea of "therapeutic regression," Balint wished to reclaim from drive theory the idea of the value and even the necessity of clinical regression, not just "in the service of the ego," but as the expression of a needed return to unmet needs at more archaic levels of organization and a "new beginning" from that point. Like each therapist in Ghent's paper, Balint notes that the somersault was totally unexpected and "proved to be a great breakthrough."

It is worth considering the function of such a story for the reader. What is its impact on the reader? We too feel something unexpected. We are also taken by surprise, and this opens us up to the possibility of new emotional experiencing. Very much like the Zen koans I had the pleasure of discussing in seminars with Mannie, these psychoanalytic stories continue to operate on us over time, working quietly and unseen from within to create the possibility of new areas of awareness or new clinical sensibilities.

It is easy to trace the influence of Eastern thought on Ghent's idea of the "bell sounding," a moment that comes after much long and hard work has been done and that requires a receptivity or responsiveness that one might describe in a more traditional language as "unconscious." This moment of insight comes unbidden, with no obvious relationship to cause and effect. One senses the influence of the kinds of stories that come from Buddhist and other contemplative traditions, in which enlightenment comes in this way—not easily, usually with great preparation, but also with a spontaneity, surprise and unpredictability.

I recall Mannie retelling one such story about the way enlightenment comes: there is a door at which one knocks and knocks, until a moment comes when one realizes that there is no door, and there never has been. I think it is safe to say that Ghent was impressed and influenced by these ideas of personal transformation, but always in a relational context. The role of the therapist, like the role of the "guru," is essential.

Ghent brings in a decidedly relational bent in his expressed goal of finding a place for the idea of "need" in a post-drive psychoanalytic theory. He draws on theoretical ideas of Winnicott and Kohut, while also introducing systems theory and ideas about the organization of complex living systems. He establishes the concept of "need" on the basis of something that is relational at the core. He differentiates need from the instinctualized wish of drive theory and finds a place for such yearnings in the clinical process. He identifies "good needs" as understandable developmental imperatives such as those identified by Winnicott or Kohut, and he identifies "bad needs," such as the apparent need for impingement and/or neglect that appear in clinical enactments and self-destructive trends (more fully elaborated in his most famous paper, Masochism, submission, surrender (Ghent, 1990)).

The flip side of need is gratification, and Ghent revisits this latter concept as well. The concern about gratifying infantile wishes as an impediment to therapeutic progress in classical Freudian theory provides an opportunity for Ghent to offer a different perspective on the idea of gratification. Gratification does not always signify "acting out" on the part of the analyst in response to the pressure of the patient's infantile wishes, nor is it always a resistance to awareness of the transferential origins and sources of the patient's wishes. Rather, the clinical vignettes illustrate the importance and even necessity of certain kinds of "gratifying" responses that lead to therapeutic breakthroughs such as those he describes. Perhaps the heart of this paper is expressed in the following sentence:

> Might it be said that at least on some occasions the analyst was responding to a "need" of the patient's, one that even the patient did not know existed … until the analyst, by his spontaneous action, "gratified" it as a need, thereby allowing the patient to become aware of, and acknowledge it as, a wish and so begin the process of rehabilitating some repudiated or dissociated need?"
>
> (p. 483)

Ghent's use of quotation marks here, and also when he describes Hoffman's "gratification" of his patient's need, is clearly intended to ensure that we do not confuse his use of the term with its more literal origins in drive theory.

What is critical is the idea that yearnings and longings—not just instinctual wishes—can be buried and lost to awareness, and while such needs may respond to interpretation, Ghent wants us to consider how often we find that it is some piece of therapeutic interaction—a therapeutic response—that brings them to light, as opposed to interpretations. In this, we see Ghent's reworking of the concept of repetition compulsion: here it is not the compulsion to repeat or reenact past traumas, but the use of provoking impingements as a defensive expression of the yearning for some need to be met by an appropriate response. He expresses this idea explicitly:

> behind the manifest need for self-thwarting and the "invitation" to neglectful impingement as appeared in varying degrees of intensity in these illustrations, there lies another need-system whose goal is the reverse of the repetition compulsion.
>
> (p. 484)

Ghent postulates the existence of another motivational system, one that acts in opposition to that which is often described in Freudian terms as the "compulsion to repeat." This system represents a tendency to "seek out a new quality of experience or to destabilize the smooth functioning of the old, constrictive system" (p. 486)—a system Ghent associates with *hope* for a different response from the environment than the "expected" one. While Ghent wishes to be able to speak about motivational systems, he also seeks to avoid the usual error of reifications. Here too we see the influence of Eastern philosophy, as he expresses a view about motivation within a framework of flux: nothing is fixed, nothing is separate, and our conceptualizations to that effect are illusory and self-deceptive:

> We have come to recognize that not only is there no such thing as a baby, there is no such thing as an individual, only matrices of individuals in constant interactive flux.
>
> (p. 481)

Multiple readings of this paper have made it clear that it is a deceptively rich and wide-ranging discussion of some of the central themes of relational theory and practice. Ghent's voice is clear and personal, and one cannot help but feel his presence. And, while it is easy enough to locate Ghent's argument in a particular historical context—as part of a dialogue reflecting some of the concerns of the early years of the relational movement—this paper's poetry, subtlety and warmth raise it to the level of a true and enduring psychoanalytic classic.

References

Balint, M. (1968). *The basic fault*. Evanston, IL: Northwestern University Press.

Ghent, E. (1990). Masochism, submission, surrender. *Contemporary Psychoanalysis, 26*, 108–136.

Interaction in the psychoanalytic situation[1]

Emmanuel Ghent

Interaction in the psychoanalytic situation

In this age of the here-and-now of psychoanalytic interaction, a discussion about the place of need in psychoanalysis may seem strangely anachronistic, like rummaging among the dregs of a one-person psychology that is fast losing fashion. Having myself (Ghent, 1989) contributed to the cause of slaying the one-person dragon, I feel somewhat entitled to suggest now that a reconsideration of the question of need, rather than compromising the gains made by a thorough-going admission of the dimension of interaction into the psychoanalytic process, will augment and reinforce those gains.

To begin with, let me state my view of psychological need. The neonate comes equipped with a set of biases or preferences, such as a preference for warmth over cold, or for the edible over the inedible, and a quite amazing nervous system with a formidable array of built-in capabilities, central among them being an intrinsic capacity for organizing experience. Capacities, as for example, the ability to recognize invariants in recurring situations—tend to acquire a new feature, a quality one might think of as a *need to exercise the capacity* and gradually to expand its range of efficacy. Capacities, then, under the systematizing influence of experience, very soon graduate into needs, or motivational systems. To continue the illustration, the ability to recognize invariants before long evolves into the capacity to abstract or generalize from experience and, in time, the capacity, indeed the need, to "make meaning." This will ultimately expand vastly, in interaction with experience, to include increasingly complex organizations of meaning. The making of meaning, or the push for coherence, ultimately itself becomes an elaborate motivational system. All need-systems have their origin in creative response to their immediate environment.

Circumstances both internal and external activate needs in the developing person—neonate, infant, child, adult—in successive tiers of complexity.

By the time we encounter the neonate, it has already evolved an absolutely unique neural constellation, rooted partly in genetic givens and partly on the basis of the natural selection of neural "circuitry" in the fetus, such that even in identical twins there are substantial differences in neural patterning. Here I am referring to Edelman's (1987, 1992) theory of neural group selection or "Neural Darwinism" (see also Sacks, 1993).

My point in articulating this preamble is twofold: (1) to stress the role of experience—particularly interactive human experience—not only in the dynamic evolution of styles of perception, memory, affect, and action but also in the very nature of need, and (2) to alert you to my usage of the term need. Although in the vernacular the word need is sometimes used to suggest an intensity of wish or desire, I am using it to signify the thrust, tendency, or goal of a motivational system, without regard to whether the system is progressive or growth oriented on the one hand, or conservative or defensive on the other.[2] I find it valuable to think in terms of motivational systems and their thrusts or goals. Historically, need crept into psychoanalysis because yearnings were encountered that had no place in drive theory. In this usage—Winnicott, Balint, Kohut—the term need was used largely in connection with "good needs." But "bad needs" were at times also elevated into prominence as, for example, in Winnicott's (1950–55, p. 212) discussion of the need for impingement in false self organizations of personality. The terms good needs and bad needs were, of course, never made explicit, but their very presence has been, to me, an invitation to reconsider the entire question of need: its developmental origins, its functional relations to the organism as a whole, its systematization. Removing the term need from the sphere of implicit value judgments frees us to consider need afresh and conceptualize any particular need as a resultant of a highly complex mix of conflicting constituent needs—*interactive* systems of motivational pushes or pulls.

As one studies the workings of living organisms, it soon becomes clear that everything living is interactive, be it at the molecular level, the molar level, or the level of interaction with other living beings. Even this formulation, however, is insufficient. *Everything* is in flux, which means that *everything*, living or not, is interactive. When the rate of change—the rate of interaction—is rapid we call it process; when it is very slow, we refer to structures. In the early years of psychoanalysis, there were structures galore: the unconscious, the instincts, the subdivisions of mind, concrete memories and fantasies, all were looked upon as entities. There was the patient and the analyst, the observed and the observer, each in its separate corner of existence. All this (like everything else) is changing. We have come to recognize that not only is there no such thing as a baby, there is no such thing as an individual, only matrices of individuals in constant interactive flux. Sullivan (1940/1966, p. 11) was among the first to recognize this and coined the phrase "participant observation," a term that, after some 50 years, was recently reinvented by Charles Brenner (1987). Erich Fromm, long ago anticipating the current trend toward social constructivism, changed it to "observant participation." Now it is called, simply, interaction.

Out of the vast arena of interaction in psychoanalysis, I would like to carve out a tiny morsel as a focus for discussion. The crux of my concern on this occasion lies at the intersection of two quite different levels of interaction: (1) the relation between analyst and patient as sentient, responsive human beings, and (2) the complex relationship between perception and response and their roles in modulating one another. Clearly, these matters have relevance for the still open question of the nature of the therapeutic effect of psychoanalysis. I would like to emphasize at the outset, however, that my selection of topic is in no way intended as a claim on what is primary in therapeutic efficacy. Instead, I offer this discussion to suggest that among the *many* factors that may contribute to the healing, wholing, and mending of the human soul, the one that I am about to articulate plays a role on occasion, and probably only in certain types of analyst-analysand dyads. First, a few illustrations.

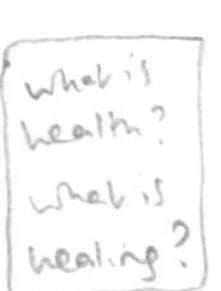

Many years ago I had an office on the ground floor of a Greenwich Village brownstone. As it faced out on a large garden and much open space, the office was quite susceptible to chilly drafts on windy winter days. One such day a woman patient was haltingly recounting, as was her wont, the details of some event that had recently occurred; I cannot now recall the content. She was sitting in a chair at right angles to me, about 15 feet from the windows. Suddenly, but not abruptly, I got up, went over to where a Scottish throw was folded on the couch, picked it up, covered her lap and legs with it, and returned to my chair. As I sat down I noticed, *to my surprise*, that she was sobbing silently. It was the first time in our work, by then over two years in duration, that there was any indication of distress, pain, or even sadness. After some time, her first words were, "I didn't even know I was feeling cold," and then she wept profusely. The event was a turning point.

A second example. In discussing the analyst's natural, spontaneous reactions to patients during the work, Irwin Hoffman (1992) has drawn attention to how often it turns out that such an event has enormous therapeutic value. Hoffman recounts how, at one point in an analysis, he yielded to the temptation to engage a patient in a political debate regarding an issue about which they both had strong but opposing feelings. Jumping to the last session, when analyst and patient were reflecting on the ways in which the therapy had helped her, Hoffman comments, "[S]he said, *to my surprise*, that if she had to select one event in the whole therapy that she thought had the most impact it was probably that time when we discussed politics. She said … it had something to do with allowing herself and being allowed by me to step out of the role of the patient, if only momentarily, something to do with regarding herself and being regarded by me as a peer" (p. 12). Reflecting on such situations, Hoffman adds, "What a therapist [actually] does at [moments of deciding among a variety of alternative actions,] although it may reflect a great deal of clinical and theoretical sophistication, is also invariably personally expressive and cannot be understood merely as the application of a principle of technique. … Moreover, the full nature of what is expressed by the action is not transparent to the therapist, the patient or anyone else" (pp. 2–3).

Although Hoffman's focus in his presentation was on the dialectic of repetition as against new experience, his material lends itself as well to another question, one that informs all my illustrations. Might it be said that at least on some occasions the analyst was responding to a "need" of the patient's, one that even the patient did not know existed—the unthought known (Bollas, 1987)—until the analyst, by his spontaneous action, "gratified" it as a need, thereby allowing the patient to become aware of, and acknowledge it as, a wish and so begin the process of rehabilitating some repudiated or dissociated need?

Darlene Ehrenberg (1992) offers us a wonderful illustration. Her patient, Sara, was an extremely anxious patient; she "was profusely apologetic about her state and extremely solicitous of" her therapist. At one point, Ehrenberg writes,

> there were some seemingly inexplicable moments with Sara when I would find myself becoming distracted despite her apparent great

> pain. One time when she began to cry and I found my attention wandering I felt horror at my own insensitivity. Though she seemed barely to notice, I told her that I did not understand what had happened. I felt the least I owed her was an apology. She brushed this off. I persisted and noted that as far as I was aware, this kind of insensitivity was not typical of me. I tried to engage her as to her ideas about what had happened. *To my surprise* she replied matter of factly, saying that this was the typical way her mother had responded to her whenever she had tried to talk to her about anything. She reiterated her feeling that it was no big deal to her now. I replied that as far as I was concerned it *was* a big deal, and that from my perspective her failure to understand that it was and her willingness to accept this kind of treatment from me—or from anyone—without a protest seemed to be part of the problem. She said nothing.
>
> (pp. 53–54, italics added)

Ehrenberg then goes on to show how valuable this experience was in alerting her to the quality of interaction so that the next time something similar arose she was able to catch it early and use it as a basis for microscrutinizing and clarifying, as she puts it, "who was doing what to whom, and in what order—then with her mother, now with me" (p. 54).

I would like to suggest an extension of this focus, that behind the manifest need for self-thwarting and the "invitation" to neglectful impingement as appeared in varying degrees of intensity in these illustrations, there lies another need-system whose goal is the reverse of the repetition compulsion. In another context, I (Ghent, 1990) have referred to one expression of this type of need system as the yearning for surrender. Winnicott (1950–55) insisted that, where environmental impingement has played a major role in one's early life, "[t]he 'individual' develops … as an extension of the impinging environment" (p. 212). In this pattern, he adds, "it is only through environmental impingement that the motility potential becomes a matter of experience. … [T]he individual *must* be opposed [—I would add '*needs* to be opposed'—], and only if opposed does the individual tap the important motility source" (p. 212). In the case of Sara, clearly the neurotic need was to evoke a reenactment of an old familiar pattern of impingement and not being recognized. Ehrenberg, however, recognized her own participation in the as yet unclear scenario as she became aware that her attention was wandering just when the patient began to cry. But she would not allow it to rest at this level of interaction. Despite the patient's protestations, Ehrenberg was responding to—gratifying, so to speak—Sara's deeply dissociated need, her unconscious yearning for a caring, responsive attunement, and Sara could only respond with silence. Had the yearning been less deeply buried, less entwined with a dread of betrayal, it is possible that she would have wept, much as in the first illustration. While, on this occasion the *response* did not bring out the yearning (as a derivative of the need) into focal awareness, it nonetheless had something of a stunning effect and was an experience that paved the way for more work in the direction of integrating her need for recognition and tenderness.

In the first example, the patient's first words, "I didn't even know I was cold," are telling. I read these words to mean something like, "I am not in touch with my need for warmth, and I am certainly not aware of a need for someone to recognize my state of being, and especially to be sensitively responsive to it. But immediately I felt you place the throw over me, I felt overwhelmed with a feeling I can only call pain, a pain that tells me of the intensity of a longing I barely knew was there."

Note, by the way, that in none of these examples was there any question of demand, the shibboleth of the neediness that often masquerades as need but in actuality is organized as a defense against—a blackwashing of—the need for caring responsiveness.

Like a bell sounding in each of the illustrations, the phrase "to my surprise" was part of the therapist's reaction. It is as if the therapist's attention has been claimed by something unexpected, a loud hint that a new vista, a new *insight*, is brewing.

Of special moment in each of the examples is that, along with the old pattern of behavior, *something new* was happening, and it is impossible to say, nor does it much matter, whether the trigger for the new element was something in what the patient was doing or how she was doing it, or in the therapist's response; certainly it was in the interaction. The need to repeat some old, well-established pattern of interaction does not mean that the patient "wishes" to repeat (although that may be there as well); it means that a motivational system (with perceptual expectations, memory, affect, and action built into it), once established, tends to perpetuate itself; this is in the very nature of many centripetally organized systems, systems that we commonly think of as defensive. It is this conservative *tendency of the system* that I am referring to as a species of need. The form it takes may be some version of a repetition compulsion, a need to grind out some rendering of an old and usually self-defeating pattern, a pattern that works best if it can get the other member of a dyad to participate actively in the consummation of the pattern.

But mixed in with the apparent need to repeat, another (and opposing) motivational system, or need, is operating as well, one that is usually much weaker and less developed; it is an expansive rather than a conservative system, one whose tendency or need is either to seek out a *new* quality of experience or to destabilize the smooth functioning of the old, constrictive system. Winnicott (1956/1958), speaking of the antisocial tendency, recognized that the delinquent act was (*also*) an expression of hope—an act that compels the environment to respond, hope that the therapist will respond "in terms of management, tolerance, and understanding" (p. 309). Many types of acting out likewise are expressions not only of a repetition to avoid remembering, as Freud (1914) put it, but an action designed to elicit a *new* and more growth-enhancing quality of interaction.

The point that I am trying to bring into focus is that, among the various modes of interaction that can have mutative impact, one is the "gratification" or, perhaps a better term, the validation, of a need that has as yet not surfaced into awareness and certainly has not been integrated into the self. The more general point is that *response can change perception*. I emphasize this because it is the reverse of what most of us, as analysts, have come to believe.

Usually when we use the word interaction we are referring to the interaction between individuals. But there is another interactive circle, the interaction between perception and response within an individual. In the three vignettes the interventions are primarily aimed, however spontaneously or unintentionally, at the response end of what might be called the perception-response loop. And yet one can recognize that a change is taking place at the perceptual end; the patient is beginning to see, or feel, or experience something about herself and about the other person that had not been experienced before. Needs, like the need for tenderness and the need for recognition, that had long lived in the deep shadows of awareness, were given an opportunity to come into the light; at the same time, the analyst's response gave validation to a sense of agency and efficacy, however undeveloped and out of awareness, in the patient's making her needs known.

I think we tend to overlook the plurality of routes by which psychic change occurs, both within and outside of analysis. Some types of intervention focus on the perceptual pole of an interactive circle, others on the effector or response end. A change in either may, and often does, result in a change in the entire system. Classically, psychoanalysis has concentrated on the perceptual end of the loop. Interpretation is aimed at helping the patient see, or perceive, things differently, that is, from a new perspective. The implicit assumption was that changed perception would result in changes in ways of being and doing in the world, that is, that changes at the effector or response end will result. *Insight* will lead to change. That this has, by no means, been the universal result has caused great problems for psychoanalysis, problems often spoken of under the rubric of the uselessness, even counterproductiveness, of "intellectual insight."

Insight itself is another way of referring to perceptual change. Even in those instances where it seems that insight has made for change, one is often left with the lingering suspicion that substantial, perhaps critical, change had already occurred and that the insight was made possible as the concluding step in the long buildup of change, much like the sudden precipitation of crystals in a supersaturated solution. One might reasonably conclude that change in the system, *however it is brought about*, may *result* in insight.

When we say "however it is brought about" are we not implying that something in the *interaction* of the person with his environment (say, the analyst) has brought about the change? Is this not a way of saying that changes at the effector end, the response end of the loop, in the *interaction* with another have wrought change? It seems reasonable to infer that the nature of a relationship in and of itself could effect ameliorative psychic change—being taken seriously, being listened to with empathic sensitivity, being recognized in a meaningful human sense; all of these, incidentally, are addressed to the response end of the loop. Even an interpretation, that is, an intervention directed to the perceptual pole, always exists in an interactive context.

One might extend a familiar aphorism by saying that there is no such thing as an interpretation without a relationship. The quality of the interpretive interaction may be anything—a feed, a joyous gift, a bloodless exercise, a hackneyed recital, or a toxic assault. The envelope of the interpretation may be of greater moment than its contents, but both are inevitably present—for better or worse!

At a recent conference Arnold Cooper (1992) said:

> It is less than clear that cognitive aspects of insight are essential for psychic change. … Stanley Greenspan … has shown that better mothering or removal from an abusive situation produces powerful and lasting changes in the child, even though the child is not helped to develop insight into what is going on. … This also brings up the question of non-analytic change, and the importance for analysis of our better understanding of conversion experiences—whether St. Paul or Malcolm X—and the importance of peak affect.
>
> (p. 248)

As we look back on the three illustrative vignettes, insight seems to have been quite secondary; yet each portrayed a kind of transformative experience (on however small a scale).

There is a shift going on in psychoanalysis. Although it had its early roots in healing as an end in itself, psychoanalysis soon developed along the lines of cognitive understanding as a vehicle for psychic change. For Freud, even the matter of psychic change assumed secondary importance. The foreground was occupied by psychoanalysis as a research endeavor, a means of comprehending human nature, especially human motivation. In the matter of praxis, interpretation and insight became cardinal shibboleths. Although never expressed explicitly, the idea was that information would produce transformation.

Over the past half century, with increasing momentum, both within psychoanalysis and in the variety of "new therapies" that have sprung up around us—group therapy, family therapy, encounter therapy, gestalt therapy, behavior therapy, art therapy, primal scream, rebirthing, and so on—this notion has been challenged in different ways and for different reasons. Interestingly, the goals of these therapies were explicitly transformative, not informative. Common to all these challenges is a premise that transformation may be addressed directly, that it may be assisted by "informational" facilitation, but that information alone is probably only rarely transformative.

Within psychoanalysis, some of the thrust for this change in emphasis came from analysts who were troubled by the inefficacy, *as a therapy*, of much psychoanalytic effort. Increasingly, pioneering analysts were extending therapeutic efforts into the farther reaches of human psychopathology, areas that required new and imaginative approaches. There were Ferenczi, Winnicott, Balint, Fromm, Sullivan, Alexander, Racker, Bion, Searles, and, most recently, Kohut, among many others—each with his own perspective and each addressing somewhat different aspects of the need for a transformative focus in the analytic process. All are joined, despite their theoretical differences, in stressing the importance of the *interactive* experience in the analytic process. Many share a common perspective that recognizes a *need* in the patient for a *quality of experience* in the analysis without which therapeutic effect will be minimal. Many were, at some point, looked upon as heretics or renegades. I remember how Heinz Hartmann (1959, personal communication), speaking about Sullivan, said, "Well, he's not an analyst; from a therapeutic point of view his approach may get better results than we do, but it's not psychoanalysis."

Perhaps what I am suggesting here is that, if we are to set our sights on *therapeutic* goals, we may find ourselves considering, for some people, ancillary modes that could complement and facilitate the psychoanalytic mode. I think, for example, that meditation (with proper instruction) can function this way. Just two things to say about meditation for now. First is that I look upon meditation as interactive, but in a unique way: even when one meditates alone, one is not alone; the other, the guru, is always present as the transitional object who provides the transitional meditation space. Second, meditation raises a very interesting question: the role of self-discipline and practice in effecting psychic change. In almost every other endeavor in life, effort and practice are part of improving and developing one's skills, talents, and capacities; but when it comes to the question of psychic change in psychoanalysis, analysts have tended to assume that coming to sessions, "free associating," and receiving accurate interpretations two or four or six times a week will somehow effect the change. And sometimes it does!

By way of a coda that picks up a strand of the main theme, I would like to recount a fourth vignette. Many years ago I was working with a young surgeon who came into analysis because he had received numerous complaints from patients, and even colleagues, that he seemed totally oblivious to their feelings. Although he told me a good deal about his life, his narration was singularly devoid of affective connection. One day he came in with his usual cherubic smile and said, "Guess what! Gail called me from upstate. She said she had decided to leave this cold climate and move down south to Florida. She asked me to meet her at the airport, where she will be changing planes. It was strange to hear from her, I hadn't heard a peep from her in over a year. But it'll be kind of nice to see her again." My instant response was, "Does she have a gun?" He wheeled around on the couch, looked at me with a mixture of incredulity and scorn, and, after a short while, said, "I always thought psychiatrists were weird, but aren't you overstepping a bit? She wouldn't know which end of a gun to hold in her hand! I replied, "Perhaps I am weird, but I would like to ask you to do something for *me*—let's call it a favor for me. Please call the State gunlicensing authority and inquire as to whether she has a license." By now amused, he agreed to do this, and we proceeded to explore why I might have had such an outlandish idea. Next session, he came in, looking different than I had ever seen him; the ebullient smile had vanished. He announced grimly, "I found out that Gail got a gun license two weeks ago." Needless to say, he did not keep the airport rendezvous.

My reaction was not magic. In retrospect, the hunch was the resultant of three vectors: his history of car accidents and private-plane crashes, his remarkable skill in the art of exploiting women, and an amazing obliviousness to other people's feelings. The quality of the analysis improved significantly after this dent in the manic defense; he began to be able to *perceive* something of other people's reactions to him. Note that the action was at the response end: I *did* something; he was shocked; he *did* something (called the license bureau) and was shocked again. Had I addressed him at the perceptual pole, by interpreting his obliviousness to having exploited Gail financially, so that revenge might be in the offing, he would likely have said with a touch of scoffing, "Oh, that's interesting!"

In closing, I would like to recapitulate what I said at the outset, that what I have carved out of the vast arena of *interaction in psychoanalysis* represents but one tiny morsel, and even there—as with anything potentially useful—dangers and pitfalls abound. It would be easy to misunderstand my intention as recommending primary attention to the effector pole. Second, while my aim in therapy is transformative, this should not be construed to mean mere adaptation to social expectations. Also, I hope it is clear that my focus in this presentation is in no way meant as advocacy of behavior therapy, which not only tends toward social adaptation, but also tends to eschew any interest in understanding or clarification and by and large seems to work largely through suggestion and manipulation. At the same time, I am aware of, and have respect for, the more enlightened forms of behavior therapy, as for example Wachtel's (1977) efforts to couple it with a psychoanalytically informed therapy. Finally, I would like to add a few words of caution in relation to another danger that ill-conceived use of the concepts discussed here could lead to. I am referring to a type of therapy characterized by a simplistic and highly manipulative reductionism, one that I have come to call "Bolshevik therapy." An example may be found in the perversion of Sullivan's epigenetic scheme into a programmatic cult experience that became wildly destructive, the very opposite of what one would hope for from psychoanalysis.

Notes

1. First presented at a *Symposium on Interaction in the Psychoanalytic Situation*, sponsored by the National Institute for the Psychotherapies, April 24, 1993; also presented at the spring meeting of the American Psychological Association, Division 39, Washington, DC, April 16, 1994.
2. My reasons for this usage, and its relation to "Neural Darwinism," will be discussed in a forthcoming paper.

References

Bollas, C. (1987). *The shadow of the object: Psychoanalysis and the unthought known*. New York, NY: Columbia University Press.

Brenner, C. (1987). Notes on psychoanalysis by a participant observer: A personal chronicle. *Journal of the American Psychoanalytic Association*, *35*, 539–556.

Cooper, A. M. (1992). Psychic change: Development in the theory of psychoanalytic techniques. *International Journal of Psycho-Analysis*, *73*, 245–250.

Edelman, G. M. (1987). *Neural darwinism*. New York, NY: Basic Books.

Edelman, G. M. (1992). *Bright air, brilliant fire*. New York, NY: Basic Books.

Ehrenberg, D. B. (1992). *The intimate edge*. New York, NY: Norton.

Freud, S. (1914). Remembering, repeating and working-through. *Standard Edition*, *12*, 145–156.

Ghent, E. (1989). Credo: the dialectics of one-person and two-person psychologies. *Contemporary Psychoanalysis*, *25*, 169–211.

Ghent, E. (1990). Masochism, submission, surrender. *Contemporary Psychoanalysis*, *26*, 108–136.

Hoffman, I. Z. (1992). Expressive participation and psychoanalytic discipline. *Contemporary Psychoanalysis*, *28*, 1–15.

Sacks, O. (1993, April). Making up the mind. [Review of the book *Bright air, brilliant fire:On the matter of the mind*, by G.M. Edelman]. *New York Review of Books*, 42–52.

Sullivan, H. S. (1966). *Conceptions of modern psychiatry*. New York, NY: Norton. (Original work published 1940)

Wachtel, P. L. (1977). *Psychoanalysis and behavior therapy*. New York, NY: Basic Books.

Winnicott, D. W. (1950–55). Aggression in relation to emotional development. In *Through paediatrics to psycho-analysis* (pp. 204–218). New York, NY: Basic Books. (Original work published 1956)

Winnicott, D. W. (1958). The antisocial tendency. In *Through paediatrics to psycho-analysis* (p. 306–315). New York, NY: Basic Books. (Original work published 1956)

Chapter 5

The butterfly in the consulting room

Barry Magid

In this, his last published paper, Ghent attempted a radical re-thinking of our basic analytic metaphors, inspired by the revolution in developmental systems theory of Esther Thelen and the neurobiology of Gerald Edelman's Neural Darwinism. Edelman and Thelen were part of a larger paradigm shift that included new, mathematically rigorous theories of chaos theory (Lorenz, 1972) and fractal geometry (Mandelbrot, 1983). This shift can be dated back to 1972, when meteorologist Edward Lorenz gave a lecture entitled "Predictability: Does the flap of a butterfly's wings in Brazil set off a tornado in Texas?" which was the starting point of what became known as the famous butterfly effect.

Progress in the sciences is usually thought of in terms of research and the acquisition of new data. However, the greatest impact of a scientific discovery may be how it reshapes our metaphorical view of ourselves and our world. It made no practical difference whatsoever to Renaissance man whether the earth revolved around the sun or vice versa; it made an enormous difference whether he, and his Church, saw himself as the center of God's universe or whether he was a de-centered occupant of an infinite cosmos indifferent to his existence. This shift in perspective is, on the one hand, a shift in the understanding of the basic *causal* mechanisms at work in the universe; on the other, it involves a shift of *meaning,* the substitution of one explanatory frame for another. When we speak of causes, we are inclined towards a mechanistic and deterministic picture of events; the realm of meaning, however, brings us back to a sense of human agency and the possibility of alternate stories, by which we can make sense of our experience. A purely Newtonian picture of causality seems to preclude the possibility of free will and agency; the world of reasons and meanings is reduced to the totally deterministic language of physics. The only alternative appears for us to act as if the mind operates in a separate sphere of freedom, across a Cartesian divide designed to allow mind and will to be somehow transcendentally free of their physical constraints.

However, with the advent of what became known as dynamic systems theory, a model of recursive systems and emergent properties was proposed as an alternative to linear, teleological and causal systems, and the old Newtonian "billiard ball" model of causality was itself shown to be a picture that very poorly approximated how nature works. Physical systems were no longer paradigms of determinism and predictability; rather, randomness, complexity and unpredictability were shown to be irreducibly part of the natural world.

Along with Lorenz and his followers, Benoit Mandelbrot's *The Fractal Geometry of Nature* (1983) provided the mathematical basis for complexity theory that in many ways underpins Thelen and Edelman's work in biology and neurology. Mandelbrot wrote, "Classical mathematics had its roots in the regular geometric structures of Euclid and the continuously evolving dynamics of Newton." Nature, however, as Mandelbrot was to show, was intrinsically irregular and discontinuous, and was poorly modeled as variations on regular angles and smooth curves. He coined the term "fractal" from the Latin verb frangere (adj. fractus), meaning to break into irregular fragments. Like chaos theory, fractal geometry demonstrated how very small variations in initial conditions could give rise to unpredictably complex outcomes.

Taken together, these revolutions—dynamic systems theory, neural Darwinism, chaos theory and fractal geometry—radically overturned our linear understanding of cause and effect. Ghent's reconfiguring of our thinking about drive, need and wish can be seen as a contribution to this Kuhnian paradigm shift, bringing the insights of complexity to the language of psychoanalysis.

Ghent quotes Thelen: "Although behavior and development appear structured, there are no structures. Although behavior and developmental appear rule driven, there are no rules. There is complexity." (If "rules" seems an unlikely word, think how automatically we refer to the genetic "code.") "Structure" and "rules" were concepts so basic to our understanding of function, that we no more could imagine a way of talking about minds and brains and language and development without using these words than we could omitting "the," "and" and "is." Concepts like "design" and "program" we could recognize as metaphors; after all, we no longer believed in a divine designer or programmer. But the gene had subtly replaced God in our metaphors; perhaps we should have begun spelling "Gene" with a capital G, to reflect its apotheosis. Design, purpose, and, most importantly for us as psychoanalysts, drive, need and motivations, were "built in" biologically, that is, genetically predetermined functions that could emerge, be blocked, expressed or sublimated, but whose essential nature was a given.

Ironically, this shift took place just as another metaphorical wave was cresting—the wave of the computational model of the mind, which gave us pictures of the "hardwiring" and "programming" of the brain, which was to be mimicked in the burgeoning project of artificial intelligence. It was this picture of the brain as "hardwired" that Edelman specifically challenged, demonstrating that neural connectivity was not predetermined, but instead was dependent on environmental stimulation, not just for its emergence, but its very architecture. Doubly ironically, Ghent was simultaneously a pioneer in computer science and in its application to musical composition. But Ghent recognized that the metaphor of the computer as a model of the mind was one of the most persistent and pernicious carriers of linear thinking. A computer is the quintessential Cartesian isolated mind (Stolorow and Atwood, 1992), certain only of its inner programming and "knowing" the world only through coded inputs to which it responds in a predetermined manner. John Searle (1980) illustrated the deficiency of the computational picture with the metaphor of the Chinese Room. Imagine you are in a sealed room with only a single small window, through which a piece of paper can be passed back and forth. A slip comes in. On it are written Chinese characters. Behind you is a giant reference book, in which you can look up the characters on the paper. But your reference book only indicates that when a particular character is given to you, you are to write another particular character on a new slip of paper and pass it through the window in response. An observer outside the room would see questions in Chinese being asked and correctly answered. But you do not know a word of Chinese. Searle maintained that understanding Chinese belonged not to the room or its occupant (i.e. the computer), but solely to the programmer who complied the reference book. And no amount of increased complexity in the programming could ever result in the room being considered either intelligent or conscious.

In line with Thelen's perspective on dynamic systems, we can instead see consciousness along a spectrum of evolving capacities and motivations at every evolutionary stage of life. Building on Thelen, and echoing Ghent's notion of evolving capacities creating the underpinning of motivation, Maxine Sheets Johnson (2011) writes,

> A creature's corporeal consciousness is first and foremost a consciousness attuned to the movement and rest of its own body. … Kinetic spontaneity may be analyzed in terms of kinesthetic motivations … a repertoire of what might be termed "I cans"—a sense of agency. (p. 62)

This sense of bodily knowing and agency permits us to place consciousness on an evolutionary continuum, rather than have it appear, suddenly, mysteriously, with the advent of language or Cartesian self-awareness. Agency originates in bodily capacity, not with an inner self (and "free will") pulling the levers that make the physical body move. As such, the responses of a single-cell organism moving and responding in its surround offer a closer approximation of consciousness than do the actions of the most sophisticated super-computer.

The turn to non-linearity in systems theory can be seen paralleling the turn to multiplicity in psychoanalytic theories of the self (Bromberg, 1996). Rather than envisioning a unified and unifying overarching "self," as in Kohut's (1976) Self Psychology, the relational turn led to a picture of multiple, competing selfstates, and multiple, competing systems of motivations, which increasingly defied hierarchical sorting. Psychological development was no longer seen as proceeding step-wise through a predictable linear sequence (Ogden, 1989); rather, multiple needs, once thought to represent different "stages" of maturation, could co-exist, combining or conflicting in ways that had no predictable pattern or outcome. Multiplicity was no longer a sign of pathological fragmentation or disintegration (Slavin and Kriegman, 1992), but a description of the healthy dissociation that allowed an individual to maintain a sense of personhood and continuity, while at the same time experiencing an ever-shifting set of subjective realities.

The non-linear approach to development led Ghent to reconceptualize motivation as arising from the self-evolving emergence of capacities or functions. Drawing an analogy with Thelen's description of the multiplicity of ways by which a child develops the capacity for reaching for an object, Ghent hypothesizes that emergent capacities, met with varying facilitating and thwarting circumstances, gradually coalesce into stable motivational systems, which in turn are experienced, consciously or unconsciously, as "needs." In this model, the organization of defensive behaviors to avoid shame or disappointment have, for Ghent, "as much claim on the word as the need for exploration, though from the outside they appear to us to be antithetical to what we think of as an intrinsic need of the child." Seeing needs as nothing more than organized motivational systems removes them from the realm of values, including health values. Needs are not a priori classifiable as good needs or bad needs, healthy or defensive. Confusion between need and wish at both the colloquial and theoretical level allowed unexamined value judgments to enter into their alleged distinction, typically with the analyst knowing what the patient "actually" needed despite what they consciously expressed a wish for. Ghent's perspective also allows us to drop the distinction between wishes—motivations that could be accounted for in a drive-based model—and the kind of needs, postulated by Winnicott, Balint, Kohut et al., for self regulation and self cohesion. Both transference and what had been seen as resistance are equally expressions of need, that is, of powerful motivational systems developed early in life that are highly resistant to change, neither of which can a priori be deemed superordinate to the other. Eschewing value judgments, we instead see a highly complex interaction of entwined systems.

This stepping back to a non-judgmental observation of the multiplicity of motivational systems, Ghent likened to the introspective process of Buddhist meditation. The meditator observes the ephemeral nature of the mind's contents, and over the course of much practice, dis-identifies with the ever-shifting amalgam we are used to calling "I." "Needs" from this perspective are not to be repudiated, as Buddhism is sometimes misunderstood to be advocating, but seen as empty of intrinsic value or foundational meaning. However, the meditator's non-goal-directed observation of the flow of thought and emotion potentially reveals something more than is indicated in Ghent's brief description here. We might also see, for instance, that the flow is actually constituted by an ongoing dynamic struggle that seeks to avoid shame and vulnerability, to exercise control over the flow and quality of our experience, and attempts, through concentration, to reinforce preferred states of calm, thought-free silence or even bliss. Thus what we observe is anything but free-flowing. Its particular patterns of turbulence are continually re-created and re-enforced by conscious and unconscious attempts at controlling our mind. Ghent's description foregrounds the de-shaming that can take place from a stance of detached observation. Another important aspect of de-shaming occurs in the basic acceptance of the uncontrollable flow of multiple self states. This is not because we distance or detach ourselves from them—rather, in a way more parallel to psychoanalysis, we allow ourselves to feel what has been hitherto warded off; we stay with what we habitually avoid; and tolerate precisely those aspects of the mind we probably came to meditation to eliminate.

Meditation leaves everything just as it finds it (to echo Wittgenstein's (1953) description of his philosophical position). But doing nothing is profoundly disruptive to the dynamic system of a mind perpetually engaged in control and avoidance. "Just sitting" and leaving the mind as is, is itself a powerful perturber of the system. This provides us with a better dynamic systems view of what happens in meditation than Ghent was able to offer at the time, and one which draws it closer to the analytic process.

Furthermore, Ghent's model of meditation is of a one-person system; the meditator, through a prolonged process of meditative introspection, observes and de-centers himself from the repetitive content of his thought patterns. This allows both de-shaming and the opportunity for "choice" regarding other potential patterns of thought or behavior in the future. Contrast this to the Zen story of the monk who asks his master, "What is the highest truth of Buddhism?" In response, the master hits him. Here we clearly have a scenario where the master's intent is to radically perturb the monk's system of thought. After being hit multiple times, the monk may suddenly realize that he is not being chastised; he is being given an answer. What kind of answer? The highest truth of Buddhism is to be found in the immediacy of this present moment, prior to any conceptualization. What could be more immediate and attention-getting than being hit?

Whatever you think about this as technique, we are being presented with a systems approach to transformation. Yet, in the realm of complex systems, it becomes extremely difficult to specify or predict the results of a perturbation in the system. If the proverbial flutter of a butterfly's wings can set off a hurricane, how are we to understand the potential consequences of any of our interventions, let alone control or predict them?

Ghent's concern in this paper lies primarily within the realm of validation, and the underlying assumption that therapeutic action resides in the recognition of the equal legitimacy of all motivational systems. From the perspective of dynamic systems theory, to the extent that the patient's psychodynamics have been organized around an implicit or explicit repudiation of some aspect of their own needs, acknowledgment, rather than rejection, will in and of itself constitute a perturbation in that system. The implications of this re-formulation of therapeutic action are part of what we might have anticipated in Ghent's future work. This perspective parallels the more recent formulations by Bromberg on the overcoming of dissociation by the validation of the claims of conflicting selfstates. Further, we can imagine Ghent moving towards a recognition of the analyst's participation in the establishment and perpetuation of a particular relational matrix, as well as the impact of the patient on the analyst's system and the role of mutual influence. All are emergent dimensions, which, following Ghent's challenging leads, we are now endeavoring to explore.

References

Bromberg, P. (1996). Standing in the spaces. *Contemporary Psychoanalysis, 32*, 509–535

Edelman, G. (1992) *Neural Darwinism: The theory of neuronal group selection*. New York, NY: Basic Books.

Kohut, H. (1976). *The restoration of the self*. Madison, CT: International Universities Press.

Lorenz, E. (1972) Predictability: Does the flap of a butterfly's wings in Brazil set off a tornado in Texas? *American Association for the Advancement of Science.*

Mandelbrot, B. (1983). *The fractal geometry of nature*. San Francisco, CA: W. H. Freeman.

Ogden, T. H. (1989). *The primitive edge of experience*. Northvale, NJ: Jason Aronson.

Searle, J. (1980) Minds, brains and programs. *Behavioral and Brain Sciences, 3*, 417–457.

Sheets-Johnstone, M. (2011). *The primacy of movement*. Philadelphia, PA: John Benjamins Publishing Company.

Slavin, M. O. and Kriegman, D. (1992). *The adaptive design of the human psyche*. New York, NY: Guilford.

Stolorow, R. D. and Atwood, G. E. (1992). *Contexts of being: The intersubjective foundations of psychological life*. Hillsdale, NJ: The Analytic Press.

Thelen, E. and Smith, L. (1994). *A dynamic systems approach to the development of cognition and action*. Cambridge, MA. MIT Press.

Wittgenstein, L. (1953). *Philosophical investigations*. London, UK: Blackwell.

Wish, need, drive

Motive in the light of dynamic systems theory and Edelman's selectionist theory[1]

Emmanuel Ghent

Historically, wish, need, drive, impulse, instinct, defense, resistance, motive, among other neighboring conceptions, have mingled in an uneasy existence with one another, sometimes contrasting and in opposition and, at other times, overlapping in the territory they cover. My ultimate goal in this essay is to reevaluate these conceptions and to advocate a more generic way of dealing with the phenomena that each reflects and expresses. I believe that thinking in terms of process rather than structure, evolving *motivational systems* of varying types rather than structure-like entities, will do much to dispel the confusion in this area of psychoanalytic thinking and theorizing.

My initial goal is to explore such questions as how such motivational systems first come into being and take shape in the developing human being. Subsidiary to this question are such issues as (1) whether or not there are innately organized regularities in this developmental process and, if so, whether or not they then lead to predictable motivational patterns. (2) To what extent do environing circumstances, relative to innately organized givens (if, indeed, they can ever be separated) play a role in the establishment of motivational systems on both a microscopic and a macroscopic level? (3) Is there a more fruitful way of thinking about development, one that transcends the nature-nurture controversy and the contest between a one-person as against a two-person psychology? My approach to many of these questions is informed by conceptions derived from dynamic systems theory, with emphasis on the groundbreaking work of Esther Thelen and her colleagues, and by the seminal contributions of Gerald Edelman, in particular his Theory of Neural Group Selection (TNGS).

The second portion of this paper is devoted to a consideration of need, wish, defense, centripetal versus centrifugal systems, and other topics related to motivational systems. In this context I touch on the question of the usefulness, from a clinical point of view, of thinking in terms of motivational systems. Throughout this essay my use of the term motivational systems is to be distinguished from that of Joseph Lichtenberg (1989), whose brilliant work on this subject, counts as the most systematic alternative to the dual-drive theory of classical psychoanalysis. My usage focuses more generically and far less specifically by accenting a new, and perhaps speculative, way of thinking about the organization and development of motivation.

Since the beginnings of psychoanalysis, motivation has been expressed as wish, need, drive, impulse, instinct. What all these terms have in common is the implication of a force, either a particular driving force (*vis a tergo*) or a goal-driven force (*vis a fronte*). A further implication was that these forces were either innately organized and subsequently underwent an elaborate series of prescribed, stagelike differentiations modulated in part by experience or were organized on the basis of the interaction of genetic givens as biological substrate, with experience, largely interhuman experience, providing specificity of shape to the biological underpinnings. Although much ink has been spilled over Freud's shift from trauma theory to drive theory, what is easily overlooked is that "*in neither of these propositions [innate vs. experiential organization] is the individual regarded as the active agent*" (Stechler, 1997, p. 2; italics added). In current psychoanalytic thinking, no less than in Freud's time, the focus has remained on whether a person is *reacting* to internal or to external forces or some combination of both. Occasionally, a voice has been heard to cry out in challenge as, for example, when Isadore Chein (quoted in Holt, 1965, p. 165), in his 1962 presidential address to the Society for the Psychological Study of Social Issues, declared that "psychology must choose between two images" of man—two basic conceptions of man's nature, which he found implicit in all theories of behavior.

> The first is that of Man as an active, responsible agent … a being who actively does something with regard to some of the things that happen to him … who insists on injecting himself into the causal process of the world around him. … The contrasting, and among psychologists whose careers are devoted to the advancement of the science,

> the prevailing image of Man is that of an impotent reactor, with its responses completely determined by two distinct and separate, albeit interacting, sets of factors: (i) the forces impinging on it and (ii) its constitution (including … momentary physiological states).

Gill (1983) was approaching a similar question when he asked whether the appropriate point of view for psychoanalysis was to be energy discharge or a person-centered point of view.

Some years ago, in a paper ridiculed by Holt (1981) for its "bad philosophy" and applauded by Wallerstein (1976, 1986) among others for distinguishing between *causes* and *reasons*, Home (1966) wrote:

> Science asks the question how does a thing occur and receives an answer in terms of causes, whereas a humanistic study asks the question why and receives an answer in terms of reasons.
>
> (p. 44)

> In discovering that the symptom had meaning and basing his treatment on this hypothesis, Freud took the psychoanalytic study of neurosis out of the world of science into the world of the humanities, because a meaning is not the product of causes but the creation of a subject.
>
> (p. 43)

While there is much to be critical of in Home's rigidly stereotyped notion of science, I draw attention to his looking on meaning as a *creation* of the subject.

What stands out for me in Chein and Gill and Home, and, from another point of view, Winnicott, among many others, is their struggle to find a way to emphasize the centrality of agency and creativity in human activity. Alas, often enough it has seemed that the sacrifice of science was a necessary requirement. I believe we have, fortunately, arrived at a point at which science can provide the beginnings of a deeper understanding of these uniquely human qualities, by groping into the territory of their developmental origins in the infant. Although the tendency has been to see human beings as *designed* this way, perhaps we will discover that such precious qualities as the quest for meaning and the act of creation or agency arise not out of design but, in a manner of speaking, spontaneously, almost as a fire can begin by spontaneous combustion given the right circumstances. It is exactly in response to what so often appears to be the mystery of a spontaneous process (as in weather configurations, the onset of turbulence, pathological heart rhythms, the shape of a leaf), that the power of dynamic systems theory has come to be recognized. Illustrative of the then-prevailing view of development, Holt (1976), wrote:

> The human being is *designed* [italics added] and functions so as to process and produce meanings. That being the case, so long as the person is alive and well, he cannot help but deal with meanings and make meaningful sense out of his experience. To say that he has a *need* to find meaning is thus no more accurate than, and is as misleading as, to say that an automatic knitting machine has a need to knit or a seed has a need to germinate. … I believe that the human nervous system, in its organismic setting, makes the generation of meanings as natural as the generation of sweat from sweat glands.
>
> (p. 192)

That is a most interesting paragraph. It highlights the ubiquity of the notion, even when drives are eschewed, that all manner of higher functions are built in, designed into the organism. Who, then—or what, then—is the designer? Certainly there is no gene for making meaning. On the other hand, from very early on, a human being *is* centrally involved in making meaning (cf. Stern's, 1985, p. 97 notion of RIGs—Representations of Interactions that have been Generalized). In effect we learn to be motivated to make meaning; it provides great predictive and survival value. Making meaning, or what Edelman (1992) refers to as recategorization of experience, is intrinsic to perception and action. The very success of this operation as a contingent response becomes an inducement to seek more of this type of activity—to categorize and recategorize experience, to make meaning on an ever-more complex level. Is this not the beginnings of motivation as a process?

But there is more in Holt's paragraph: he brings in the question of *need*. Of course a knitting machine has no need to knit; it is a nonliving, highly linear, cause-and-effect, closed system; what comes out is proportional to what goes in. But a need to find meaning is quite another matter: a human being seeking meaning is motivated. Seeking meaning often invokes a constellation of other processes—action, perception, memory—all of which interact with one another in a nonlinear way, and with never fully predictable results. When it comes to the "need to sweat," we are dealing with a homeostatic system, a type of essentially linear system that is very different from most nonlinear dynamic systems. There are, of course, some systems, for example, the need for food or the need for sleep, that, on one hand, have some features of homeostatic regulation and, on the other, become imbricated in complex, nonlinear motivational systems.

The power of dynamic systems theory lies in its transcendence, by virtue of its insistent focus on process, of such age-old controversies as nature versus nurture, mind versus body, causes versus reasons, and so on. Until very recently all theories of development were embedded in an often covert fabric of teleology wherein the organism was assumed to have a preordained direction of development often marked by a sequence of stages. Similarly, in all theories, life is driven by some basic "drives," be they the classic drives of sex and aggression, or the need for attachment, the quest for satisfaction and security (Sullivan, 1953), the needs for safety and effectance (Greenberg, 1991), the five motivational systems of Lichtenberg (1989), the five biologically rooted behaviors of Bowlby (1988), or some other collection of basic, nonnegotiable urges. The question of how these drives originated—for me a matter of great interest and concern—is usually bypassed, or else it is assumed that they are somehow built into the design of the organism. At best, some effort is made to account for the development of motivation in terms of the "interaction" of external experience with the biologically given. I enclose the word interaction with quotation marks to emphasize how much this buzzword is used to gloss over ignorance as to what actually happens in terms of process. *How* interaction operates is never examined.

Over the past two decades, Esther Thelen and her colleagues have been working on a new way of thinking about infant motor development. Although the words motive and motivation seldom appear in her writings, I believe a careful study of her approach will provide us with a new and useful way of thinking about the development of motivation. Before exploring how her ideas may be relevant to the question of the development of motivation, let me touch on some of the main features of her point of view and of the findings with regard to motor development that this new way of thinking has spawned. In the light of very significant recent work in motor development and in neurobiological selectionist theory, I do believe a new way of thinking about motivational development is in the offing.

Thelen (1995) opens her discussion of motor development with these words:

> The study of the acquisition of motor skills, long moribund in developmental psychology, has seen a renaissance in the last decade. Inspired by contemporary work in movement science, perceptual psychology, neuroscience, and dynamic systems theory, multidisciplinary approaches are affording new insights into the processes by which infants and children learn to control their bodies. In particular, the new synthesis emphasizes the multicausal, fluid, contextual and self-organizing nature of developmental change. Studies are concerned less with how children perform and more how the components cooperate to produce stability and engender change. Such process approaches make moot the traditional nature-nurture debates.
>
> (p. 79)

What about dynamic systems theory? What is it? How is it relevant to our concerns about development in general and motivation in particular? Some confusion is apt to arise from the almost interchangeable use of terms denoting this theoretical approach: complexity theory, chaos theory, nonlinearity, self-organizing systems theory, and synergetics, among others. The variety of designations derives from the fact that the field developed simultaneously from many different quarters of science (see Gleick, 1987). Stechler (1997) asks, "What if there is a totally different way of viewing how emerging structures come into being? What if we don't have to search for the template or blueprint that forms the necessary substrate of every phenomenon we observe?" (p. 2).

Prigogine (1983), one of the founders of this new view of science, specifies some of the features characteristic of self-organizing systems. Given a source of energy, all open systems, of which all living beings are a prime example, can create internal organization without the need for a pattern or design. Such a system is characterized by both stability over time and instabilities that lead to new state properties within the existing organization. The more stable states are referred to as "*attractor* states" as if the system is attracted to those "preferred states." Perturbations of the system are likely to destabilize it and thereby, provide the opportunity for change. The situation most pregnant with the possibility for change is a system poised on the edge of chaos. To afford a visual representation of attractors, the image of a landscape with a variety of hills and valleys is invoked; the deeper the valley or trough, the more stable the attractor is likely to be, in the sense that a ball in a deep valley would require a great perturbation to move it up the hill and over into some other valley. By contrast, a ball situated at the crest of a hill would be vulnerable to the slightest perturbation; any slight change in the system, even an accidental one, might set the ball in motion with relatively unpredictable result. It is the spiraling sequence of complexity to simplicity to complexity that, as Thelen and Smith (1994) put it, "captures the essence of dynamic systems whatever the material substance of the elements … photons, biological molecules, cells, tissues, organs, networks of neurons, organisms, or social systems" (p. 51).

All living systems are self-organizing systems that receive a variety of inputs, such as the input from genes, metabolites, the physical surround (including the force of gravity), and the vast number of experiences especially, in the case of human beings, of interhuman experiences encountered in living. From these ingredients the system creates its own states and structures and patterns of action, which are not totally predictable from the array of inputs (pp. 204ff., for a simple example—infants' mobile kicking). These principles of self-organization apply not only in moment-to-moment activity, but on every time scale, including the ontogenetic (p. 63). Regarding the meaning of nonlinearity, Gleick (1987) provides a simple example: "Without friction a simple linear equation expresses the amount of energy you need to accelerate a hockey puck" (p. 24). The moment you include friction (as in the real world) the relationship gets complicated.

> Nonlinearity means that the act of playing the game has a way of changing the rules. You cannot assign a constant importance to friction because its importance depends on speed. Speed, in turn, depends on friction. That twisted changeability makes nonlinearity hard to calculate, but it also creates rich kinds of behavior that never occur in linear systems.
>
> (p. 24)

Over the last few years the power and generality of dynamic systems theory has created a revolution in science. There has been an explosion in applications to real-world problems, in areas as diverse as weather, laser beams, galaxy formations, leaf patterns, biological rhythms, lung tissue morphology, morphogenesis, nerve impulse patterns, neural network behavior, heart rhythms, motor coordination, perceptual systems, to mention a few (Thelen and Smith, 1994, p. 50). In Gleick's (1987) words, "Now that science is looking, chaos seems to be everywhere" (p. 5).

> It is a relatively new science that discards simple cause-and-effect models, linearity, [ordinary] determinism and reductionistic analysis. Instead, it is a science for systems with a history, systems that change over time, where novelty can be created, where the end-state is not coded anywhere, and where behavior at the macro level can, in principle, be reconciled with behavior at the microlevel.
>
> (Thelen and Smith, 1994, p. 49)

With regard to cognition, Thelen and Smith (1994) propose

> a radical departure from current cognitive theory. Although behavior and development appear structured, there are no structures. Although behavior and development appear rule-driven, there are no rules. There is complexity. There is a multiple, parallel, and continuously dynamic interplay between perception and action, and a system that, by its ... nature, seeks certain stable solutions. These solutions emerge from relations, not from design. When the elements of such complex systems cooperate, they give rise to behavior with a unitary character, and thus to the illusion of structure. But the order is always executory, rather than rule-driven, allowing for the enormous sensitivity and flexibility of behavior to organize and regroup around task and context.
>
> (p. xix)

Notice the sentence, "These solutions emerge from relations, not from design." It reminds me of "the words of the French mathematician, Henri Poincaré, the discoverer of what we now call chaos, that 'the aim of science is not things themselves, as the dogmatists in their simplicity assume, but the relations among things; outside these relations there is no reality knowable'" (Kelso, 1997, p. 97). To my mind it is in *this* meaning of relational, rather than its more superficial usage as the relations

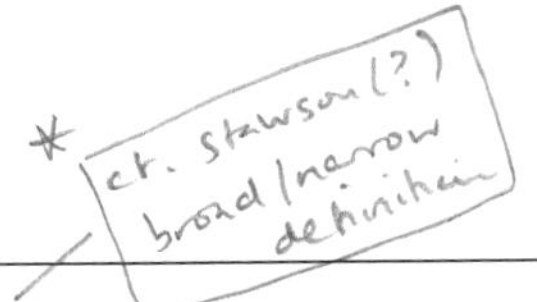

between people, that gives power and significance to the term relational psychoanalysis.

It would take us far beyond the scope of this paper to illustrate the specific applications of dynamic systems theory. You are encouraged, however, to refer to Thelen and Smith (1994), which goes beyond description by providing empirical instantiations of the principles. A second way the authors go beyond description and structural concepts is by suggesting a neurologically plausible mechanism for the ontogeny of cognition and action and, I believe, motivation, one that is entirely harmonious with general dynamic principles. Gerald Edelman's (1987, 1989, 1992) Theory of Neuronal Group Selection (TNGS), or "Neural Darwinism," fits the "basic requirement for a plausible account of ontogeny that there be no homunculus in the brain or the genes directing the process" (Thelen and Smith, 1994, p. xxi).

Other authors have dipped into the world of dynamic systems theory to better explain the phenomena of change in the psychotherapeutic situation (see Stechler, 1997; Stern et al., 1998; Fajardo, 2000). Barry (2000) invokes Edelman's work in her study of self-organizing aspects of learning in the clinical situation. Shane, Shane, and Gales (1997), making use of dynamic systems theory, have mated self-psychology and attachment theory into a new and fruitful synthesis. Stolorow (1997) has made use of these principles as metaphors for many of the phenomena described in intersubjectivity theory. Craig Piers (1999) has written a fascinating study on character as self-organizing complexity. Adrienne Harris (accepted for publication) is completing a book titled, *Gender as a Soft Assembly: Developmental Process in the Light of Relational Psychoanalysis.* A significant focus of her work is on the radical constructionism implied in dynamic systems—an extension of constructionism from a macro level to a micro level. Stanley Palombo (1999) makes extensive use of complexity theory in creating a way of viewing the psychoanalytic process as an emergent evolutionary process. For a more general discussion of dynamic systems theory in relation to psychoanalysis, see also Moran (1991), Spruiell (1993), and Galatzer-Levy (1995). Pally and Olds (1998, p. 981ff) make extensive use of Edelman's work in their study of neural aspects of consciousness. My guess is that a cascade of articles and books will follow as the power and significance of nonlinear dynamic systems theory and "Neural Darwinism" begin to take hold in our field.

Need, Drive, and Edelman's Theory of Neuronal Group Selection

Where do such familiar concepts as drive, wish, and need fit into this scheme of things? I look upon all these motivational concepts as highly complex derivatives of very primitive biases, or preferences, that, after eons of honing in evolutionary time, are built into the human infant.

The term *drive* has two distinct meanings as used in psychoanalysis, one customary and virtually an emblem of classical psychoanalysis, the other uncommon but significant. In its standard usage, drive is a metapsychological term. Since the development of the second instinct theory, drive refers to the life and death instincts—manifested clinically in sexuality and aggression—as the basic motivational forces in the human being. Built into this package are the assumptions that the two drives are the only source of psychic energy, that they are pre-experiential, that all human motivation, no matter how remotely related, ultimately derives from these drives, and that individuals differ constitutionally in the strength of the drives (see Greenberg, 1991, pp. 37–41). Greenberg, citing his agreement with Strachey's views regarding drive, writes: "What becomes crucial for Freud's drive theory is that what is represented initially is simply a need and not a need *for* something. Life's accidents (borrowing Freud's term) sooner or later provide something suited to satisfy the need, and that something achieves the status of an *object*" (p. 54).

But there is another meaning of the term drive. If we can conceive of a certain divestiture of drive theory, the term drive—with a little "d"—could remain and be used independently of its association with instinct theory. On this basis it would be fair to say that even those psychoanalytic theories that eschew drive theory nonetheless retain some notion, however disguised, of drives, be they called object-seeking needs (Fairbairn, 1963), needs for a facilitating environment (Winnicott, 1965), selfobject needs (Kohut, 1977), needs for satisfaction and security, (Sullivan, 1940), trends toward autonomy and homonomy (Angyal, 1965/1982), the five basic motivational systems proposed by Lichtenberg (1989), the five root behaviors of Bowlby (1988), a set of five basic human needs proposed by Fromm (1955), or, most recently, the drives for safety and for effectance (Greenberg, 1991).[1] It would take us too far afield to examine the specifics of these various systems of hypothesized needs. As I see it, however one chooses to parse basic motivational systems, however one positions which motives are superordinate and which subordinate, or even if there need be any hierarchical ordering, there must be some as yet unnamed pre-experiential influences; and, while these influences are innately organized, the specificity of their patterning and organization, even at the anatomical level is contingent on experience. At some point in early development, we may choose to think of these emergent neural organizations as drives or needs or, as I prefer, motivational systems. What these organizations are and how they develop into needs or motivational systems is, to my mind, the challenging question. In an effort to approach this and related questions, I believe it is timely to consider what recent developments in neuropsychological thinking can contribute.

The proposal advanced by Edelman (1987, 1989) that neural and psychic structure develops not by instruction or prescription, but by selection, has far-reaching consequences. In lieu of either a psychology based on innately prescribed drives and developmental systems or one that eschews any psychological significance to innately given organization and instead replaces it by a psychology rooted entirely in the human relational matrix, Edelman's theory of neuronal group selection proposes two kinds of (natural) selection of interactive neuronal patterns in the evolution of each individual nervous system: developmental and experiential. Fortunately for us human beings, our brains are not organized like computer circuitry, for, if they were, our entire nervous system would have to be controlled by a system of instructions. Instead, it seems that, with a neural system organized more like a tropical rain forest with vast and ever-changing connections and relations among the myriads of organisms residing in ecological balance, dendritic circuitry and high-level mapping and inter-connections are likewise in constant developmental flux subtended largely by survival of the fittest, by the most adaptive, neural connections. It is this sensitivity to environmental circumstances—and by environmental I am referring not only to direct human influences but also to all manner of physical and chemical influences in fetal development—that makes possible, indeed predicts, that each individual (even identical twins) will have an absolutely unique neural system of connections that came into being on the basis of "natural selection."

Earlier, when I referred vaguely to preexperiential influences as innately given precursors to the formation of functional neuronal patterning and, ultimately, motivational systems, I was hinting at what Edelman referred to as "values" or biases. A brief excerpt from Oliver Sacks's (1993) elegant summary of Edelman's work will help situate its relevance to the present endeavor, the ontogeny of motivational systems and the place of need in psychoanalysis.

Clearly there are some innate biases or dispositions at work; otherwise the infant would have no tendencies whatever, would not be moved to do anything, seek anything, to stay alive. These basic biases Edelman calls "values" [not to be confused with the customary meaning of human values]. Such [biases or] values are essential for adaptation and survival; some have developed through eons of evolution, and some are acquired through exploration and experience. Thus if the infant instinctively values food, warmth and contact with other people (for example), this will direct its first movements and strivings. These "values"—drives, instincts, intentionalities—serve to differentially weight experience, to orient the organism toward survival and adaptation, to allow what Edelman calls "categorization on value," e.g., to form categories such as "edible" and "non-edible" as parts of the process of getting food. It needs to be stressed that "values" are experienced internally as *feelings* ....

At a more elementary physiological level there are various sensory and motor "givens," from the reflexes that automatically occur (for example, in response to pain) to innate mechanisms in the brain, as, for example, the feature detectors in the visual cortex which, as soon as they are activated, detect verticals, horizontals, boundaries, angles, etc. in the visual world. Thus we have a certain amount of basic equipment, but in Edelman's view very little else is programmed or built in. It is up to the infant animal, given its elementary physiological capacities, and given its inborn values, to create its own categories and to use them to make sense of, to *construct* a world—and it is not just a world that the infant constructs, but its *own* world, a world constituted from the first by personal meaning and reference.

[Daniel Stern (1985) in describing an "emergent self" notes how infants] "have distinct biases or preferences with regard to the sensations they seek. ... These are innate. From birth on, there appears to be a central tendency to form and test hypotheses about what is occurring in the world ... [to] categorize into ... patterns, events, sets, and experiences" (p. 44).

Here again, a detailed explication of Edelman's work is vastly beyond the scope of this essay, but I suggest a variety of valuable sources:

Edelman (1992), Edelman and Tononi (1995), Sacks (1995), Thelen and Smith (1994), Rosenfield (1988), Pally and Olds (1998), Migone and Liotti (1998), Fajardo (2000), and Barry (2000). I am dwelling on Edelman's work only because it is, to my mind, the only meaningful attempt to relate the growing body of neurophysiological knowledge to my particular area of interest, the ontogeny of motivational systems.[3] The theory of neuronal group selection allows us to transcend the nature-nurture dichotomy insofar as it provides a window into how the brain integrates, by a process of self-modification, all levels of experience from the genic to the behavioral. I include the genic inasmuch as we know that gene expression, the turning on and off of the activity of a particular gene, is at least as important (if not more so) as the presence of the gene. And, in turn, gene expression is a function of all manner of environmental influences from the activation or turning off of other genes, to hormonal, to behavioral.

By applying three basic tenets, the idea of neuronal group selection constrained by values or biases, the process of reentry, and global mapping, Edelman (1992) has proposed a theory that offers analysts a way of thinking about the development of memory, perception, conception, motivation, and, ultimately consciousness.

Edelman's selectional theory of brain function includes proposals as to how both, initially, developmental neuronal group selection and, secondarily, experiential group selection develop "repertoires," which, in turn, form vast numbers of brain maps that interact by a process called reentry. Developmental selection refers to the processes of self-organizing microanatomical selection that occur in embryological time and lead ultimately to the formation of the large-scale neuroanatomy characteristic of any given species. Experiential selection refers to the selective strengthening or weakening of populations of synapses as a result of behavioral experience, thereby "carving out" a variety of functional "circuits" from the anatomical network. A set of such functional circuits is called a secondary repertoire. Considering that there are about one billion synaptic connections in a section of the brain the size of a match-head, it is not difficult to imagine the degree of complexity of connections, repertoires, maps of repertoires, and maps of maps that evolve in the course of experience. These maps and circuits automatically adapt their boundaries, sometimes quite dramatically, on the basis of lived experience. Edelman adds that "brains contain multiple maps interacting without any supervisors and yet bring unity and cohesiveness to perceptual scenes" (p. 69). Note here the parallel to Thelen and Smith's (1994) reference to general systems theory, as quoted earlier: "although behavior and development appear rule-driven, there are no rules" (p. xix).

The maps that Edelman is describing

> are connected by massively parallel and reciprocal connections. The visual system of the monkey, for example, has over thirty different maps, each with a certain degree of functional segregation (for orientation, color, movement, and so forth), and each is linked to the others by parallel and reciprocal connections. Reentrant signaling occurs along these connections. This means that as groups of neurons are selected in a map, other groups in reentrantly connected, but different, maps may also be selected at the same time.
>
> (p. 85)

Using these basic tenets, Edelman is able to explicate "how the ability to carry out categorization is embodied in the nervous system" (p. 87). He continues, now evoking in my mind a parallel with Stern's (1985) concept of RIGS,

> Brains contain multiple maps interacting without any supervisors, yet bring unity and cohesiveness to perceptual scenes. And they let their possessors (pigeons, for example) categorize as similar a large if not endless set of diverse objects, such as pictures of different fish, after seeing only a few such pictures.
>
> (p. 69)

A major question that has direct relevance to the subject of the ontogeny of human motivation remains for further research: What *are* the innate values[4] or biases in the human infant? Edelman and his associate, Giulio Tononi, have indicated

> that it is not yet known how [simple or] complex these values are in the neonate and how predictably these values progress into motivational systems. It is known that the values include a repertoire of around 100 inborn reflexes, including such value-based behaviors … as rooting, sucking, startle, reaching, and grasping. [There may]

> also be more complex values inherent in earliest life, including, for example, attachment per se, but that as of now, such inclusion of complexity in developmental theory is not possible.
>
> (quoted in Shane et al., 1997, p. 41).

It is thus entirely possible that values for touch, warmth, feeding, for example, along with a variety of inborn reflexes, lead, from the earliest moments of postnatal life, to successive categorizations of experience such that attachment very soon becomes valorized into a motivational system in its own right.

Even genetically organized values may be subject to environmental (prenatal) experience. It is very easy to forget that behavior that appears convincingly instinctual may be dependent on environmental experience at some point in the life cycle. The susceptibility to audiogenic seizures in a highly inbred strain of mice can be altered by transplanting the fertilized eggs from the uterus of a susceptible mouse to the uterus of a nonsusceptible mouse. Under such conditions the susceptibility of the young to fatal seizures is reduced, although their genetic characteristics are unchanged (Ginsburg and Hoyda, cited in Beach, 1955). Such studies emphasize that prenatal experience may well have an impact even on such stable attractors as primitive value systems.

Although he refers to them as basic infant motivations, it seems to me that Emde (1988) is in the territory staked out by Edelman as phylogenetically organized values. Emde points to four such basic infant motivations: activity, self-regulation, social fittedness, and affective monitoring, the propensity to monitor experience according to what is pleasurable and unpleasurable. Clearly many of these motivations are interactive: that activity is better than nonactivity, for example, depends in part on the self-regulatory state of the infant. Activity is viewed as a basic motive having nothing to do with tension or drive reduction. Among its resultants are such motivations as exploration, curiosity, effectance, and mastery.

By social fittedness, Emde is referring to the variety of inborn

> capacities for initiating, maintaining and terminating interactions with other humans. Many of these capacities are present at birth and include a propensity for participating in eye-to-eye contact; a state responsivity for being activated and soothed by human holding, touching and rocking; and a propensity for showing prolonged alert attentiveness

> to the stimulus features contained in the human voice and face. … Several researchers have pointed out how the integrative capacities of the young infant (for processing sequential information, for generating complex patterns of motor activity, for cross-modal perception, for an early form of social imitation and for orienting—to note some of these) can be thought of as magnificent pre-adaptations for the complex dynamic circumstances of human interaction.
>
> (p. 30)

If I were to add anything to this formulation it would be to lay special emphasis on the value of perceptual coherence (which later develops into a need for conceptual coherence). I think a value or bias of this nature must underlie the tendency of neural networks to categorize and recategorize successive experiences along the lines suggested by Edelman. Take, for example, Stern's (1985) conception of RIGS, whereby infants are able to generalize a coherent averaging of similar but nonidentical images, a kind of primitive capacity for abstraction. An infant's capacity for cross-modal perception may be another outgrowth of a very fundamental value— coherence is better than noncoherence. In the light of the work by Thelen and her associates discussed earlier, many, if not all these propensities, will turn out to be self-organized and emergent on the basis of an infant's activity under the limitations of still more primitive values or predispositions. These, in turn, are constrained, of course, by the evolutionary givens of the infant's anatomy and physiology and the limits imposed by the physical surround as, for example, gravity, in relation to motor learning.

Throughout the discussion of Edelman's selectional or "Darwinian" theory, I find myself wondering, particularly in the context of so much groundbreaking work being done in dynamic systems theory, whether another factor besides selection plays a very important role in development—the spontaneously emergent and relatively unpredictable patterning that is independent of experience. I cite Kauffman's (1993) reflections on the relation between selectionism and spontaneous emergence over evolutionary time and would not be surprised that the same considerations apply as well at the level of somatic time (ontogeny):

> What makes the present stage of biological science so extraordinary is that molecular biology is driving us to the innermost reaches of the

> cell's ultimate mechanisms, complexity, and capacity to evolve. At the very same time, work in mathematics, physics, chemistry, and biology is revealing how far-reaching the powers of self-organization can be. These advances hold implications for the origin of life itself and for the origins of order in the ontogeny of each organism....The order inherent within the busy complexity of the cell may be largely self-organized and spontaneous rather than the consequence of natural selection alone. …
>
> We must understand how … self-ordered properties *permit, enable*, and *limit* the efficacy of natural selection. We must see organisms in a new light, as the *balance found*, the *collaboration achieved*, when natural selection acts to further mold order which preexists. In short we must integrate the fact that selection is not the sole source of order in organisms.
>
> (p. xiv)

The recognition that self-organization plays such an important role in biological processes holds great significance for the age-old question of the relation between determinism and free agency. Nonlinear complexity theory, at last, opens for us a way of integrating notions of classical determinism with creativity, agency, and free will. While the spontaneous emergence of structure at the cellular level may seem a far cry from what we ordinarily think of as agency or creativity, I do mean to put forward, albeit with a little hesitation, the hypothesis that it represents the basis, at the most primitive level, of what later in life becomes genuine expressions of agency and creativity—in the form of the spontaneous emergence of new patterns of thought or behavior. Earlier in this essay I referred to Stechler's (1997) comment that in neither of the propositions about the development of psychic structure (innate versus experiential organization) is the person regarded as the active agent. This new way of conceptualizing psychic ontogeny does indeed provide a means for understanding the roots of agency and even creativity without the need to invoke shades of entelechy. A further corollary to this way of thinking is that the current controversy between one-person and two-person psychologies (Modell, 1984; Ghent, 1989; Aron, 1990) is now further complicated, (or simplified, depending on one's outlook) by the advent of a new form of one-person psychology having nothing to do with its classical homonym, but everything to do with the infant's intrinsic capacity to integrate outer experience with inner constraints and create solutions sui generis.

The Relation Between Functional Capacity and Need

A question that I frequently find myself pondering is the relation between functional *capacity*[5] and *need*.[6] Once a capacity has been self-organized, it is intrinsic to the nature of such a system to exhibit new properties of its own. It seems to me that given the nature of emergent systems there will arise a need, underpinned by such values as the bias for coherence, to exercise and develop the functional capacity to greater efficiency, complexity, or both. In other words, the acquisition of a new capability is in itself a perturbation that destabilizes the existing state of motivational organization. To the extent that the use of a capacity (1) provides pleasure or satisfaction, (2) diminishes pain or distress, or (3) in some way enhances survival, there will, barring inhibitory circumstances, emerge a *need* to execute and develop this capacity. Here is the beginning of desire, the beginning of motivation, whether one is aware of it or not.

The evolution in each person of new capacities and, with them, new motivations is emergent and nonlinear, a function of a complex array of inputs and environing circumstances that are actively engaged by the developing person. What appears to be a regularity in development, a maturational sequence of prescribed stages is, instead, the resultant of a vast number of individual microcosmic solutions and achievements, leaving room for a great range of variability from one individual to another in the acquisition of capacities and motivations. Of course, on a macroscopic level, many regularities will be found. Just as most infants learn to talk and to walk, so too do most infants elaborate macroscopically similar sets of capacities and motivations. If we look more closely, we see that profound variation in detail is the rule.

In the earliest stages of life, the term capacity is coequal with value or bias. As early experience accumulates, capacities develop that are presymbolic and involve procedural memory. An illustration from studies in visual learning in infants and monkeys conveys a sense of how capacity (capability), activity, perception, and motivation are all intertwined. Hebb (1949) described how an infant learns to perceive a triangle. Perception is not a passive act of reception, but an active participatory phenomenon. The infant first has to move its eyes from point to point, and, eventually, after many repetitions of this motoric act, he or she becomes able to relate the points to each other and thereby perceive an entity called a triangle. Schilder similarly tied motility with perception: "Primitive perception is a state of motion. … Development is in the direction of the elimination of the inner motion of the perception" (quoted in Nass, 1984, p. 482). Unpacking this process, we might say that at some point in development the infant acquires the capacity to organize eye movements in an increasingly coherent manner. This new capability makes possible a kind of visual reaching and, just as with tactile reaching in infant development (Thelen, 1998), it is both motivated and motivating. The infant now is motivated to search out motorically the points that constitute a triangle. With much practice these movements become integrated as a perception of a triangle, a great accomplishment. In brief, a capacity evoked a motivation to explore with the result that a new capacity came into being. It is not difficult to imagine how ever more complex versions of this scenario ultimately lead to the capacity for rapid perception of symbols such as those used in text.

The recent discovery of mirror neurons (Rizzolatti et al., 1996) in monkeys (and presumably humans) provides a fascinating illustration of the imbrication of response, perception, the creation of new function, and motivation. When a monkey watches a specific movement (as, for example, the grasping movement of an arm) in another monkey, the motor neurons that would evoke the identical movement in the observing monkey are stimulated. Many studies of this phenomenon suggest that evolutionary changes that resulted in the functional presence of mirror neuron systems have had far-reaching consequences (see Vihman, 1993; Rizzolatti et al., 1996; Williams et al., 2001). The new capacity has led to new motivations: for imitative perception, which in turn lead to the ability to "read another's intention," as well as the motivation to do so since the capacity would confer evolutionary advantage on the person. It is likely that other new motivations and capacities have come into play in humans as, for example, the capacity for empathy, and perhaps even such a vital human capacity as the infant's acquisition of speech by imitative perception of adult speech patterns.

In later life, the capacity for complex symbolization emerges and with it the acquisition of higher consciousness (Edelman, 1992). The equation between capacity and motivation is still there but now greatly influenced by the tangle of conflicting and complementary capacities and needs, together with the welter of symbolic meanings and associations (categorizations and recategorizations) that have become attached to one's capacities and related motives. One may have the capacity, for example, to venture into strange, unfamiliar places, but the execution of that capacity may have become associated with shaming or frightening experiences at the hands of the primary caretaker. The capacity may still be there, but pleasure is minimal and distress maximal. In time the desire is extinguished and, with it, even the capacity and the skills involved in exploring new situations wither.

To my mind this is a very important issue since, if it can be shown that capability and need each stimulate the further development of the other, we have a basis for understanding the origins of motivational systems as part of the self-evolving processes of the expansion of function or, in a word, psychological growth. I am not aware of any empirical research bearing on this issue, so that I am reduced to hypothesizing that such a relation exists.

Before going on to consider need, wish, and defense at a later stage of development, that is, motivational systems that have already emerged as nameable and recognizable entities, let us summarize briefly. Clearly there exist innately organized primitive values that prepare the organism, in our case the human infant, to prefer certain types of stimulation over others. Ultimately, governed by the constraints of genic activity, physical development of the infant, and environmental experience, there emerges, without rules or a blueprint as a guide, a more complex array of biases. This nonlinear emergent process continues—in time leading to ever-more complex biases and values. At a certain point we, as observers, begin to categorize these into systems of motivation. Depending on the observer's frame of reference, certain motivational systems are held to be superordinate to others; these then are held up as basic motives.

I believe that we psychoanalysts currently find ourselves in a situation of competing organizational systems vying for prominence. The current multiplicity of such systems speaks to the uncertainty and the need for further developmental research to clarify issues such as: Does a singular hierarchy of motivational systems develop as a regularity in the human infant and child? If so, how can this development be best described? If not, is there a variety of such developmental outcomes discernable in human development? Is the variety limitless, such that no generalizations can be made? Do cultural factors play such a large role that what emerges as a characteristic organization of motivational systems in one culture would seem remarkably alien in another culture? Clearly we do not yet have the answers to these questions. Until we are in a better position to understand the breadth and scope of early motivational development, the psychoanalytic scene will necessarily be occupied with competing hierarchies of motivational systems.

Need, Wish, and Defense in Relation to Motivational Systems

Some years ago I wrote a paper (Ghent, 1993) on the subject of the place of need in psychoanalysis in which I went to great lengths to try to distinguish between need and wish. I decided against publishing until the ideas found a suitable mold in which to gel. At this point I believe that the work in dynamic systems theory and Edelman's (1987, 1989, 1992) selectionist theory provides a suitable scaffolding for an exploration of needs, wishes, and defensive patternings.

In the earlier presentation I was at pains to avoid the historical dichotomy between "good needs" and "bad needs"; I hoped to formulate need without regard to whether a motivational system is growth oriented, on one hand, or conservative or defensive, on the other. In effect, I was trying to transcend the tight boundaries between impulse and defense, between progression and regression, between what I have referred to as "surrender" (Ghent, 1993, 1995) and resistance.

In that paper I noted that, for a variety of reasons (which I discuss presently), I preferred the term *motivational system* to the terms *need* and *wish* or *drive, impulse, defense*, and such like terms. The term motivational system, however, seemed unwieldy, uneuphonious as well as disturbingly impersonal, so that I kept returning to the more familiar phrases, often adding "motivational system" as a parenthetical appendage. I think the time has come to make the case for thinking (or training ourselves to think) in terms of motivational systems of diverse types and levels of complexity.

I am not proposing that we dispose of colloquial terms like need and wish, but that we *think* in terms of motivational systems and do our best to not use the everyday terms in such a way as to obscure our thinking. Whether a particular motivational system is expressed as a wish, a need, or a defensive stance is a separate issue that merits further exploration.

Throughout the history of psychoanalysis, wish and need have vied for *prominence*. Freud first saw the roots of motivation in infantile psychological needs, needs that today we would refer to as self-regulatory needs (see Akhtar, 1999, for a fuller treatment of this issue). Need, according to Freud (1915/1953), arose from an inner tension and was "the psychical representative of the stimuli originating from within the organism" (p. 121). "Wish, in contrast, was indissolubly bound to memory traces of a previous gratification" (Akhtar, 1999, pp. 115–116). Early on, then, need gave way to wish as the motivational engine. From a psychoanalytic point of view, in the beginning there was *wish.*

> Freud worked productively for his first fifteen years as a psychoanalyst without the concept of *Trieb*, relying primarily on wish as his motivational term. … The main dynamic concept in *Studies in Hysteria* … —affect-charged, repressed memories—has the major defining properties of wish. … The principal motivational concept used in the brilliant case history of *Dora* (Freud, 1905/1953) and in Freud's (1900/1953) masterpiece of combined clinical insight and theoretical elaboration, *The Interpretation of Dreams*, is wish.
>
> (Holt, 1976, p. 179)

By forsaking the two-person seduction theory, Freud built the towering edifice of drive theory, in which the *drives* were the source of all motivation and the notion of drives and the defenses against drives or their derivatives were among the pillars that held up the edifice. Yet even with regard to the question of drive and defense there has been an undercurrent of disquiet. For over three decades, Gill (1978; see also Hoffman, 1985) drew attention to Freud's questionable division of motivations into opposing categories: those having to do with impulse and those designed to oppose impulse. Gill presented the case very clearly:

> Though [Freud, by shifting from the topographic to the structural theory,] had thus disposed of the error of assuming that defensive processes had ready access to consciousness, while the processes defended against did not, he was still left with a class distinction between processes seeking expression and processes seeking to prevent such expression. An alternative scheme would have been to conceptualize the contending processes as equally striving for expression and to sever the idea of processes seeking expression from any special relationship to the body, but such a scheme would have violated [Freud's] conception of a hierarchy of psychic processes with the base of the hierarchy constituted by the somatic "drives."
>
> (cited in Hoffman, 1985, pp. 149–150)

Historically the notion of *need* crept back into psychoanalysis only because yearnings were encountered that had no place in drive theory. In this usage—Winnicott, Balint, Kohut—the term "need" was largely used in connection with "good needs." By this ungainly term I mean to signify needs not only that had to be met to afford physical and psychological survival, but also that conduce toward growth, the enhancement of functional capacities. The need for recognition would be one example. Nonetheless, "bad needs" (in the sense of defensive, self-stifling or antigrowth needs) were at times also elevated into prominence as, for example, in Winnicott's (1950–1955/1975) discussion of the *need for impingement*[7] in false self-organizations of personality. The terms good needs and bad needs have, of course, never been explicit, but their implicit presence has been, to me, an invitation to reconsider the entire question of need: its developmental origins, its functional relations to the organism as a whole, its systematization. Removing the term need from the sphere of implicit value judgments frees us to consider need afresh and conceptualize any particular need as a resultant of a highly complex mix of conflicting constituent needs—*interactive* systems of motivational pushes and pulls.

What, then, is a need? Should it be employed on the basis of the *feeling* of need, its urgency, peremptoriness, demand? Or should it be seen as denoting a *requirement* for the healthy well-being and development of the person? Or, then again, should it be looked upon as denoting a person's motivational subsystem, organized physiologically, psychologically, or both, but *without regard to what is healthy?* The first meaning of need, based on the *feeling* of need, is relatively arbitrary and, as has been pointed out by Mitchell (1991) and by Myerson (1981), is, much like the distinction between need and wish, often a function of who is looking at what particular piece of behavior and in what context. The second meaning, bound to health values, will clearly be affected by one's view as to what constitutes basic human needs, one's value system, as well as one's view of the nature of psychopathology.

The third conception of a need as nothing more than an organized motivational system, or the resultant of an aggregate of motivational systems, is the one that I am here advocating. It has the advantage of putting aside questions of health values and the disadvantage of requiring us to find a new way of thinking that addresses the question of human values. A need so defined *may* be felt subjectively as a "need," in which case it *may* be expressed as a need or as a wish or longing. On the other hand, it may not be felt as a need or even as a wish; instead it may be felt very indirectly as, for example, dread, or even fury. Or, yet again, it may not be felt at all; there may not be any corresponding awareness of need. The specific experience or expression of a need is probably a function of its interaction with other, conflicting or complementary needs (motivational systems).

As suggested earlier, functional capacities, as for example, the ability to recognize invariants in recurring situations, tend to acquire a new feature, a quality one might think of as a *need to exercise the capacity* and gradually to expand its range of efficacy (growth). Capacities, then, under the systematizing influence of experience, soon graduate into needs, or motivational systems. The ability to recognize invariants, for example, evolves into the capacity to abstract or generalize from experience, and in time the capacity, indeed the *need*, to "make meaning." This sequence will ultimately expand vastly with experience to include increasingly complex organizations of meaning. The making of meaning, or the push for cognitive coherence, then itself becomes an elaborate motivational system, one that may have little conscious representation as *wish*, even though it inevitably becomes a fundamental need.

All need-systems have their origin in creative response to their immediate environment. Circumstances, both internal and external, activate needs in the developing person—neonate, infant, child, adult—in successive tiers of complexity. Depending on circumstances in a person's life, basic needs will develop in unique ways, reflecting (1) the potential talents and skills, as well as handicaps, that were organized on the basis of genetic programming and prenatal experience and (2) the facilitative and thwarting environmental influences in postnatal life. The adaptive capacities of the developing human are enormous.

In this connection it should be noted that the word adaptive is shorthand for tendencies that are intrinsic to neural tissue to find creative solutions to new situations. From this point of view, the gradual organization of complex motivational systems is likewise the consequence of emergent creative neural synthetic activity. Although experimental work in motivation is sorely lacking, an excursion into the exciting work of Thelen and her colleagues provides a glimpse into what I believe is an analogous area of development. As a result of extensive studies in the microanalysis of developing motor skills in infants—walking, reaching for objects—Thelen (1990) states that developmental theorists have not met the challenge of individual differences because those differences have been regarded as extraneous, as noise in the system. From her point, of view, on the contrary, it is precisely such differences, the huge variations between individuals, that allow the evolution of unique motor patterns.

> Thelen found that the development of such skills, as Edelman's theory would suggest, follow no single programmed or prescribed pattern. Indeed there is great variability among infants at first, with many patterns of reaching for objects, but there then occurs over the course of several months, a competition among these patterns, a discovery or selection of workable patterns, or workable motor solutions. … Each child, Thelen showed, explores a rich range of possible ways to reach for an object and selects its own path, without benefit of any blueprint or program. The child is forced to be original, to create its own solutions.
>
> (cited in Sacks, 1993, p. 50)

In my view, what Thelen has shown in relation to motor individuality very likely applies equally to the development of unique qualities of needs or motivational systems in each individual.

As unique modes of adaptation to the mix of facilitating and thwarting circumstances begin to emerge, systems of motivation develop. These systems, by virtue of the general tendency of many systems toward stability, once established, become what we call *needs* and what I am here referring to simply as elaborate motivational systems. The unique formatting or patina that any need, say, the need for exploratory behavior, acquires during its evolution, will reflect the experiences of that particular individual. But, perhaps more important, there likely will have developed a congeries of needs in association with the specific need under scrutiny, say exploratory behavior. For example, an infant may have developed strategies for testing the waters to see if shaming will be forthcoming; or he or she may have discovered that it is safer to conceal exploratory behavior from a particular adult, or that it is wise to find some way of propitiating the adult by clowning behavior before revealing the exploratory actions. These defensive activities soon also become "needs"; they have just as much claim on the word as the need for exploration, even though from the outside they appear to us to be antithetical to what we think of as an intrinsic need of the child.

This illustration highlights the advantage that accrues from thinking of needs as value-free motivational systems rather than grouping them into categories of needs as against defenses. Much like trying to divine the location of the ocean by extrapolating from the direction of flow at any given point in a highly meandering river, there is often no way of knowing whether what appears to be a defensive need at one point in life may become the basis for a highly creative self-expression at another. The need for very private exploration or, to continue the illustration, the need for clowning or theatricality may turn out in the end to have invaluable consequences for later development.

There are, I believe, other advantages to uncoupling built-in human values from the notion of need as a motivational system. By including the quality of "good" or "healthy" (or, conversely, bad or needy) into the very term need, we not only forgo clarity as to what need means, we also glide imperceptibly into making judgments about what is healthy or unhealthy on the basis of the word we have chosen to use. Thus, a self-psychologist using the term need is usually implying "good need"—something that requires a particular kind of response. When a conflict analyst (whether classical Freudian or interpersonal) uses the word need, it generally connotes something bad and defensive.

In contrast to both of these outlooks, where need is thought of as an organized motivational system that is exerting pressure on the person, it presents us with a person who is the container of a vast array of such systems—needs—some of which are healthy, others pathological; but they are not healthy or pathological on an a priori basis. I much prefer this more complex view of the nature of need; it forces us, (or offers the opportunity) to seek out explicitly the complex relations among the various needs (motivational systems) rather than using terms that make some of those decisions for us without our being aware of it. Need defined this way carries a more accepting, less judgmental tone. Not having values built into need, we are encouraged—perhaps forced to deal with human values independently of need.

A further benefit, one with important clinical relevance, deserves mention. Therapeutically, at least for some people, the recognition that some repetitive pattern of experience is really an expression of an organized system operating to maintain its own stability—a kind of internal Frankenstein—can provide the leverage for one to become acutely aware of the system, a kind of consciousness-raising as to some aspect of one's inner workings. One is then in a position to do something about the repetitiveness of a pattern by exploring its origins and associated affects, and even by risking alternative ways of being. Recognizing that one is the unwitting and involuntary bearer of a long-since organized motivational system facilitates a sense of intensified ego-dystonicity and diminishes the sense of shame or personal inadequacy about being inhabited by wishes that feel unacceptable to oneself. One is likely to feel a sense of humiliation at one's awareness of, say, a recurrent masochistic patterning of interaction with a loved one, but not feel humiliated at being hostage to an impersonal internal motivational system that is driven to self-perpetuation. The very awareness provides a conception of an alternative; one can begin to imagine what life might be like without the demands and seductions of this autonomously organized system, a valuable first step in furthering the analytic process and enhancing the possibilities for change. It facilitates the realization that, while one was not responsible for the system having become organized, one now does have the responsibility for dealing with its presence.

This brings us to consider the relation between the view of need in terms of motivational systems and a central feature of Buddhism, *anatta*, or no-self. One of the most compelling features of Buddhist psychology is the cultivation of the capacity for nonjudgmental self-reflection through intensive meditation. The goal of insight meditation is not to gain insight into the contents of one's thinking; rather, it is to gain insight into the way the mind works, to cultivate mindfulness, and ultimately to have the experience of what has been called naked awareness. The means toward the attainment of this capacity is a profound immersion in a state of awareness in which one observes, and disidentifies with, the contents of one's mind. Needs, one might say, simply become motivational systems, phenomena to observe. In so doing, the meditator, after much practice, becomes acutely aware of the ephemeral nature of his or her thoughts, wishes, and feelings of need. They begin to take on a remarkably impersonal quality; one has become the finely attuned observer of the incredible panoply of one's motivational systems, operating now in tandem, now in conflict. In time the meditator may become so aware of the illusory nature of one's self, or the multiplicity of selves that one had thought of as "I," that the sense of selfness dissolves. Although we all are not likely to achieve this level of attainment, that it can happen offers another incentive to thinking of needs and wishes as motivational systems.

As I noted earlier, there is a price to pay when thinking of need simply as a motivational system without regard to its health value. This way of thinking requires of us that we remain aware of the differences in function of different types of motivational systems and find ways of designating those differences. Where such functional differences are not recognized, major confusion can arise. In Buddhism three types of needs are recognized, each with a different word. Unfortunately all three have been rendered in English as *need.* One type of need has to do with the need to exercise one's functions of everyday existence, perhaps including that sense of "going on being" (Winnicott, 1960/1965a, p. 47). A second type is the need for expanding one's functions, developing skills, learning new ways of being, transcending one's everyday being. The third is closer to what we refer to as craving. When we, in the West, think of Buddhism as advocating the repudiation of need as the solution for man's suffering, *we* mix up and lump together all three meanings of need.

The Buddha's meaning is altogether different and distinguishes among the three. The first two types of need are actively encouraged—husbanding one's resources and feathering one's nest, and, second, the need for growth and transcendence, the pursuit of which need is highly valued (unless it has become a craving). Craving is an altogether different type of need. Its origins arise in one's misguided efforts to heal one's existential suffering. By its very nature, it cannot accomplish its mission and so results in frustration and further suffering, which, in turn, intensifies our ever-more desperate efforts at self-healing by seeking the satisfaction of what we might call alienated needs, no matter how powerfully they are felt. And so continues the spiral of suffering. It is this spiral that the Buddha was addressing when he advocated the repudiation of need. Seeing all the futile ways by which we seek to assuage our existential suffering, the Buddha discovered a way of detaching oneself from the vicious spiral We, in the West, tend to crunch together all three meanings of need because of the way we have come to use the word. We then end up thinking either that need is bad and should be repudiated or that need is good and one should live the sybaritic life of self indulgence.

Wish and Need

What, then, is the relation between need and wish? We have postulated a hierarchy of structuring that begins with built-in biases and preferences. Then, as experience interacts with these biases or, in Edelman's (1989, 1992) language, "values," an increasingly complex array of motivational systems, or needs, comes into being, each level building on and modulating what has preceded it. Needs make themselves known through feelings, through wishes, through action, as well as through their influence on perception, memory, and thought processes. If we could stick to this kind of formulation, the relation between need and wish would be reasonably clear. Confusion, however, comes about from several sources. One is that, both in vernacular and in professional usage, the word need is often used as almost synonymous with wish or want. Need differs then from want largely in its implication of a feeling of intensity or even urgency in connection with the wish or a certain justification for the wish on the basis of some standard of necessity: "I need a vacation," meaning, "I have a strong wish to have a vacation." Or "I need a new dress for the dinner party," meaning, "I want (wish for) a new dress for the occasion lest I appear there in a dress everyone has seen before."

Another source of confusion is that the word need is used to express a judgment about what someone else is purported to need in his or her best interests. An occupational hazard of caretakers and psychoanalysts is their proneness to this form of interaction. My point here is not whether or not the purported need is valid, but that it is an external assessment of someone else's developmental status. Analysts are always making decisions like, "What this person needs is clear and persistent interpretation," or "What this person needs is affirmation and mirroring." As an illustration of how readily the word need slips into this mode, Lichtenberg (1989), whose efforts in the study of human motivation I greatly admire, implicitly articulates this usage.

> I distinguish between needs and wishes. Need satisfaction is fundamental to the maintenance of self-cohesion and is the source of selfobject experience. Wishes are manifold conscious and unconscious motivations derived from each [of the five basic systems], often competing with another. Wishes and needs may coincide, as they do in the wish and need of toddlers to have the caregiver put them to sleep with a reassuring kind word. Wishes and needs may not coincide, as in a toddler's wish to follow a lost ball into the street and yet need protective restraint. (p. 12)

Although we may well agree that a toddler needs protective restraint in this circumstance, it is a judgment that *we* are making about the child. If it were an adult analysand whom we judge to need a "holding environment" rather than interpretation, we would more clearly recognize that it is the analyst who is deciding what the analysand needs.

The passage from Lichtenberg also illustrates a third source of confusion surrounding the term need. In his usage, needs have to do with self-cohesion, whereas wishes have to do with motivations stemming from the five systems that he delineates, "each [of which] is built around a fundamental need" (p. 1).

> My hypothesis is that for each of the five basic motivational systems ... there are specific needs and that when these needs are met, the result is a selfobject experience [... a particular affective state characterized by a sense of cohesion, safety, and invigoration].
>
> (p. 12)

What I find curious about this formulation is that self-cohesion is not accorded the status of a fundamental need, perhaps one that is even more fundamental and primitive than "the five basic needs." Are not coherence and the maintenance of self-cohesion, much like self-regulation, the superordinate need? Why would one want to make a distinction between an implied *need* for self-coherence as against the *wishes* that stem from five motivational systems? I believe we have stumbled on an important root of the problem surrounding the word need. Lichtenberg, in this context, is using "need" to mean something like *drive*, as used in classical psychoanalysis; whereas the need for self-coherence does not fit in the framework of classical metapsychology and is, therefore, assigned a different category in much the same way as Balint (1968) and Winnicott tried to resolve the problem. It is worth noting that Winnicott (1966/1987), half a century ago, drawing attention to a similar distinction between wish and need, at that time also used the term need to denote something quite different from wish, where wish was tied to the concept of drive:

> It may seem rather strange that I should make this big distinction between desire [wish] and need. ... I was constantly in a state of frustration ... because in the Scientific Meetings. ... I constantly heard references to wishes [drive derivatives], and I found that this was being used as a defense blocking the study of need. ... I have tried to enumerate the

> psychotic- type anxieties which cluster around the word need. These have nothing to do with instincts. They have to do with such things as disintegration, depersonalization, the opposite of progress in emotional development, that is to say annihilation, falling for ever. …
>
> (p. 156)

Thinking of needs in terms of motivational systems enables us to transcend these distinctions between needs, on one hand, and wishes or drive derivatives, on the other, and encourages us to think afresh about motivations, rather than falling prey to the vestiges of classical metapsychology.

If we pause for the moment to consider how, in the clinical situation, one distinguishes between needs having to do with self-cohesion and other types of needs, we find that there is no ready-made, theory-given answer. I believe the resolution lies in the empirics of clinical practice, rather than in a distinction between need and wish or desire. In those circumstances where consistent and perspicacious interpretation seems counterproductive and results in the analysand's feeling increasingly isolated, misunderstood, attacked, and humiliated and where the analysand's functioning deteriorates such that one senses that self-fragmentation and feelings of annihilation are in the making, one is likely to recognize that the need for self-cohesion is in the foreground. With experience, one is likely to recognize the signs long in advance of major deterioration or futile impasse.

Winnicott (1962/1965) discovered that in certain patients' needs that were interpreted as deriving from instinctual need really had nothing to do with instinctual need, but instead stemmed from inadequate or distorted self-integration. Balint (1968), too, recognized that there was a whole category of need, such as what he referred to as the "need for recognition," that had no place in drive theory. Both analysts recognized that this new category of need was refractory to interpretation and, instead, required the analyst to accommodate, in some significant degree, to the patient's need. This recognition left only two alternatives, either (1) to revise radically the dual-instinct theory to include another set of centrally important motivations or (2) to leave the theory unquestioned and find a way to introduce this other level of need as a sort of auxiliary theory. Both Winnicott and Balint opted for the latter; hence, I believe, the origins of their distinction between need and wish or desire. Need was to be for those needs that did not fit into classical theory, and wish or desire would be retained for those that could fit into the theory. This strategy also had the advantage that need could be responded to by noninterpretive means, without challenging the supremacy of interpretation as applied to the kind of need that was called desire and could be related to "the instincts."

To return to the broadened meaning of need to signify motivational systems in general, the "healthy need" conception may be seen now as merely a way station in the evolution of psychoanalytic thinking, a notion that at one time served a useful function in furthering the decline and fall of drive theory. My sense is that the wish-need dichotomy that has carried over into self-psychology and into Lichtenberg's usage is a vestige of another era. The time has arrived when, in keeping with the broadest sweep of Stern's (1985) and Lichtenberg's (1989) work, needs are needs, though they may differ in their manifestations, their pathology, and in the means of mending problems that have accrued from their faulty evolution. From this point of view, resistance and transference are expressions of needs, expressions of elaborate motivational systems that evolved early in life and powerfully resist change; they represent the centripetal needs whose central thrust is to perceive new situations in terms of well-honed ancient systems or find or create new enactments that are consonant with those systems.

There is yet a fourth source of confusion in the use of the term need, one that is commonly overlooked. Because, as noted earlier, the word need is at times used popularly to signify a feeling of intensity or even urgency in association with a wish, it lends itself to being confounded with what I would call neediness rather than need (Myerson, 1981; Ghent, 1992). Shabad (1993b) describes how

> the child attempts to forestall … psychic injury by perpetually crushing the wishes that led only to endless disillusionment. … With a sense of resentment and righteous indignation, [the person] may then, with a vengeance, seek to retrieve those wishes from their exile in the unconscious—by giving them a "rebirth" as entitled demands or "needs" that must be filled and indulged through action, immediately and repeatedly.
>
> (pp. 484–485)

What Shabad is describing is a perspicacious and important insight into the pathological nature of neediness and provides a valuable avenue for therapeutic influence. The problem, for me, arises out of the dichotomous view of need and wish and the notion implicit in this view that need requires some type of gratification, such as a holding environment, whereas wish is to be dealt with through interpretation. This view requires that the analyst choose one or other package. Although Shabad opts for the latter, either choice would reaffirm that the issue is between wish and need. My concern is not with the clinical value of his insight, but with the underlying conceptual issue.

As I see it, the choice is not between need and wish, but between different orders of need. What the patient is yearning for is appropriate response to appropriate needs. Those needs and, with them, the wishes that were object-specific expressions of them have gone underground. In their place have appeared "entitled demands or 'needs' that must be filled and indulged through action, immediately and repeatedly" (Shabad, 1993b, p. 485). Need, in this usage, however, carries a quite different aura of meaning than would accompany a value-free denotation of the term, in which need signifies nothing more than "motivational system." In Shabad's usage, need refers to a feeling of subjective urgency and peremptoriness; it has the ring of manipulation, importunity, entitlement. "Need" now connotes demand and reflects as much the feelings of the beholder as of the beheld. Using a non-judgmental conception of need, one might configure the patient as dealing with a superset of needs (a complex amalgam of motivational subsystems), which both reveal and express, however indirectly, an underlying need, while simultaneously covering it over, blackwashing it with a complex of interwoven derivative and defensive needs. What appears as demand is a mix of an underlying thrust to experience a quality of responsiveness that was severely flawed at some earlier point in life and now imbricated with other needs: for example, the need to scream out in fury at the depriving parents; to remain embedded in the parental matrix; the need for revenge; the need to alienate the other and confirm the parental diagnosis of the patient's being the hateful repository of unreasonable demands; the need to force goodness out of the other so as to confirm the expectation that nothing will be forthcoming out of a sense of caring; the need to make the transition from object relating to object usage, and, above all, the need to forestall recognition that the other is indeed caring, lest such awareness threaten the entire system of needs, disorganizing it and evoking intense anxiety. Note that I am using the term need here rather than wish. Conscious or unconscious wishes are the expressions or manifestations of needs, the resultants of a web of interacting motivational systems

What Kinds or Categories of Needs?

Having arrived at a working hypothesis about the nature of need as a shorthand for motivational system, we may now embark on issues that may be of more direct clinical interest. What kinds of needs do we commonly encounter in our work as psychoanalysts, either in our practice or in our theorizing, and what is the relation between particular kinds, qualities, or intensities of need to psychoanalytic therapeusis?

First, the question of what kinds of needs bring themselves to our attention whether by their presence or their apparent absence: in their most general form I would say they fall into two broad categories, the old and the new. You will recognize that this is just another way of specifying two broad classes of motivational systems, those that generally were organized early in life and that tend toward self- perpetuation, and, on the other hand, those that tend to disrupt the status quo and promote the integration of new experience. These latter systems probably also had their earliest beginnings in infancy and childhood, but being less explicit and visible in their outward expression, perhaps existing only in dissociation, have tended to be thought of collectively as the expansive or growth thrust.

Building on Edelman's (1987) theory, it does not seem at all implausible that under many circumstances experience is simultaneously organized around two or more mappings, leading to the simultaneous development of quite different motivational systems. One such mapping would be based on what is consistent and readily compatible with systems that are already well organized and accessible to consciousness; and another is organized on the basis of the same experience but without the need to be integrated with other conscious systems. This latter system of motivation would be expansive, centrifugal in nature, always seeking the expansion of self-experience even at the risk of being disruptive of the more conservatively organized centripetal systems, particularly if it broke through into consciousness. Here we enter into the province of such notions as Winnicott's (1960/1965b) true and false self-organizations and, by extending the level of complexity, dissociative processes and multiple personality syndromes.

I believe that in all human beings these two types of needs, those organized around maintaining homeostatic safety and those that tend toward expansion of function, are always operating and in some degree of dynamic balance. As one ages, the balance seldom remains static; one either grows in breadth and inclusiveness, or one constricts and becomes narrower and more rigid. Perhaps the extreme expression of the need for growth is enlightenment, and its opposite extreme is the paranoid solution.

In analysis we encounter the "old needs" in the multifaceted forms of resistance, transference[8] and repetition; and the new needs as the feelings of distress about one's state of being, coupled with a wish to change, an urge to expand one's sense of potential, a wish to feel whole rather than a bundle of contradictions, a wish to enhance one's skills in the human and nonhuman world, a yearning for transcendence or for surrender of a sense of falseness to one's life, and so on. Here, too, we recognize Winnicott's (1960/1965b) true-self needs, Kohut's (1977) need to realize one's nuclear design, and Bollas's (1989) personal idiom. Clearly there is some risk in making generalizations such as the foregoing, since we all know that in the complexity of an actual life there is vast opportunity for one motive being coopted in the service of another, so that masquerades, feints, and disguises, for better or worse, ever complicate the relation between appearance and substance.

Earlier I said that the very notion of *self* not only implies need *states* (motivational systems)—both the need to expand its structure and the need to resist change—but also that its very nature can be thought of as a high-level system of systems, itself characterized by a bootstrapping operation wherein needs develop capacities and capacities beget needs. Even such a high-level function as the faculty of consciousness—awareness itself—becomes a need in the sense of having a motivational valence. Lichtenberg (1989) implies something similar when he defines "the self as an independent center for initiating, organizing, and integrating. While self, person, and identity are all related terms, *self* as defined here [by Lichtenberg] emphasizes motivation (initiating) and its function with regard to experience (organizing and integrating)" (p. 12).

Greenberg (1992) is less than enthusiastic about what he calls multiple drive models, such as those proposed by Lichtenberg or Pine (the "four psychologies") among others, and makes a persuasive case for a return to a dual-drive model. But he replaces the drives of sex and aggression with "effectance" and "safety."

> I believe there are two quite different feeling states that can usefully be thought of as aims of fundamental drives. One is the sense of physical

> or emotional well being—freedom from the pressure of any urgent need and the absence of unpleasant affects of which anxiety is the prototype. … I call the search for this feeling state the "safety drive." The second feeling state, in contrast, involves the sense of vitality and vigorousness; the sense is of being alive and active ... when we have achieved a goal, overcome an obstacle, felt that we have used ourselves well. It is a feeling of being effective, stimulated, perhaps excited. … [I] call the search for this feeling state the "effectance drive."
>
> (pp. 129–130)

Subsumed within these basic drives would be all manner of needs (motivational systems). Among the appeals of this conception is that it suggests that there are two basic thrusts, one a centripetal, conservative one, the other a centrifugal, risk-taking, expansive one. Since I view all living systems as in a balanced flux between maintenance and expansion (growth), Greenberg's conception is inviting. Note, however, that his formulation also subsumes human values in the conception of drive or need. Both the safety and the effectance drives represent organizations or systems of need that serve our well-being and fulfilling development.

Freud's drives (fundamental motivational systems) are, by contrast with Greenberg's and Lichtenberg's models, *value free.* Since Freud's are conceived of as biologically given, genetically programmed, life and death instincts (whose usual expressions are through sex and aggression), they are intrinsically neither good nor bad for the organism, although they must have evolutionary advantage. In fact, in Freud's system it is society that imposes order and human values on the instincts, to tame their unruliness. It might be thought that the value-free conception of need that I am advocating is in some fashion a return to classical drive theory. Not so. Early on in this essay I tried to convey the idea that all that is built into the organism is a collection of primitively organized preferences amplified and modulated by hormonal influence and primitive reflexes; and that it is out of lived experience in the context of these preferences that motivational systems, needs, arise by an ever-more inclusive process of neural natural selection and the self-emergent properties inherent in this very complex nonlinear system. There are no preprogrammed drives; needs that, by their ubiquity, may have the appearance of universal drives owe their origin to the ubiquity of some form of infant caretaking to insure survival.

Probably every analyst is occupied by an implicit belief system having to do with the basic needs of the members of our species. Such a belief system is often unarticulated and, even when articulated in the form of theoretical propositions, axiomatic assumptions often remain unrecognized or unacknowledged. The very nature of the theoretical position—often spoken of as a model of mind—is in itself an expression of the private conception or belief system having to do with the nature of man's needs (see Stolorow and Atwood, 1979). Certainly any model of therapeutic action is also an expression of how one conceives of the bringing into being of a degree of balance, integration, flexibility, and expansibility among one's needs. Indeed, the need for a belief system, a system that aims at cognitive coherence and integration of a vast variety of one's own motivational systems, has itself become a basic need by the time one has reached a certain stage of development. It would be extremely valuable to study, in extenso, this question of how the many different theoretical positions in psychoanalysis reflect different conceptions both of the nature and ontogeny of human needs and the nature of the best means of facilitatively influencing those needs. We may then be able to discover some broad principles underlying the nature of psychic therapeusis, principles that may transcend and be inclusive of such issues as conflict and deficit, abstinence and gratification, insight and "intouch," information and transformation, interpretation and relationship, here-and-now as against then-and-there, and so on.

There is much to be explored regarding the place and meaning of need in the many theoretical systems that have appeared since Freud. To name a few arbitrarily, consider, Fairbairn (1963), Sullivan (1953), Fromm (1955), Kohut (1977), and more recently, Lichtenberg (1989) and Greenberg (1991). I mention Fromm because it is not commonly known that Fromm (1955) outlined five "basic needs" of man. It will also be of advantage to explore a wide variety of more specifically articulated needs that have assumed particular importance in the work of particular authors: needs for physiological self-regulation, for attachment-affiliation, for exploration and assertion, for aversive reaction, for sensual enjoyment and sexual excitement (Lichtenberg, 1989); the dual needs for effectance and safety (Greenberg, 1991); the needs for autonomy and homonomy (Angyal, 1965); the need for recognition (Balint, 1968); the need for the vitalization of true self (Winnicott, 1960/1965b); needs for empathic attunement and for the realization of one's nuclear design (Kohut, 1977); the need for the expression of personal idiom (Bollas, 1989); the conflicting needs for recognition and autonomy (Benjamin, 1988); the need to exhume and give proper burial to childhood wishes that have reappeared as peremptory neediness (Shabad, 1993a, 1993b); the need to have an impact on one's environment, or "efficacy" (Broucek, 1979); the need to be helpful or have a healing influence on one's therapist or parents (Searles, 1975/1979); the need to integrate oppositional states, as in the attainment of the depressive position (Klein); needs for the maintenance of self-cohesion and self-esteem (Kohut, 1977; Sullivan, 1953); the need to move beyond object relating to object usage (Winnicott, 1969/1971); various types of transitional needs such as the need for surrender (Milner, 1958/1959; Ghent, 1990); the need for experience of nascent intensity (Alberoni, 1983); the need for transcendence (Fromm, 1955); and so on (see also Akhtar, 1999). Needs to exercise capacities that are maturationally developing, to exercise functions that are already integrated, and to expand functional capacity (growth) are often taken for granted and thus overlooked as vital needs. So too with the need for creating meaning, as well as the need to deconstruct meaning as a feature of creativity.

I have chosen a few illustrative needs that traverse a wide range of hierarchical levels. Clearly many could be subsumed in the more generic system of one or another systematizer of the ontogeny of motive. I believe, however, that exploration of the origins and evolution of specific needs will cast light on the nature of need systems and their interactions in general.

Another category of needs as motivational systems is the type of need that ordinarily we think of as having to do with resistance and transference, defensive activities, security operations, the repetition compulsion, whether thought of as a mysterious compulsion rooted in the death instinct or as a need to fixedly maintain patterns of human interaction. Severely maladaptive needs are nonetheless needs in the sense that the organism is likely to experience a degree of disorganization if the need is not satisfied. An addict's need for a fix is perhaps the extreme form of this type of need, but a believer's reaction to a challenge to a vital belief system is not much less disorganizing. A compulsive hand washer "needs" urgently to repeatedly wash his hands. An anorectic "needs" not to eat; indeed, feels threatened by food. A phobic person "needs" desperately to get away from the phobic situation. Perhaps the single compelling distinction between defensive, maladaptive needs and what we have referred to as healthy needs is to be found in the degree of rigidity or inflexibility that characterizes maladaptive needs. Even this is not clear cut. One need only recall how some highly creative artists feel compelled almost constantly to exercise their creative gifts, at times to the point of what appears to others to be a form of madness.

A fitting place to close this discussion would be to turn inward, to look into the workings of the field we all devote so much of our life to—psychoanalysis—and reflect on how the need to make meaning—by now so highly elaborated from its primitive beginnings in selectional biases—can serve the need for leaps of creativity and growth and yet, given a slight perturbation, ever so subtly glide into a need to cling to a defensive and constrictive belief system. Every day in our practice we pay homage to, and stand back in awe of, the marvels of the human mind caught up in the struggle to heal and transcend itself, while holding back in fear, jousting with itself in dread of walking through the valley of the shadow of death.

Notes

1. Emmanuel Ghent, M.D. is Clinical Professor, Postdoctoral Program in Psychotherapy and Psychoanalysis, New York University, where he was founding chairman of the Relational Track. He is a Supervising Analyst at the William Alanson White Institute. This paper is a version of a paper written originally in 1998 for a book that never materialized. It was presented at the Washington (DC) School of Psychiatry, November 6, 1999 and, in abbreviated form, at the American Academy of Psychoanalysis, New York, January 8, 2000; the New York University Postdoctoral Program Colloquium, January 27, 2001; and the Institute for Specialization in the Psychoanalytic Psychology of the Self and Relational Psychoanalysis, Rome, October 6, 2001.
2. Greenberg (1991) points out that such formulations as the need for contact, attachment, or object-seeking are inadequate descriptors of the nature of a fundamental need. The very use of such terms as "good object" as against "bad object" or "good breast" or "good mother" as against "bad breast" or "bad mother" means that infants have a need for some other quality, be it pleasure or security or affirmation or stimulation, than the mere contact with or attachment or connection to the object. As I see it, Greenberg's critique does not disqualify the notion of object seeking—after all, consider the vast efforts that people engage in to seek "bad objects"—but points to the necessity of refining the nature and complexity of the needs that characterize attachment behavior. Perhaps what is at work here is both a need for attachment, which may have had its origins in an earlier bias favoring warmth and soft touch, and needs that

originated experientially in connection with specific caregivers and that may or may not have traumatic overtones.

3. Shortly after this paper was written, a paper by Migone and Liotti (1998) appeared in which the authors suggest that many years after the abandonment of the seduction or trauma theory, we are today "facing a second trauma in the history of psychoanalysis that we might call the 'abandonment of drive theory'" (p. 107). The authors go on to make extensive use of Edelman's (1992) theory as an alternative basis of exploring the origins of motivation.
4. In order to study how simple or complex such values need to be, Edelman (1992) has constructed a series of robots based on simulated neural networks. In sharp contrast to work in artificial intelligence, these robotic "organisms" are programmed with only a very few preferences or values, such as light is better than no light and contact is better than no contact. It is fascinating to witness how this organism-like device is able to interact with the surround by categorizing and recategorizing experience—the fundamental processes involved in both perception and memory. Edelman "called the study of such devices *noetics*, from the Greek, *noein*, to perceive. Unlike cybernetic devices that are able to adapt within fixed design constraints, and unlike robotic devices that … [are] under programmed control, noetic devices act on their environment by selectional means and by categorization on value" (p. 192).
5. In keeping with traditional usage in psychoanalysis, I use the word capacity to connote capability. At times it borders on achievement, even skill or ability. As French (1999) puts it, "A capacity … is not predetermined, fixed or static; rather, it is a potential that is only realized in use. A capacity develops through action or shrinks through neglect." It may also be inhibited or eroded by excessive anxiety.
6. The more complex the capacities that have developed, the more complex and differentiated the needs. It may seem puzzling that need arises out of capacity (the reverse is, of course, also true). The more common conception of need as deriving from developmental deficit would suggest that need develops out of *in* capacity, functional deficiency. The contradiction, I believe, is only apparent. Capacities and faculties, I believe, evoke the need to exercise those capacities, much as the functional capacity of muscles begets the need to use the muscles, else the functional capacity, even the anatomical structure, tends to atrophy. As I see it, deficit arises when capacities have begun to develop, that is, have had sufficient experiential input to initiate their development but, in some significant way, have been thwarted in the exercise and expansion of the relevant functions. The type of need that results from deficit is one among many types of need systems. Perhaps the difference between needs that arise out of deficit as against needs that arise out of expansion of functional capacity is, in the end, only a matter of degree. The more consequential and clinically significant difference may be the likelihood that needs derived from deficit coexist and are intertwined with a variety of compensatory and defensive needs that confer a particular

flavor to the syndrome, in contrast to needs that have not been grossly interfered with and are, therefore, free to continue relatively uncomplicated development.

7. Although Winnicott usually used the word need to mean good or healthy need, on occasion he did employ the term in a value-free way, as, for example, in the following quotation, in which he described how, in an extreme form of environmental impingement, the "'individual' develops … as an extension of the impinging environment. … [In this pattern] it is only through environmental impingement that the motility potential becomes a matter of experience. Here is ill health. To a lesser or greater degree, the individual *must* be opposed, and only if opposed does the individual tap the important motility source. … Environmental impingement must have a pattern of its own, else chaos reigns since the individual cannot develop a personal pattern" (Winnicott, 1950–1955/1975, p. 212).
8. Clearly this formulation is an oversimplification. At various points in the paper I have stressed that any particular clinical expression is always a resultant of many motivational systems, some complementary and some at odds with each other. Transference, for example, is usually not merely the expression of "old needs" but is often at the same time an expression of centrifugal needs seeking some environmental cooperation in perturbing the "old needs."

References

Akhtar, S. (1999). The distinction between needs and wishes: Implications for psychoanalytic theory and technique. *Journal of the American Psychoanalytic Association*, *47*, 113–151.

Alberoni, F. (1983). *Falling in love* (L. Venuti, Trans.). New York, NY: Random House. (Original work published as *Innamoramento e amore*, 1981)

Angyal, A. (1982). *Neurosis and treatment: A holistic theory*. New York, NY: Wiley. (Original work published 1965, New York, NY: Da Capo Press)

Aron, L. (1990). One person and two person psychologies and the method of psychoanalysis. *Psychoanalytic Psychology*, *7*, 475–485.

Balint, M. (1968). *The Basic fault: Therapeutic aspects of regression*. London, UK: Tavistock.

Barry, V. C. (2000). Reflections on interactive and self-organizing aspects of learning in psychoanalysis. *The Annual of Psychoanalysis*, *28*, 7–20. Hillsdale, NJ: The Analytic Press.

Beach, F. (1955). The descent of instinct. *The Psychological Review*, *62*, 401–410.

Benjamin, J. (1988). *The bonds of love: Psychoanalysis, feminism, and the problem of domination*. New York, NY: Pantheon Books.

Bollas, C. (1989). *Forces of destiny: Psychoanalysis and human idiom*. London, UK: Free Association Books.

Bowlby, J. (1988). *A secure base*. New York, NY: Basic Books.

Broucek, F. (1979). Efficacy in infancy: A review of some experimental studies and their possible implications for clinical theory. *The International Journal of Psychoanalysis*, *60*, 311-316.

Edelman, G. M. (1987). *Neural Darwinism*. New York, NY: Basic Books.

Edelman, G. M. (1989). *The remembered present: A biological theory of consciousness*. New York, NY: Basic Books.

Edelman, G. M. (1992). *Bright air, brilliant fire: On the matter of the mind*. New York, NY: Basic Books.

Edelman, G. M. and Tononi, G. (1995). Neural Darwinism: The brain as a selectional system. In J. Cornwall (Ed.), *Nature's imagination: The frontiers of scientific vision*. New York, NY: Oxford University Press.

Emde, R. N. (1988). Development terminable and interminable- I. Innate and motivational factors from infancy. *International Journal of Psycho-Analysis*, *60*, 23–42.

Fairbairn, W. R. D. (1963). Synopsis of an object-relations theory of personality. *International Journal of Psycho-Analysis*, *44*, 224–225.

Fajardo, B. (2000). Breaks in consciousness in the psychoanalytic process: A dynamic systems approach to change and a bridge to Edelman's mind/brain model. *Annual of Psychoanalysis*, *28*, 21–45. Hillsdale, NJ: The Analytic Press.

French, R. (1999). The importance of capacities in psychoanalysis and the language of human development. *International Journal of Psycho-Analysis*, *80*, 1215–1226.

Freud, S. (1953). Fragment of an analysis of a case of hysteria. *Standard Edition*, *7*, 3–124. London, UK: Hogarth Press. (Original work published 1905)

Freud, S. (1953). Regression. *Standard Edition*, *14*, 141–158. London, UK: Hogarth Press. (Original work published 1915)

Freud, S. (1953). The interpretation of dreams. *Standard Edition*, *4 & 5*. London, UK: Hogarth Press. (Original work published 1900)

Fromm, E. (1990). *The sane society*. New York, NY: Henry Holt. (Original work published 1955)

Galatzer-Levy, R. M. (1995). Psychoanalysis and dynamic systems theory: Prediction and self-similarity. *Journal of the American Psychoanalytic Association*, *43*, 1085–1113.

Ghent, E. (1989). Credo: The dialectics of one-person and two-person psychologies. *Contemporary Psychoanalysis*, *25*, 169–211.

Ghent, E. (1990). Masochism, submission, surrender. *Contemporary Psychoanalysis*, *26*, 108–136.

Ghent, E. (1992). Paradox and process. *Psychoanalytic Dialogues*, *2*, 135–159.

Ghent, E. (1993, May). *The place of need in psychoanalysis*. Presented to Chicago Association for Psychoanalytic Psychology, Chicago, IL.

Ghent, E. (1995, April). *Need, action, interaction and enactment in psychoanalysis*. Presented to Appalachian Psychoanalytic Society, Knoxville, TN.

Gill, M. M. (1978). Freud's concepts of unconsciousness and the unconscious. In A. S. Prangishvilli, A.E. Sherozia and F. V. Bassin (Eds.), *The Unconscious* (Vol. 1). Tbilisi, USSR: Metsniereba.

Gill, M. M. (1983). The point of view in psychoanalysis: Energy discharge or person. *Psychoanalysis and Contemporary Thought*, *6*, 523–551.

Ginsburg, B. E. and Hoyda, R. B. (1947). On the physiology of gene-controlled audiogenic seizures in mice. *The Anatomical Record*, *99*, 65–66.

Gleick, J. (1987). *Chaos: Making a new science*. New York, NY: Penguin.

Greenberg, J. (1991). *Oedipus and beyond: A clinical theory*. Cambridge, MA: Harvard University Press.

Harris, A. (2012). *Gender as soft assembly*. New York, NY: Routledge.

Hebb, D. O. (1949). *The organization of behavior*. New York, NY: Wiley.

Hoffman, I. Z. (1985). Merton M. Gill: A study in theory development in psychoanalysis. In J. Reppen (Ed.), *Beyond Freud* (pp. 135–175). Hillsdale, NJ: The Analytic Press.

Holt, R. R. (1965). Ego autonomy re-evaluated. *International Journal of Psycho-Analysis*, *46*, 151–167.

Holt, R. R. (1976). Drive or wish? A reconsideration of the psychoanalytic theory of motivation. In M. M. Gill & P. S. Holzman (Eds.), *Psychology versus metapsychology: Psychoanalytic essays in memory of George S. Klein*. New York, NY: International Universities Press.

Holt, R. R. (1981). The death and transfiguration of metapsychology. *International Review of Psycho-Analysis*, *8*, 129–143.

Home, H. J. (1966). The concept of mind. *International Journal of Psycho-Analysis*, *47*, 43–49.

Kauffman, S. A. (1993). *The origins of order: Self-organization and selection in evolution*. New York, NY: Oxford University Press.

Kelso, J. A. S. (1997). *Dynamic patterns: The self-organization of brain and behavior*. Cambridge, MA: MIT Press.

Kohut, H. (1977). *The restoration of the self.* New York, NY: International Universities Press.

Lichtenberg, J. D. (1989). *Psychoanalysis and motivation*. Hillsdale, NJ: The Analytic Press.

Migone, P. and Liotti, G. (1998). Psychoanalysis and cognitive-evolutionary psychology: An attempt at integration. *International Journal of Psycho-Analysis*, *79*, 1071–1095.

Milner, M. (1959). Psychoanalysis and art. In J. D. Sutherland (Ed.), *Psychoanalysis and Contemporary Thought*. London, UK: Hogarth Press. (Original work published 1958)

Mitchell, S. A. (1991). Wishes, needs and interpersonal negotiations. *Psychoanalytic Inquiry*, *11*, 147–170.

Modell, A. H. (1984). *Psychoanalysis in a new context*. New York, NY: International Universities Press.

Moran, M. G. (1991). Chaos theory and psychoanalysis: The fluidic nature of the mind. *International Review of Psycho-Analysis*, *18*, 211–221.

Myerson, P. G. (1981). When does need become desire and desire need? *Contemporary Psychoanalysis*, *17*, 607–625.

Nass, M. L. (1984). The development of creative imagination in composers. *International Review of Psycho-Analysis*, *11*, 481–492.

Pally, R. & Olds, D. (1998). Consciousness: A neuroscience perspective. *International Journal of Psycho-Analysis*, *79*, 971–989.

Palombo, S. (1999). *The emergent ego: Complexity and coevolution in the psychoanalytic process*. Madison, CT: International Universities Press.

Piers, C. (2000). Character as self-organizing complexity. *Psychoanalysis and Contemporary Thought*, *23*, 3–34.

Prigogine, I (1983). Interview. Omni, 5(8), 85–121.

Rizzolatti, G. and Arbib, M. (1998). Language within our grasp. *Trends in Neuroscience*, *21*, 188–194.

Rizzolatti, G., Arbib, M., Fadiga, I., Gallese, V. and Fogassi, L. (1996). Premotor cortex and the recognition of motor actions. *Cognitive Brain Research*, *3*, 131–141.

Rosenfield, I. (1988). *The invention of memory*. New York, NY: Basic Books.

Sacks, O. (1993, April 8). Making up the mind. *New York Review of Books*, *40*, 42–52.

Sacks, O. (1995). Making up the mind. In J. Cornwall (Ed.). *Nature's imagination: The frontiers of scientific vision*. New York, NY: Oxford University Press.

Schilder, P. (1964). *Contributions to developmental neuropsychiatry*. New York, NY: International Universities Press.

Searles, H. (1979). The patient as therapist to his analyst. In *Countertransference and Related Subjects*. New York, NY: International Universities Press. (Original work published 1975)

Shabad, P. (1993a). Intergenerational transmission of traumatic themes. *Psychoanalytic Psychology*, *10*, 61–75.

Shabad, P. (1993b). Resentment, indignation, entitlement: The transformation of unconscious wish into need. *Psychoanalytic. Dialogues*, *3*, 481–494.

Shane, M., Shane, E. and Gales, M. (1997). Intimate attachments: Toward a new self psychology. New York, NY: Guilford.

Spruiell, V. (1993). Deterministic chaos and the sciences of complexity: Psychoanalysis in the midst of a general scientific revolution. *Journal of the American Psychoanalytic Association*, *41*, 3–44.

Stechler, G. (1997, March). The anatomy of change in psychodynamic psychotherapy. Presented at *Developmental Process and the Enigma of Change in Psychodynamic Therapy*, Boston, MA.

Stern, D. N. (1985). The interpersonal world of the infant. New York, NY: Basic Books.

Stern, D. N., Sander, L. W., Nahum, J. P., Harrison, A. M., Lyons-Ruth, K., Morgan, A. C., Bruschweiler-Stern, N. and Tronick, E. Z. (1998). Non-interpretive mechanisms in psychoanalytic therapy: The "something more" than interpretation. *International Journal of Psycho-Analysis*, *79*, 903–921.

Stolorow, R. D. (1997). Dynamic, dyadic intersubjective systems: An evolving paradigm for psychoanalysis. *Psychoanalytic Psychology*, *14*, 337–364.

Stolorow, R. D. and Atwood, G. E. (1979). *Faces in a cloud: Subjectivity in personality theory*. New York, NY: Aronson.

Sullivan, H. S. (1940). *Conceptions of modern psychiatry: The first William Alanson White memorial lectures*. Washington, DC: The William Alanson White Psychiatric Foundation.

Sullivan, H. S. (1953). *The interpersonal theory of psychiatry*. H. S. Perry (Ed.). New York, NY: Norton.

Thelen, E. (1990). Dynamical systems and the generation of individual differences. In J. Colombo & J. W. Fagan (Eds.), *Individual differences in infancy: Reliability, stability and prediction*. Hillsdale, NJ: Lawrence Erlbaum Associates.

Thelen, E. (1995). Motor development: A new synthesis. *American Psychologist*, 50, 79–95.

Thelen, E. (1998, October). *Dynamic mechanisms of change in early perceptual-motor development*. Paper presented at the 29th Carnegie Symposium on Cognition. Mechanisms of Cognitive Development: Behavioral and Neural Perspectives, Pittsburgh, PA.

Thelen, E. and Smith, L. B. (1994). *A dynamic systems approach to the development of cognition and action*. Cambridge, MA: MIT Press.

Vihman, M. (1993). Variable paths to early word production. *Journal of Phonetics*, *21*, 61–82.

Wallerstein, R. S. (1976). Psychoanalysis as a science: Its present status and its future tasks. In M. M. Gill & P. S. Holzman (Eds.), *Psychology versus metapsychology: Psychoanalytic essays in memory of George S. Klein* (pp. 198–228). New York, NY: International Universities Press.

Wallerstein, R. S. (1986). Psychology as a science: A response to new challenges. *The Psychoanalytic Quarterly*, *55*, 414–451.

Williams, J. H. G., Whiten, A., Suddendorf, T. and Perrett, D. I. (2001). Imitation, mirror neurons and autism. *Neuroscience & Behavioral Reviews*, *25*, 287–295.

Winnicott, D. W. (1965a). The theory of the parent-infant relationship. In *The maturational processes and the facilitating environment* (pp. 37–55). New York, NY: International Universities Press. (Original work published 1960)

Winnicott, D. W. (1965b). Ego distortion in terms of true and false self. In *The maturational processes and the facilitating environment* (pp. 37–55). New York, NY: International Universities Press. (Original work published 1960)

Winnicott, D. W. (1965). Ego integration in child development. In *The maturational processes and the facilitating environment* (pp. 56–63). New York, NY: International Universities Press. (Original work published 1962)

Winnicott, D. W. (1965). *The maturational processes and the facilitating environment* (pp. 140–152). New York, NY: International Universities Press.

Winnicott, D. W. (1971). The use of an object and relating through identifications. In Playing and reality (pp. 86–94). London, UK: Tavistock. (Original work published 1969)

Winnicott, D. W. (1975). Aggression in relation to emotional development. In *Through paediatrics to psycho-analysis: Collected papers* (pp. 204–218). New York, NY: Basic Books. (Original work published 1950–1955)

Winnicott, D. W. (1987). Letter to Lili E. Peller, 15th April 1966. In F. R. Rodman (Ed.), *The spontaneous gesture: Selected letters of D. W. Winnicott.* Cambridge, MA: Harvard University Press. (Original work published 1966)

Part II

Early writings

Chapter 6

Psyche and eye[1]

Emmanuel Ghent

"Eyes are bold as lions—roving, running, leaping here and there, far and near, they speak all languages. They wait for no introduction; they are no Englishmen; ask no leave of age or rank; they respect neither poverty nor power, nor virtue nor sex, but intrude, and come again, and go through and through you in a moment of time. What an inundation of life and thought is discharged from one soul into another through them." With these words did Emerson (1886) pay tribute to the potency and pervasiveness of the eye, the almost magic eye, the window of the soul. We have only to recall the innumerable uses to which the word "eye" is put to perceive how closely it is twined into the fabric of our daily speech. One says "keep an eye on her—she is the apple of my eye," or, "he eyed her keenly"—often so with an "eye to the future." On another occasion one may "give her the glad eye" only to feel "daggers from her escort's eyes." I am sure that you can supply many more examples from the museum of your "mind's eye;" but at least these serve as "eye-openers," unless you prefer to consider them "so much eye-wash." One last one is interesting because it transgresses the borders of our own language: we say he is "ogling her," meaning, he is "making eyes" at her. Curiously, "to ogle" is derived from the German *äugeln*, (to eye) or *Auge* (eye).

The history of mankind is replete with examples of practices which emphasize the status of the eye as the identity of the person, the focus of his being. When we look at someone, we are, in fact, looking at their eyes; so that we behave as though the eye is truly the deputy of the "self." We say "he looked him right in the eye," meaning that there was no evasiveness in his glance; he looked directly at him. A favorite way of losing identity, at least for play, is to cover one's eyes—for example in the masquerade. Machover (1949) has observed that the common expression "to knock the living daylights out of you" suggests that one kills a person by depriving him of the use of his eyes. Greenacre (1926) has drawn attention to our practice of closing the eyes of the dead, and to the rituals of certain tribes in putting out the eyes of slain animals immediately after death, in order to insure the death of the animal and protect the slayer from revenge.

No survey of the folklore of the eye (Rolleston, 1942) would be complete without at least brief mention of the "evil eye" and the couvade. The belief that the eyes of some persons are peculiarly able to inflict harm on the objects of their attention is an extremely widespread and ancient superstition. The significance of the eye as an organ of aggression is attested to by the great prevalence of the belief in the evil eye. Hart (1949) remarks of the evil eye, "No science, religion or law has been able to eradicate it. Incantations and references to it go back to the early records of Egyptian, Assyrian and Chaldean civilisations." Plutarch said that the Thebians could destroy with a glance not only infants but strong adults (Hart, 1949), and Montaigne likens its influence to a contagion (Greenacre, 1926). In Proverbs 22:6 it is said, "Eat not thou the bread of him who hath the evil eye." Arabs believed that if a stranger admired his horse, it would waste away. In the middle ages, epidemics such as the Black Death, smallpox and cholera were attributed to the evil eye (Hart, 1949). Belief in it was said at the turn of the century to exist in the highlands of Scotland, in Greece and Italy, and even now exists in isolated communities throughout Europe and Asia (Greenacre, 1926). Even today one of the most common expressions among Jews is *kein ayin hora* (no evil eye), which is uttered parenthetically whenever praise is given, in order that the evil eye should not cause harm to fall. Amulets such as swastikas, thorns, stars and even the eye itself were used to protect against such influences. Perhaps herein lies the explanation for the eye printed on the U.S.A. $1 bill, which, indeed, so often is the object of praise for its power and potency.

The relation between ocular symptoms and the couvade, by which it meant the imitation by a man of various aspects of a woman's sexual life, was brought to light a few year ago by Inman (1943). Frazer, in *The Golden Bough*, long ago described various types of couvade, for instance the one which aims ostensibly at a magical transference of the mother's labor pains to the person of the father, the father pretending to undergo what the mother experiences in reality. Likewise, there is the post-natal couvade when the father keeps to his bed and refrains from eating certain foods. Some compelling evidence has been gathered by Inman that albeit, in more subtle form, the couvade operates even in this sophisticated age. Most remarkable was his patient who developed a stye, ear abscess, corneal ulcer or some such trouble just at the time of his wife's labor. But this is not all; it had long been a standing joke in the family that a little scar on the tip of the husband's nose always bled for a few minutes during his wife's menstrual period. In this connection Inman (1943, 1946) has developed a most intriguing hypothesis that the sty practically always occurs in a person unusually concerned with childbirth in some way. Apropos of the Couvade, Abenheimer (1946) recently reported the dream of a patient, who, prior to his wife's pregnancy had been under treatment for great anxiety lest his wife become pregnant, which event he feared would put him in a constant state of panic. Three days following his wife's successful delivery the patient had a single dream in which his eye (baby) was displaced and lying on his cheek. He seemed to be conscious of a comparison with the yolk of an egg (baby). A doctor, in whom he had confidence, finally succeeded in replacing the eye (successful delivery). The author interpreted the dream as a symbolic vicarious pregnancy. Curiously, the German word for fried egg is Ochsenauge (ox-eye), and in English we speak of it as a "Bull's Eye." I will leave more to be said about this fascinating subject until later.

With this introduction as our point of embarkation let us now plan our course across the sea of symbol and symptom. We will pass many an island laden with choice symbolic harvest, and will cast anchor in not a few psychosomatic ports and hysteric harbors. Lastly, let us leave as our terminus those few havens where neurology and psychology share a quay.

I have already mentioned some of the symbolic uses to which the eye has been partner, not only in our daily speech and during the analytic session, but also in the customs of our ancestors and relatives. Many more such illustrations will crop up during the discussion of symptoms, but for the meanwhile let us stop to consider the eye as a genital symbol. The hollow pupil with its sphincteric iris covered over by the hair-bearing lip-like eyelids permits its easy translation into the female genitalia. As far back as 1913 Ferenczi (1913) reported such symbolism in several cases—for example a woman who had the marked phobia that her eye was going to be injured by sharp pointed objects, and who turned out in analysis to be suffering from great fear that she would be torn during coitus. Curiously, she continually inflicted minor wounds to her eye with knitting needles and similar objects. Hart (1949) relates that the god Indra, because of sexual transgression, has his whole body covered with vulvae which later turn into eyes. It would appear that many of our ancestors noted such a symbolic connection since *pupilla* in Latin, *nina* in Spanish, and *kori* in Greek mean both pupil (of the eye) and maiden. Even in English we speak of the eye of a needle, the hook and eye (or eyelet) of clothing, and refer to a dead-end street as a "blind alley."

The eye, as an emitter of magic looks, "daggers," tears, etc., has also been used as a male genital symbol. Hart (1949) has collected numerous cases from anthropological data. Ferenczi (1913) described five cases in which the eye was used as a male genital symbol, sometimes representing the penis sometimes the two testicles with the nose (=penis) in between. Reitler recorded the case of a psychotic patient who gouged out both his eyes and screamed that he had one more which was next in line. It is interesting that in medieval England a modification of Alfred's Laws prescribed emasculation and enucleation of the eyes as 'Punishment for the deflowerer of a virgin. With tongue in cheek, I should like to read to you two lines from Shelley's "Prometheus Unbound" (Act VI scene 4).

> "Think ye by gazing on each other's eyes
> To multiply your lovely selves?"

By way of such symbolism I will take leave of the principle theme for a moment to digress to the symbolism of spectacles, or even of glass itself. Inman (1940) has presented us with considerable clinical data which suggest that the breaking or losing of glasses is often associated with ideas of marriage, or at any rate, defloration. Such an event, as in the case of the 49-year-old girl who was presented with probably her last opportunity to lose her long cherished but now fading treasure, can often be decoded by applying the symbolic equation glass = hymen. There is a well-established Jewish wedding custom in which the bridegroom breaks with his foot a glass. Shakespeare on at least two occasions used "glass" with similar connotations: In "Pericles" (Act IV Scene 5) (Inman, 1940) Marina is sold to a brothel where her chastity proves such a barrier to the custom of the place, that the bawd cries out to the pander's servant,

> "Boult, take her away; use her at thy pleasure: Crack the glass of her virginity and make the rest malleable."

Again, in the "Passionate Pilgrim" (stanza XI)

> Beauty is but a vain and doubtful good,
> A shining gloss, that vadeth suddenly;
> A flower that dies when first it 'gins to bud;
> A brittle glass that's broken presently:
> A doubtful good, a gloss, a glass, a flower,
> Lost, vaded, broken, dead within an hour.

In addition to the particular symbolism to which Inman has alluded, the breaking of glasses may have other significance as has been suggested by various analysts (Hart, 1949; Jelliffe, 1926).

Scopophilia or voyeurism, the terms applied to the libidinous investment of the sensations of looking, might well be called the shibboleths of ocular parlance. So let us now polish our credentials with a few thoughts on this subject. Elements of scopophilia can probably be found in all individuals in our culture, but in some it is of such a degree as to have symptomatic repercussions. How does it arise? I think it not too unpardonable a simplification to draw a parallel between its origin and that of the better recognized drives such as the oral and anal. We could say, as Freud did, that the first organ through which the infant can discharge its generalized sexual energy is the mouth because the baby is so vitally concerned with food-getting. Later anal function becomes the prepotent focus of attention and the infant uses this organ for the expression of his libidinous urges. On the other hand, there has been a tendency to think of these stages as arbitrary events in the developmental sequence of the infant's interpersonal relations, so that in the oral phase, for example, his relation to mother, her love or rejection, approbation or displeasure, are all condensed into the function of feeding. If psychic trauma occurs in particular relation to one or other of these stages the infant may become fixated at, or later regress to, that "level" of infantile sexuality and thence develop sublimations and reaction-formations to this excessive drive. It may so happen in the child's development that the function of looking may be invested with libidinous feelings, or to use an analytic term, overcathected, be it from traumatic visual events, punished peeping experiences or "you must never watch little Mary taking a bath."

Very often sadistic impulses are tied up with scopophilia: the desire to see something in order to destroy it, or gain reassurance that the object is not yet destroyed. It is as if they are saying "I did not destroy it; I merely looked at it" (Fenichel, 1945).

Like other sexual components, scopophilia may be the object of repression and now inhibitions of looking come to the fore. Occasionally one encounters extreme cases—in shy, inhibited persons who dare not behold their environment. In less severe cases the patient may be unable to face certain classes of objects and turn away when these remind him of facts that once aroused castration anxiety, or anxiety over loss of love (Fenichel, 1945). In this connection it is remarkable to note the close relation between repressed scopophilia and unconscious castration anxiety. Recently I saw a patient with early schizophrenia in whom scopophilic trends were quite marked. Throughout his adolescence, whenever he met a girl he would experience an overpowering impulse to shut his eyes firmly, or even put his hands over them, using the excuse that a particle of dust got in his eye. His eyes would become itchy and he would rub them for some time. When I saw him he had a moderate blepharospasm and his eyes were always red from rubbing. I have already mentioned the eye as a genital symbol, and Ferenczi (1914) long ago described cases of eye-rubbing as a masturbation substitute. This patient also masturbated to great excess which again served to allay the underlying castration anxiety. Much guilt was connected with this practice and the patient felt that people could see in his eyes that he masturbated. The connection between scopophilia and castration fears is brought borne by the oft-quoted dream, or, perhaps fable, of another patient well known for his voyeuristic and pornographic interests. One night he was awakened suddenly by his wife who wanted to know why he was sitting up in bed and vigorously pulling up the covers from the end of the bed. He was able to summon up enough wits to tell her that he had been dreaming he was on a ship and was hastily and vigorously pulling up anchor. The dream, in actual fact was that he was looking out the window of his room when suddenly he noticed a beautiful girl seductively disrobing and displaying her wares from her window directly across the street. He became so excited by this aphrodisiac exhibition that his penis, displaying Pinocchio-like propensities soon emerged from his window-sill, down the wall, across the street and up the side of her building. Just as it was about to enter her window a tram-car came into sight whereupon he feverishly began "pulling up anchor."

The counterpart to scopophilia is an exhibitionism, the two usually appearing together. However, in the *perversion* of exhibitionism the individual derives assurance against underlying castration anxiety (Fenichel, 1945). For example, he may be saying (unconsciously) to his audience, "Reassure me that I have a penis by reacting to the sight of it."

At last we have arrived at a point where we can talk of symptoms and syndromes. A most astute experimental study was devised a few years ago by Wolf (1943) to demonstrate the dynamics of the specific loss of function in neurosis. He divided 44 rats into three groups. The members of the first group had their eyes sealed, and those of the second group their ears sealed just one day following the onset of function, thus allowing each animal only one day's normal function before depriving it of that modality of sensation. At a certain date the sealings were removed, after which each rat was isolated for two weeks. Then the rats of all groups were conditioned to associate a *light* signal with the presence of food. After the rats had been adequately trained, a competition period followed, in which a previously-blinded rat was made to compete with a previously-deafened animal for food. The same *light* stimulus was used. It was soon apparent that the previously-deafened rats were quite superior. Now, however, a similar experiment was run, in which the rats were trained and competitively tested, this time using an *auditory* stimulus (buzzer). The results were completely reversed so that now the previously blinded ones were the more successful. Results among the controls together with certain other observations led to the author's conclusions which merit quotation:

> Integrated capacity to cope with reality is maintained until a rat reaches a competitive impasse. At this point mature responses disintegrate. The animal retreats to an immature previously-conditioned response which formerly secured mastery over the environment. In the process of withdrawal it loses adult functions which were underdeveloped in the nursing period. An analogy can be drawn with human neurotic behaviour in which adults lose highly developed skills in retreating to outmoded but previously serviceable forms of adaptation and are left with inadequately evolved and incoordinate resources. The experiment illustrates the dynamics of the selective inhibition of particular function.

Interestingly, Fenichel (1945) from clinical observation alone, has observed that "frightening sights often result directly in subsequent inhibitions of looking, and frightening sounds in subsequent inhibitions of hearing."

Symptoms of the eye in which psychogenic factors play a role fall into two broad classes: conversion symptoms (usually hysterical) and organ neuroses. In the former the problem could be formulated as: "What is the patient's symbolic gain by having such a disability?" (e.g. Hysterical blindness, or in the gastro-intestinal tract, hysterical vomiting), whereas the situation in the latter could be paraphrased as: "What changes, usually somatic, have resulted from the organ's being used for libidinal purposes?" (e.g. myopia or stye; or in the GI tract, peptic ulcer).

I am not implying that all myopia or styes are psychogenic, nor that any case is solely psychogenic, just as you surely have inferred that not all vomiting is hysterical, nor all peptic ulcers organ neuroses. Nor is it to be understood that the distinction between organ neurosis and conversion symptom is always clear cut. My aim is to deal first with some conditions which seem to fit most comfortably in the category of organ neurosis, and then to pass on to the hysterical disorders. This will bring us ultimately to the threshold of neurology where some recent developments will, I am sure, arouse your interest.

Stye (Hordeolum)

The common stye at first sight appears to be a classical example of organic disease with the well-known Staphylococcus aureus as the etiologic agent. But why is it that we so often forget the factor of tissue resistance, albeit somewhat less tangible? And what are the factors that control it? Certainly all are not known, but equally certain it is that psychological influences can profoundly alter tissue resistance. We need only recall the common knowledge that ordinary skin warts (a virus disease) can be "wished away" by hypnotic, or other, suggestion. In fact, it is often possible to abort a stye in its earlier stages by this means. Inman (1943, 1946) has gathered considerable evidence suggesting a frequent relationship between a stye and thoughts, either conscious or unconscious, concerning childbirth. One of his many cases may whet your interest in this subject and I shall quote it in full:

> A young colleague, newly introduced to my theory, expressed incredulity; it was altogether too fantastic. He was worth convincing and

accordingly I offered to bet on the next case that presented itself. He himself was to be the judge of the value of the evidence obtained, and the odds were to be liberal. I offered eight to one. As luck would have it, within a few minutes a young man of 28 came into the room showing an unusually large painful-looking stye which, he said, had begun to develop a few days before, on May 6. In reply to my stock question he said, 'I have not been interested in birth in any way; I am not married.' A reminder that even bachelors could be interested in babies met with no greater success; the subject had not concerned him in the slightest degree. Not daunted I asked, 'Do you know anyone who has had a baby in the last few months?'

'Well yes!' he answered. 'An old sweetheart of mine had one last March, but she lives a hundred miles away and I have not seen her for months.'

'Then how did you know?'

'My sister wrote in April and told me.'

'I suppose you sent your congratulations?'

'Yes, and the girl wrote to thank me.'

'When did the letter come?'

He looked startled, and blushingly said, 'That is strange! It came just three days before the stye.'

I made a sign to my colleague to move away—third persons are not conducive to intimate confidences— and then said to the patient, 'You see that my theory works. Now help me further. How is it that you, a strong healthy young man, cannot hear from your old sweetheart without getting an abscess in your eyelid? When did you last see her?'

He replied, 'Last September.'

'Was she married then?'

'No, I expected her to marry me.'

'But from September to March is much less than nine months; did you know she was pregnant?'

'No.'

'How far did your love-making go?'

'As far as it could.'

'Then isn't that baby yours?'

His silence was more eloquent than words could have been.

Not content to have already so boldly jolted his fellow ophthalmologists, Inman (1946) titles his next paper "Styes, Barley and Wedding Rings." His case for the relation of styes to childbirth is fortified by the enormous folklore associated with this little infection. In many parts of England and western Europe, and even as far off as Hungary and Russia, the rubbing of a *golden wedding ring* on the stye is still one of the commonest remedies, at least among the less sophisticated. This, at first blush, appears quite ridiculous, but in the language of symbols what could be better treatment for an unconscious desire to have a baby than a wedding ring? In the same symbolic light the apparently irrational rituals recorded by Rolleston (1942) for the cure of styes begin to make sense; for example, "it is to be rubbed with a *tom*-cat's tail;" "A *house of feathers* is made and *set on fire*."

The rubbing on of barley has often been used as a cure of stye. It is almost unbelievable that so many languages have virtually the same word for stye as for barley: in Greek it is *krithe*; in German, *Gerstenkorn*; in Polish, *jencmien*; in Hebrew, *Sh'oira*. In Latin, *hordeum*—barley, and *hordeolum*—stye; French uses a derivative *orge*—barley; and *orgelet*—stye. Is it that so many peoples have likened the yellow buttoned stye surrounded with eye-lashes to the golden barley-kernel resting in its hairy nest? Curiously, one of the earliest tests for pregnancy, as recorded on an ancient Egyptian papyrus, was to be carried out in the following manner: "The women is to take two sacks, one containing barley, the other wheat, and to soak each in her urine for one day. If the cereals germinate then she is pregnant; but if not, she has not conceived. If only the wheat sprouts, a boy will be born; if, on the other hand, only the barley buds, it will be a girl" (Ploss, 1897).

Myopia

Pseudomyopia implies spasm of the ciliary muscle as the cause of the ametropia, whereas true myopia is usually the consequence of an anatomically overlengthened eyeball. Both of these disturbances have been under barrage from the psychosomatists if not, in fact, from the psyche! It has been repeatedly stressed that pseudo-myopia is not rare, especially among adolescents and young adults (Huebsch, 1931; F. Mohr, as cited in Dunbar, 1946; Poos, 1948; Walker, 1946). The ciliary muscle of adolescents has unusually great tone so that it is often not completely paralysed by the routine use of homatropine in refraction studies. The ciliary spasm may be either continuous or of the paroxysmal type. In the latter event it may last for from minutes to hours and is usually brought on by an emotionally charged situation (Harrington, 1947). If a person observes that variations in the intensity of his myopia occurs, it is practically certain that some degree of pseudomyopia exists. Some years ago, Huebsch (1931) reported that in such cases, vision is often perfect or improved following sexual performances which result in orgasm.

Regarding the pathogenesis of true myopia no one is pretending to deny the soma its rightful place but at the same time how shallow of us it would be to bury our heads in the sands of the soma in order to escape the storms of the psyche. Fenichel (1945) suggests that the disorder results from the eye being overcathected and, as it were, indulging in more than its normal share of libidinous activity. He disagrees with Jelliffe (1926) who regards the incapacity of the eye to see at a distance as a conversion symptom. A preliminary Rorschach study at the University of Montreal has attempted to draw attention to scopophilia in myopes (Brunet, 1947).

In considering the pathogenesis of myopia, is it not a distinct possibility that prolonged nervous stimulation of the ciliary muscle, as in pseudomyopia could result in a gradual elongation of the eyeball? Remember that the insertion of the ciliary muscle is largely into sclera and choroid. Consider also that even bony tissue can elongate when subjected to prolonged pull. The bony processes and tubercles (e.g. mastoid process, tibial tubercle) that develop as a result of muscle traction furnish good object lessons. Another possibility, as Jelliffe (1926) has suggested, is that persistent and long continued tension of the extrinsic muscles of the eye could, by their excessive traction, account for this anatomical elongation. Just as in the cases of other organ neuroses (e.g. peptic ulcer) functional changes usually long foreshadow the anatomical lesion. Hypermotility long anticipates ulceration. It would be an interesting experiment to see if certain hypothalamic lesions would result in pseudo-and/or true myopia, just as such lesions have been shown to cause peptic ulcer. To my knowledge no one has ever studied the eyes of such animals as have already been subjected to these operations.

Glaucoma

That attacks of acute primary glaucoma can be precipitated by emotional shock has long been appreciated (Dunbar, 1946). This does not intimate, necessarily, that psychological factors contribute to the causation of the condition. In fact, little has been said in the literature in this connection.

More and more evidence is being accumulated to show the relationship between intra-ocular vascular circulation, secretion of intra-ocular fluid, level of intra-ocular pressure and their control by the autonomic nervous system (Harrington, 1947). The susceptibility of the autonomic nervous system to psychic influences is well known. As an illustration, one might mention the immediate and marked rise in intra-ocular pressure that occurs after piercing cries, simulated falls or such psychic trauma (Dunbar, 1946).

Vasomotor Disturbances of the Eye

It is comparatively recently that 'physicians have begun to recognize the importance of the psyche in the etiology of such vasomotor disturbances as amaurosis fugax, central angiospastic retinopathy, Raynaud's Disease and migraine. In the latter two conditions, the eye may also be involved, as for instance in migraine, where retinal vascular spasm can often be detected during the aura. However, it is more pertinent to concentrate attention to the former. Amaurosis fugax is a condition in which dimming of vision of a few seconds' or minutes' duration occurs as a result of a spasm of the arterioles of the central (macular) area of the retina. Harrington (1947) asserts that "one of the commonest and disturbing symptoms confronting the ophthalmologist is periodic, transient 'black-outs,' 'dim-outs,' or fleeting amaurosis. In most cases it is either ignored or minimized. During the war the condition was encountered so often that the very term 'black-out' became synonymous with the desire for change of duty." Central angiospastic retinopathy is considered be a closely related disorder in which the spasm is more persistent and severe (Harrington, 1947). The first sequel to the vascular occlusion is a local edema which may become so severe as to cause local detachment of the retina. Frequently, a central scotoma remains permanently. Although von Graefe apparently recognized the condition in 1866 (Zeligs, 1947), its neurovascular nature was not appreciated until only thirteen years ago (E. Hornicker, as cited by Zeligs, 1947). Both Harrington (1947) and Zeligs (1947) have emphasized the generalized vasomotor instability of the patients affected by either of these conditions. An acute anxiety state is often associated.

Idiopathic Exudative Choroiditis or Chorioretinitis

This disease is a not uncommon affection of the choroid in which a usually circumscribed area becomes inflamed, or at least edematous, the exudation gradually subsiding, but leaving in its wake a fibrous scar to replace the choroid and subjacent retina. The onset is rapid and recurrences tend to occur, leaving a permanent scotoma at each new site. Although almost every conceivable cause has been invoked at one time or another, the current consensus (Nicholls, personal communication) is that the pathogenesis involves a neurovascular mechanism. But, as with the vasomotor disturbances of the retina, the crucial question is: "What precipitates the neurovasculor disturbances?" Probably there are many factors, among them the psyche, although to my awareness no one has officially suggested that a psychic element exists even in this remote malady! If the situation were more opportune, I should like to tell you about the role of the psyche in the one case with which I have had to deal: myself! Suffice it for now to say that I can testify that its course has followed a fascinating and consistent pattern in relation to the events of my internal and external milieu. I would guess that only now does the title make sense to those of you who, perhaps correctly, suspected there was a misspelling in the title "Psyche and Eye!"

Oculogyric Crises

Jelliffe (1929) commented on the psychologic components in postencephalitic oculogyric crises and noted that obsessive thoughts frequently occurred concurrently. Dr. Colin Russel of Montreal, in discussing his paper, recalled a patient of his who always came to the clinic with a little peaked cap on. "One day I asked him why he did this. 'Well,' he said, 'it keeps my eyes down.' And sure enough as soon as one took his cap off, his eyes turned up to the ceiling. When he put it on again they came down. I have two or three cases of this nature."

Asthenopia and "Eye-Strain"

Although cases of asthenopia and "eye-strain" of an hysterical nature doubtless occur, these symptoms, known so well to physician and laiety alike, often form part of the picture of other neuroses, anxiety states for instance. The term asthenopia, although it has been used to cover a multitude of sins in diagnosis (Poos, 1948) is generally reserved for those cases in whom, in addition to the local eye discomfort of "eye-strain," there are feelings of fatigue and reflex manifestations (e.g. tension headaches) remote from the eyes. The eye discomfort may persist for some time after close work is discontinued. In some patients the symptoms are so severe that they are unable to do close work for more than one or two minutes (Hart, 1949). The important role of emotional factors in these conditions has now been conceded by even the most conservative of medical men, although more often than not this concession appears to be little more than impotent lip-service. We must not forget that these patients are ill; they may be just as profoundly disabled as a person with a clear-cut anatomical lesion. Can we call it effective treatment to dismiss them with "There's nothing wrong with your eyes, it's all in your nerves," or else to modify slightly the formula of their glasses?

Hysteria

Ocular symptoms as hysterical manifestations have been troubling the medical sages since time began. At first the designation "hysterical" was solely applied per exclusionem; thankfully, more and more prominence is now being given to the need for establishing a positive diagnosis.

Probably the most dramatic of all eye symptoms is hysterical amaurosis. In wartime this often follows upon the witnessing of some horrible spectacle. In time of peace the dreadful sight is more often of a symbolic nature, as when a priest went blind suddenly while performing the marriage ceremony of a girl who had once been his maid (Hart, 1949). The biblical cases of blindness cured by miracles were almost beyond doubt examples of hysterical amaurosis (Burch, 1925). The folklore is replete with illustrations of blinding as punishment for lustful looking. "In the beautiful saga of Lady Godiva, all the inhabitants of the little town retire behind their shuttered windows in order to make less painful to the lady her ordeal of riding naked through the streets in broad daylight. The one man who peeps through the shutters at her nude beauty is punished by becoming blind" (Freud, 1925). In Genesis, XIX:11, you may remember how the wicked people of Sodom were struck blind because of their sins (Hart, 1949). Freud (1925) observed that in many cases of psychogenic visual disturbance in which there is a repression of scopophilia, it is "as if an accusing voice had uplifted itself within the person concerned saying, 'because you have chosen to use your organ of sight for evil indulgence of the senses, it serves you quite right if you can see nothing at all now.'" A case with interesting dream material was described by Ames (1913) in which the patient awoke one morning quite blind, and so remained for about four weeks until in psychotherapy he suddenly realized his unconscious desire not to see his wife anymore. Patients with hysterical amaurosis often exhibit "la belle indifférence" to their symptoms in contrast to the patient who is afflicted with organic blindness. Some also have an associated blepharospasm. The pupils contract to light and accommodation. The blindness can be either monocular or affect both eyes. "Tubular" vision resulting from a concentric narrowing of the visual fields has long been recognized as an hysterical conversion symptom. Even hysterical hernianopsia has been reported and apparently cured by suggestion (Cohn, 1948). I shall presently have more to say about these odd phenomena in relation to some recent work in neurology.

Blepharospasm in some cases has the features of a conversion symptom, and in such is usually of the clonic variety—really a tic of the eyelids. It often symbolizes the desire to shut out a forbidden spectacle. Hart (1949) recounts "... the case of a boy of ten with rapid closing of the eyelids, who had an obsessive fear lest his eye be put out after being hit in the eye by his mother while being punished for peeping at his parents in intercourse. Another boy … had a blinking tic after seeing the genitals of his mother and sister … A religious woman could permit herself to masturbate only to prevent her blepharospasm, and not for pleasure."

A few words about squint. Every parent and doctor who has had to do with strabismic children knows full well how readily it is aggravated by emotional stress, much as is stammering. In fact, Inman (1921) has pointed out the relation between squint, stammering and left-handedness, both in the patients themselves, and in their families. His figures are, indeed, compelling. Mohr (as cited in Dunbar, 1946), after accenting the role of the psyche in squint, discusses the case of a girl who for months following a successful operation for strabismus, complained of disturbing double images. These disappeared the moment their psychic origin had been made clear to her.

A good many other hysterical ocular symptoms have been described, among them micropsia (Bartemeier, 1941), monocular diplopia and polyopia (Dunbar, 1946), photophobia (Knapp & Schwarzmann, 1946), and epiphora (Dunbar, 1946). It is, of course, not to be supposed that these are always of psychogenic origin. On the contrary they often occur as the symptoms of well recognized somatic pathology, so that it becomes a very serious task to establish the exact nature of the derangement in each individual case.

As I approach my terminus this evening, I should like to pose an odd question and then at least attempt to soliloquize on why it is really not so odd: Have visual defects, hysteria and the diencephalon anything in common? In talking about tubular I noted that even after head injuries such visual charges have often been taken to represent hysterical phenomena. It is only fair to draw your attention to a growing body of evidence which questions, or perhaps, in a sense, supplements this view.

Bender and Teuber (1946) have been investigating the nature of these ring scotomata and tubular field defects occurring after head injury, and have established that the apparently weird nature of the field defects are not bizarre after all, but, in fact, vary in a constant and predictable fashion with variations in the technique of visual assessment. For example, in patients with a ring scotoma this can only be elicited when the perimeter target is moved *inwards*, and at that only when it is done slowly. When the movement is towards the periphery, the fields appear tubular. Tubular fields characteristically appear smaller when the target proceeds in the direction of the periphery than the reverse, and this phenomenon can be observed to a slight degree even in normal subjects. The authors have postulated that two factors are operative: (i) that the central portion of the retina is more sensitive to light than the peripheral, and (ii) that a phenomenon known as extinction[2] is occurring. At the beginning of the perimetric test the patient is able to see in the peripheral field. As the target is *slowly* moved inwards, extinction in adjacent areas becomes so pronounced that a "blind zone" is reached. As the target continues to approach the macula, the factor of increasing retinal sensitivity becomes prepotent and the patient can see again. In the reverse direction the two factors (extinction and decreasing retinal sensitivity) are obviously additive, so that tubular fields occur. When the object is moved rapidly, extinction is minimal so that field defects are less conspicuous. For this reason patients often do not notice such visual disturbances until they have become quite marked. Again, the authors point out that these phenomena can be observed to some degree even with normal subjects, and suggest that the disturbances are of a quantitative nature. The principle factor making for difference is the ease with which extinction occurs in the abnormal patients. It is likely that diffuse damage anywhere in the optic system would result in more conspicuous extinction phenomena, much as extinction of a Babinski reflex can be elicited in the presence of diffuse sensory damage (Cohn, 1948).

Knapp and Schwarzmann (1946) in addition to emphasizing the frequency of constricted visual fields following head injury, also suggest the possibility of "spontaneous" field constriction as a result of a diencephalic disorder. They present a patient as a case in point. That the diencephalon may well play a role in vision has been hypothesized by several investigators, among them W. R. Hess. Hess (as cited by Knapp and Schwarzmann, 1946) showed in cats that thermocoagulation of a certain area of the diencephalon produced an apparent contralateral homonymous hemianopsia. Bilateral thermocoagulation resulted in apparent blindness. The anatomical studies of Frey (1947) seem to indicate that there is a direct nervous connection between the retina and some small hypothalamic nuclei. The work, then, of the European school is consistent with that of Bender and Teuber, although more stress is placed on the importance of the diencephalon. Further, they hypothesize that not only head injury, poisons, etc., as have hitherto been proposed, but perhaps "spontaneous" diencephalic disturbances might result in these visual changes.

In considering all this data we are faced with two possibilities of interpretation: First that such field defects are due to neural damage and are quite different from those of hysteria. But so far they have only been shown to have a reproducible pattern; this does not disprove hysteria, especially since many such patients have been called hysterics in the past and even at present. The second possibility is that perhaps our phenotypic category "hysteria" is at this point merging over an invisible border with changes of a more neurologic character. What I am getting at, is that neural dysfunction may be due to many factors, among them the psychopathologic, which I have already stressed throughout most of this paper. On the other hand we cannot afford to forget how closely the purely psychogenic mental illnesses can be mimicked by certain organic disorders such as bromide intoxication, atypical myxedema (Asher, 1949) and even brain tumors.

Beyond the realm of such ocular disturbances as we have been discussing it is even barely possible that there is a more pervasive link between hysteria and the diencephalon. One such hint was recently given by Gasteaut (1949) in a lecture at the M.N.I. In his work on electroencephalographic photic driving he has observed abnormal responses in three groups of patients: epileptics, patients with a tumor near the diencephalon, and hysterics. Since it is now conceded that idiopathic epilepsy is a diencephalic disorder, it seems plausible that abnormal neural function in this area may from the basis for hysteria. This view is still entirely in harmony with the psychopathologic approach, and only serves to amplify it. Just as the epileptic equivalents of hysteria have an underlying symbolic meaning for the patient, so too can the true epileptic manifest unconscious drives during ictal automatic states. Indeed, Fenichel (1945) says "There is a gradual transition between genuine epilepsy and conversion hysterias, in which epileptiform seizures express a definite idea and show all the characteristics of hysterical motor symptoms (hystero-epilepsy)."

Well now, by way of pulling upon the reins, what is the meaning of all this? In view of the tenuous nature of much of the foregoing, I prefer, rather than to summarize, to merely voice a few summary questions. Are these visual phenomena hysterical or do they represent a form of neural dysfunction? Or, in fact, do such symptoms represent a phenotypic continuum with various genotypes? Further, is it possible that "hysteria" represents the final common pathway for various types of diencephalic neural dysfunction, among them the psychogenic?

I think now that we have reached our "dénouement." It has, indeed, been a strange brew that psyche and "eye" have concocted. You have sipped of symbol and symptom, and of sin and syndrome, and have perhaps been stung by the stronger spirits of some strange scotomas. Let me only hope that this desultory mixture of psyche and eye will not suffer the proverbial fate of "ye olde mixed tincture."

Notes

1. Presented before the Alpha Omega Alpha Society, January 17, 1950. Originally published in the *McGill Journal of Medicine*, *19*(2), 335–346.
2. The term "extinction" has been applied to such phenomena as the following: In visual agnosia disappearance of an image can be precipitated by intercurrent stimulation, so that a target exhibited in one region of the field becomes invisible (i.e. is "extinguished") on simultaneous stimulation of other parts. Similarly in patients with sensory defects in addition to hemiplegia, one may be able to "extinguish" the Babinski response (Cohn, 1948) by stimulating the opposite field—e.g., eliciting a plantar reflex on the other side.

References

Abenheimer, K. M. (1946). A note on the couvade in modern England and Scotland. *British Journal of Medical Psychology*, *20*(4), 367–377.

Ames, T. H. (1913). Blindness as a wish. *Psychoanalytic Review*, *1*, 55–62.

Asher, R. (1949) Myxedematous madness. *British Medical Journal*, *2*, 555–562.

Bartemeier, L. H. (1941). Micropsia. *Psychoanalytic Quarterly*, *10*, 573–582.

Bender, M. B. and Teuber, H. L. (1946). Ring scotomata and tubular fields. *Archives of Neurology and Psychiatry*, *56*(3), 300–326.

Brunet, G. (1947). *Recherche sur la myopie au moyen d' entrevues et du Rorschach* (Doctoral thesis, University of Montreal. Montreal, Canada).

Burch, F. E. (1925). Hysteric amblyopia and amarosis. *American Journal of Ophthalmology*, *8*(9), 699–712.

Cohn, R. (1948). Extinction of Babinsky sign. *Journal of Neurophysiology*, *11*, 193–197.

Dunbar, F. (1946). *Emotions and bodily changes* (2nd ed.). New York, NY: Columbia University Press.

Emerson, R. (1886). Conduct of life. In *Complete Works* (Vol. 6). London, UK: G. Routledge & Sons.

Fenichel, O. (1945). *The psychoanalytic theory of neurosis*. New York, NY: Norton.

Ferenczi, S. (1913). Zur augensymbolik [On eye symbolism]. *Internationale Zeitschrift für Arztliche Psychoanalyse*, *1*, 161.

Ferenczi, S. (1914). Reiben des auges als onanieersatz. *Internationale Zeitschrift für Arztliche Psychoanalyse*, *2*, 379.

Frazer, J. G., (1922) The golden bough. New York, NY: Macmillan Co.

Freud, S. (1925). Psychogenic visual disturbances. In *Collected Papers* (Vol. 2). London, UK: Hogarth Press.

Frey, E. (1947). Degenerationsstudien über das optische gebiet im hypothalamus des meerschweines. *Acta Anatomica*, *4*, 123–136.

Gesteaut, H. (1949). *Lecture on "photic driving."* Montreal Neurological Institute.

Greenacre, P. (1926). The eye motif in delusion and fantasy. *American Journal of Psychiatry*, *5*, 553–579.

Harrington, D. O. (1947). Ocular manifestations of psychosomatic disorder. *Journal of the American Medical Association*, *133*(10), 669– 675.

Hart, H.M. (1949). Eye in symbol and symptom. *Psychoanalytic Review*, *36*(1), 1–21.

Huebsch, D. A. (1931). Psychoanalysis and eye disturbances. *Psychoanalytic Review*, *18*, 166–180.

Inman, W. S. (1921). Emotion and eye symptoms. *British Journal of Medical Psychology*, *2*(1), 47–67.

Inman, W. S. (1940). Symbolic significance of glass and its relation to diseases of the eye. *British Journal of Medical Psychology*, *18*(2), 122–140.

Inman, W. S. (1943). The couvade in modern England. *British Journal of Medical Psychology*, *19*(1), 37–55.

Inman, W. S. (1946). Styes, barley and wedding rings. *British Journal of Medical Psychology*, *20*(4), 331–338.

Jelliffe, S. E. (1926). Psychoanalysis and organic disorders: myopia as a paradigm. *International Journal of Psychoanalysis*, *7*, 445–456.

Jelliffe, S. E. (1929). Psychologic components in post-encephalitic oculogyric crises. *Archives of Neurology & Psychiatry*, *21*, 491–532.

Knapp, P. and Schwarzmann, A. (1946). Beitrag zur frage diencephal bedingter gesichtsfeldeinschränkung. *Ophthalmologica*, *111*, 270–278.

Machover, K. (1949). *Personality projection in the drawing of the human figure.* Springfield, IL: Thomas.

Ploss, H. (1897). *Das weib in der natur- und völkerkunde* (Vol. 1, 5th ed.). Leipzig: T. Grieben.

Poos, E. E. (1948). Psychosomatic manifestations in ophthalmology. *Journal of Aviation Medicine*, *19*, 442–446.

Prideaux, E (1921). Psychogalvanic reflex in cases of mental disorder. *British Journal of Medical Psychology*, *2*, 239.

Rolleston, J. D. (1942). Ophthalmic folk-lore. *British Journal of Ophthalmology*, *26*, 481–502.

Walker, J. P. S. (1946). Myopia and pseudo-myopia. *British Journal of Opthalmology*, *30*, 735–742.

Weiss, E. and English, O. S. (1943). *Psychosomatic medicine*. Philadelphia, PA: Saunders.

Wolf, A. (1943). The dynamics of the selective inhibition of specific functions in neurosis. *Psychosomatic Medicine*, *5*(1), 27.

Zeligs, M. A. (1947). Central angiospastic retinopathy; A psychosomatic study of its occurence in military personnel. *Psychosomatic Medicine*, *9*(2), 110–117.

Chapter 7

Countertransference

Its reflection in the process of peer-group supervision

Chaim F. Shatan,[1] *Benjamin Brody,*[2] *and Emmanuel Ghent*[3]

Today, expert supervision is a cornerstone of training in both psychoanalysis and group psychotherapy, but before formal training programs arose, leaderless coffee-house supervision was a prime agency of training in these fields.[4] We can picture a situation at that time similar to the formation of our group: a few congenial colleagues in about the same stage of training and ignorance met together to discuss perplexing and anxiety-creating clinical problems. Perhaps—to complete the parallel—these discussions eventually transcended matters of technique and diagnosis and moved on to more personal material.

Few would deny that there are limitations upon any therapist's awareness of himself. He cannot be consistently free of anxiety or defensiveness when exposed to intense anxiety from patients. Furthermore, the difficulty of seeing himself in action or of hearing himself speak can be a serious hindrance in his work with patients. Even if the words are right, he may often invalidate what he says: "The words may be right, but the tune sour, and he will not even know it."[5] It is our contention that peer-group supervision is a valuable way of helping the therapist see himself, even within the present-day training framework.

This paper presents a three-year experiment that proved extremely useful in complementing the authors' formal training. We are not alone in our rediscovery of coffee-house supervision as experiments at Boston State Hospital, Chestnut Lodge, and elsewhere have shown. However, many such groups disintegrate rather quickly.[6] Perhaps our experience will help elucidate some of the factors making for the success of a leaderless peer group.

The origin of the group was quite casual. Three analysts in training, all close friends, decided to meet weekly to discuss problems concerning patients and to utilize each other's experience and skills, as though it were a case seminar, but without an instructor. In retrospect, however, the composition of the group made for an interaction and learning experience different from a case seminar. Instead of a collection of relatively chance acquaintances without much knowledge or interest in each other, we were a group with deep emotional ties and commitments. We knew each other intimately, both socially and professionally. This provided a genuine foundation of mutual trust for a learning situation of intimacy and confidence.

Over a three-year period we met once a week for two to four hours. Each week one of us discussed his work with a specific patient or presented broader issues encountered with a variety of patients. Often, this procedure was supplemented by tape recordings of actual sessions between patient and therapist which allowed the other group members to compare their own impressions with the therapist's exposition. Periodic follow-up presentations provided a fresh focus on old problems. We recorded most of our group sessions and will cite some significant examples later. Listening to these tapes proved of inestimable value in defining intragroup phenomena.

Our earliest sessions touched on most of our later problems. From the very first, we were struck by the massive importance of countertransference in those aspects of therapeutic technique which are not "learned" in the usual sense but which spring from the strengths and limitations of the therapist's personality. Our close acquaintance with the nuances of the therapist's personality differentiated this from other countertransference study groups. For example, one of us was astonished to discover that his patients were no more difficult than the patients of his colleagues, and he was casually told that this seemed in line with his usual pattern of feeling that his reality problems were the most difficult, a comforting illusion in both life and therapy. Similarly, another participant, enmeshed in a struggle of wills with a patient, learned the usefulness of an off-hand manner instead of his usual battering-ram technique, a technique which the other therapists had experienced personally with this therapist. These brief examples illustrate the spontaneity and directness with which the participant's problems in the therapeutic situation were related to his life problems.

Seldom can a supervisor achieve a comparable bond of mutuality with a candidate. The supervisor rarely knows enough about the student, nor will the student usually confide in him and interact to provide sufficient data. The fact that the supervisor is an evaluating instructor and "control analyst" must result in some lack of candor and some suppression of the student's individual style and spontaneity. The student may engage in various self-defeating maneuvers which depend on his pattern of interaction with authorities: he may conceive that putting his best foot forward will please the supervisor, or he may focus exclusively on the patient's conflicts as a defense—a development especially susceptible to peer-group analysis. When a student is working with more than one supervisor, he may move nimbly from the technique of one teacher to another, or vacillate uncertainly between them. Conflicting loyalties—and even supervisors' rivalries—further complicate the tendency to imitate supervisors' styles or to become a junior edition of one's personal analyst. Our orientation to the whole issue of style focused on removing impediments to the development of one's own style. In addition, when two group members partook of a common blind spot, the third might at times recognize it. Such shared blind spots may be overlooked in ordinary supervision because of the absence of a third person. Thus, though a group of peers has its difficulties and dangers, the stage is set, at least theoretically, for genuine consensual validation.

Our work lay somewhere between supervision in the usual sense and group analysis. We pointedly refrained from working with the participant's personality in all of its ramifications: our knowledge of each other was utilized primarily to elucidate problems with patients and to facilitate group functioning. Broadly speaking, our work embodied the three features of analysis as set forth by Freud: we investigated our unconscious motivations as therapists, we endeavored to reduce our defensive operations, and we explored our transferences to each other in an intimate collaborative atmosphere. Our chief practice was to confront each member with a cross-section of the other's views of his interaction as therapist, as group member, and in his nonprofessional life. However, our goal went further than the discovery and consensual validation of these views: we also found it fruitful to relate them to each participant's personal development. This, in particular, was facilitated by the long-standing friendship between the members. In listening to the recordings, we were struck by our frequent tenderness with each other. We consider such tenderness essential to the maintenance of group cohesion during periods of anxiety. It permits each participant to hear, and use, comments from the others which, on paper, seem extremely blunt.

Did not any of the group's advantages also presage potential drawbacks? In general, we feel that such work is limited by the participants' personalities and their modes of interaction. One trap is the danger of going the way of splinter groups. Both lack of perspective and shared blind spots due to collective inexperience are apt to limit the group's horizons. Disregard of this pitfall may foster a smug and insular attitude.

The elimination of the supervisor from the peer group carries with it another hazard in addition to the development of sectarian self-sufficiency. We refer to the substitution of the irrational authority of one of the group for the teacher's authority. If the group is so dominated by a strong autocratic member that another participant becomes passive, guarded, and noncommittal or conforms submissively, the group's real purpose is effectively sabotaged though all may seem serene on the surface. Without a formally designated authority, it is easy to be oblivious of this process. However, if uncovered, it may be turned to therapeutic advantage. In fact, in most of the exchanges in our group of three, some one member tended to stand outside of the situation as a relatively objective observer. Once group anxiety abated sufficiently for him to be heard, he was then in a position to indicate where disjunctive interaction had begun. In short, as in any analytic group, compliance and subservience are not necessary conditions but problems for analysis.

Before closing the subject of disadvantages, we are tempted to speculate about our relative freedom from the competitiveness often encountered between candidate and supervisor. Did the equilibrium of the group stem from the opportunity each member had to put a finger on the others' problems? Did this take the sting out of being on the receiving end oneself? Or did the apparent equality come from the subtle acting out of revenge and was rivalry, with its associated anxiety and hostility, so concealed?

An example will illustrate the disadvantages. Our first months of work were remarkably open, fruitful, and full of good feeling, like the initial "honeymoon period" of analysis. After a year, however, group functioning began to deteriorate. This was marked by lateness, postponement of meetings, reluctance to tape or present, flashes of irritation or accusation, and periods of detachment, boredom, and listlessness. At first, this change was met by denial, inattention, or abortive and half-hearted discussion.

Somewhat to our surprise, it finally emerged that our impasse originated largely outside the group, in changing personal relationships and extragroup contacts. Dr. Ames seemed engaged in a significant personality reorganization related probably to movement in his own analysis. He no longer looked mainly to the members of the group for friendship, support, and analysis; periods of assertiveness, willfulness, and even grandiosity replaced his old deference and self-depreciation. This sea change awakened chronic rivalry and bickering with Dr. Brennan, who countered with attention-claiming and obscurantist dust storms of trivial "facts." Initially, Dr. Calder was able to remain relatively dispassionate and serve as a mediator but as the situation mushroomed he became increasingly puzzled and eventually embittered. To him, the group had been not only a professional medium but an emotional fraternity as well, a contrast to his once isolated life. When we began to hurl accusations of paranoid behavior at each other, we knew that it was urgent to deal frankly with our difficulties if the group was to survive.

We became aware that during this period of group resistance and defensive maneuvering we had reacted in characteristic ways: Ames acted aloof, superior, guarded, and was reluctant to participate; Brennan heckled and strayed into long-winded digressions; and Calder oscillated between fearfulness over revelation of his problems and a truculent "this-is-the-way-I-am-and-damn-you-if-you-don't-like-it" attitude. By this time, we were sufficiently familiar with each other's work to relate these developments to relatively enduring patterns in each therapist's therapeutic technique: with his patients, Ames moved uneasily from seductiveness to distance and coldness or to other power operations; Brennan seemed pompous, somewhat academic, and fulsome; and Calder pressured hard for quick, dramatic improvement while comparatively threatened by the long, hard pull ending in less than hurrahs. In short, as in every analysis, our transferences to each other could be utilized toward more constructive emotional understanding, something that Freud noticed many years ago but that we painfully rediscovered.

One way to resolve intragroup friction was to play back the tape of the meeting in question. The affect-laden voices in the recording quickly recreated the original, emotionally charged situation, yet at sufficient distance to permit effective clarification. Group tapes also revealed otherwise unnoticed blind spots. In addition, we often compared a recorded therapeutic session with a recording of the group session in which the therapy tape had been presented. It frequently emerged that the therapist related to his colleagues in a manner strikingly similar to that in which the patient had related to him.

This is in line with Searles' research on the influence of the patient-therapist relationship on the intragroup functioning of a Chestnut Lodge research seminar.[7] He observed that the presenter's demeanor in the group often reflected unconsciously a problem area in his work with his patients which he could not effectively put into words. This was uncovered by noticing a close parallel between specific forms of group disorganization and the therapeutic relationship being reported at the time. Searles designated this contagion of emotion the "reflection process." One of us described it pungently: "The patient steps on the therapist's toe, the therapist steps on the supervisor's toe, and the supervisor says 'Ouch!'" As will be shown, this hypothesis helped us clarify some of our more obscure conflicts.

Our discussions encompassed a wide range of material, some traditional, some fairly new. We focused on the torpid, passive patient, a type of patient we all shared. We felt that the therapist's boredom and lack of enthusiasm were pivotal in perpetuating feelings of helplessness and inertia; periodic discussion with the group proved useful as a spark plug. Problems with supervisors were discussed in some detail, with divergent techniques and therapeutic philosophies being compared. We presented our view of ourselves as therapists and subjected this to the criticism and amendments of the others: In this way, we explored the problem of the pompous therapist, the seductive therapist, the cross-examining therapist, and the therapist in search of quick success. At times, each member deliberately enacted, in a role-taking situation, his conception of the others' functioning. Physical contact with patients was discussed, and we began to explore sexual feelings toward patients. We felt more at ease discussing this relatively unverbalized material with each other than with supervisors or colleagues.

In our experience, an accurate confrontation was often met with chagrin, outright denial, or "Yes, but. …" Such defensiveness was not necessarily a character problem of the presenter. Rather, it often indicated that the confrontation had had an impact. Once the analysis had taken root, we left its further assimilation to the presenter. We avoided endless debate about the presenter's defensiveness by viewing the countertransference a subject for inquiry rather than an obstacle to be eradicated.

Illustration 1: Alphonse and Gaston

The following brief description illustrates several steps in the clarification of a countertransference problem. These are: (1) accurate observation of what is going on between patient and therapist; (2) the relating of these observations to the therapist's behavior in other settings, and, the group in particular; (3) an attempt to link the preceding steps to the therapist's character and development.

Brennan, ordinarily firm and direct with patients, was experiencing uncommon difficulty in working with a young man, Judson. He described Judson as one of the most detached people he had ever met and felt at a loss to overcome Judson's circumlocutions, pompous formalisms, an extreme obsequiousness. Brennan believed he had made every effort cut short such maneuvers and to get Judson to curtail the verbiage.

The other participants, Ames and Calder, had the benefit, not only of the presentation, but also of a tape recording and personal knowledge of Brennan. Their impression of what he was conveying to the patient differed markedly from what he thought he was conveying. Ames suggested that the patient spoke with tongue in cheek while secretly pulling the wool over Brennan's eyes. Both Ames and Calder felt that Brennan's attempt to hurry the patient through his digressions did not get across; on the contrary, the patient had succeeded in enmeshing Brennan in his own techniques of leaning over backward. The situation had become a contest in which each was, in effect, striving to outdo the other to see who could be more charming and agreeable in going along with the other. Brennan opposed the patient's smothering tactics with long-winded speeches; he felt these embodied significant "observations" but the other two participants perceived them as counter-dust storms. It was their opinion that the therapist's indirection invited further indirection from the patient; his pomposity invited more pomposity; his pomposity invited more pomposity.

Brennan was now able to clarify some aspects of the situation in the light of this new formulation. For example, he had found it difficult to deal with Judson's polite, yet pressing, requests to enter into his private life. In fact, Brennan felt he almost had to apologize for being anything but nice to such an obliging person. As Calder put it, "He wants you to put his cream cheese and lox on his bagel for him, just like his mother does." Brennan felt not only disarmed, but also intimidated, for Judson impressed as being quite tenuously balanced, as harboring, behind his bittersweet exterior, intense and barely controllable rage.

Ames and Calder both expressed the opinion that more directness and incisiveness were required. However, they also held that Brennan had exaggerated not only Judson's detachment, but also his inner anger and fragility. The question then posed was: why did Brennan find this such a difficult case? True, Judson was rigid and detached; he did have certain techniques for rendering his therapist impotent. On the other hand, from their intimate personal and professional acquaintance, Ames and Calder could demonstrate that Brennan was quite different with other obsequious and detached patients and that he did not go in for "after-you-Alphonse" behavior in his social relations.

In a search for parallels, several of Brennan's patients were discussed, which only further emphasized the striking dissimilarity in Brennan's interaction with them as opposed to Judson. The major countertransference problem was finally narrowed down to the therapist's distorted and exaggerated view of Judson's emasculation, detachment, and hidden anger, attitudes that were particularly marked in Judson's dealings with women. At this point Brennan recognized that these were precisely the characteristics which he had cast out from his idealized image of his own father; in his own analysis, he had long struggled with his growing awareness of these same traits in himself. Brennan now saw more clearly how he had shied away from dealing with these problems in the patient lest his own anxieties be provoked. In short, Brennan had unsuccessfully tried to erase these traits from his own self-image by attributing them entirely to the patient.

An interesting commentary on the group's interaction arose from a later comparison between the recording of this group session and the recording of the therapeutic session which Brennan had presented to the group. It became evident that Brennan related to his colleagues in a manner strikingly similar to that in which the patient Judson related to him; Brennan was altogether too polite and ingratiating, yet managed in this very way to cut short many a comment, particularly with flurries of "Yes, yes, yes," reminiscent of Judson's stifling agreeableness. This is not usually a significant facet of Brennan's personal or professional behavior. More likely, it is an illustration of the reflection process described by Searles, an unconscious attempt to communicate the problem.

A related process was the repetition of information about the patient to avoid giving information about the actual patient-therapist situation.

Such evasion was a frequent group symptom. An instance with another Brennan's patients gives the feel of this conduct:

Ames: How about telling us more about the actual interplay, you know, without the notes, just what goes on and your reactions?
Calder: Yes, it's a little boresome, Brennan.
Brennan: I find it very hard to talk about her without the notes, probably an expression of my being fed up.

During the next few minutes, Calder became increasingly bored, while Ames interrupted Brennan repeatedly with a rising tide of irritation. This helped crystallize the curious fact that Brennan was reporting in a bored, grim, monotonous, and slightly complaining voice, much like the voice ascribed to the patient and which recordings corroborated. Second, his insistence on presenting more and more minutiae was similar to the repetitive nature of the patient's complaints. Despite many requests, Brennan continued to shrink from delving into the interaction between the patient and himself openly and freely. At one point, Ames spoke to Brennan in almost the very words that Brennan had used to his patient:

Ames: I don't like to keep interrupting, but my feeling about this is that it is beside the point, that is, I think we've heard most of what you're saying now and that the real issue is what's going on between you and her.

In his presentation, Brennan was unable to communicate what a "pain the neck" the patient was, except by acting as a pain in the neck himself. This raised the question of his failure to experience her as a whining nag, which turned out to be an essential scotoma deriving from a need to maintain a relationship with just such a demanding, capricious woman.

Illustration 2: Seductiveness Breeds Seductiveness

Ames had been working with a very attractive and seductive young woman whose manner was flighty and extremely superficial. He found it very difficult to break through her excessive productions of trivia and felt increasingly disturbed by the therapeutic stagnation.

Ames was asked if he really was being stern and aloof with this patient, as she asserted he was. Although he was not at first aware of this, it became increasingly clear that such was precisely the case. This insight developed in parallel with the increasing clarity of his countertransference operations in dealing with the patient's seductiveness, manipulativeness, and more basic fear of closeness. Calder insisted that Ames was both fascinated and embittered by the patient's seductiveness: "Her seductiveness breeds seductiveness on your part." Brennan and Calder both cited illustrations of Ames' similar social behavior. He soon recognized that his withdrawal and aloofness, which impressed the patient as severity, might well be a reaction against his tendency to meet seductiveness with seductiveness and bitterness of his own, both of which "ought not to be felt by the ideal therapist."

Ames recalled an hour when the patient had launched a full-scale attack on one of his most tender spots. She threatened to quit because he was "after all, very young and only beginning in practice." This occurred, not during a static period, but at a time of positive movement, with the patient coming closer to her feelings of loneliness and her desperate fear of meaningful closeness. Following this hour, Ames had a frightening dream that he was hanging by his hands from the ledge of an apartment house balcony. Brennan suggested that Ames was really made anxious, not by the patient's seductiveness, but by her "getting down to business" in a direct nonseductive and in fact closer relationship with the therapist; and that Ames was desperately hanging on to his own seductive ways—clinging to the patient's breasts or balconies—as a defense against his own fear of closeness. Brennan felt that patient and therapist shared a defensive pattern against closeness: they both were seductive. The recordings show that Brennan's point was overlooked as Calder continued to emphasize Ames' ambivalent response to the patient's seductive, teasing and coy behavior. Was it that Calder's verbal fluency was tacitly accepted by the others as proving that his view was more correct? Or was it that he too had a blind spot in the area referred to by Brennan: that the seduction as threat—which was the way the patient set it up—obscured the real threat for both patient and therapist, the fear of a closer direct relationship?

Soon after, Ames came to recognize that the patient must experience his attitude as very inconsistent, alternating between friendly seductiveness and aloof withdrawal—his characteristic defense against real intimacy. Also, it appeared that precisely such inconsistent and anxiety-fraught "warmth" in the patient's father had contributed to the origin of her own distrust and fear of closeness. Her adaptation to this was through superficial seductiveness, flighty gaiety, and preoccupation with the trivial. It was not surprising that this was exactly her response in the transference situation: she had induced Ames to reproduce with her the same pattern of interaction which had originally given birth to her own frivolity. Thus Ames had helped to evoke in the patient the selfsame response which irritated him and with which he found it difficult to cope. During the ensuing year the therapeutic situation vastly improved and the patient made real gains.

Illustration 3: A Hard Girl to Resist

Calder presented the case of a flirtatious, teasing young woman who showed no therapeutic progress. Her behavior during analytic hours was overtly provocative and her verbal productions were largely about her spicy sex life, which included the consummated seduction of a former therapist. Calder felt that his countertransference was interfering with the therapy if only because "she was a hard girl to resist." He had a vast fund of information about her sexual activities but knew little about the rest of her life.

As our discussions unfolded, two predominant themes appeared. One was Ames' and Brennan's tendency to dilate on their views of the patient's psychodynamics, that is, to fill in what they thought Calder had overlooked about the patient's problems because of his own preoccupation with the sexual. The second was an attempt to generalize the therapist's problems to include both his work with other patients and his nonprofessional interactions. Calder was not easily convinced on this score.

Much of the discussion that followed had as its focus impressions about the patient that were not at first shared by Calder. Repeatedly, attention was drawn to the patient's seductiveness as concealing and, at the same time, expressing her hatred for men, her vengefulness, her need to reduce their stature by seducing them. She warded off anxiety by precipitating that which she feared most. A complementary issue was her need to preserve her self-blaming personal image as the promiscuous "bad girl." This enabled her to avoid experiencing her hatred of her father and her transference hatred of the therapist. There was much discussion of the role of the mother, who had been given scant attention in the therapeutic work.

Conspicuously, Ames focused solely on the patient's dynamics. (We have already seen, from the previous example, that he shared a blind spot with Calder about seductiveness.) By contrast, Brennan would occasionally chime in with questions and comments typified by: "What is *your* problem with seductive women, Calder?"

A striking feature, however, was the absence of a serious attempt to understand the therapist's problem. Investigation of this marked departure from our usual practice turned up several contributing factors: Calder tended to represent the situation as: "It's not *really* a problem; it's just that I'm too healthy, too much instinct"; or "Maybe too much of a good thing isn't always for the best!" This approach lured the group into at least a partial acceptance of his view. May we hypothesize that the "reflection process" described by Searles was in operation here? Calder's seductive presentation of titillating material effectively dulled the critical faculties of both listeners, so that they overlooked his problem. This is precisely what obtained in his relationship with his patient: her suggestive anecdotes, replete with spicy detail, enticed Calder away from his therapeutic function. He had been unable to communicate this in words because he was unaware of it.

Another element in the failure to pursue our avowed goal was Ames' and Calder's overlapping blind spot about seductiveness, this time with Calder presenting. Ames directed his comments to the patient's problem and clearly veered away from the therapist's problem. Addressing his attention to the therapist's problem would have been equivalent to exposing his own.

Summary and Conclusions

In the development of psychoanalytic technique, the study of transference clarified the ways in which the patient uses the therapeutic relationship to meet his inner needs. One outgrowth of our endeavors has been elaboration of an analogous hypothesis about countertransference: *unconsciously, the therapist* (a) *maneuvers his patients into roles which best fit his needs, and* (b) *integrates his defenses against anxiety with complementary or corresponding defenses in his patients*. Freedom from this propensity is probably never completely attained, but we believe that peer-group supervision may make an important contribution to the student's awareness in this domain.

In the course of its life, our peer group suffered a number of intercurrent periods of disintegration. The roots of every such period lay in each member's characteristic defenses, defenses which corresponded to regular patterns in each member's therapeutic technique. Each specific form of group disorganization usually followed the same course as the therapeutic impasse under discussion, for the very factors which impeded a member's therapeutic functioning also impaired his intragroup functioning. The relatedness between a therapist and his peers tended to run the same course as that between the therapist and his patient (occasionally that between the therapist and his supervisor). In this way, a therapist often unconsciously reproduced, in the group, interactions which he could not otherwise describe.

A supervisory peer group is most likely to succeed if the participants already know each other well, if the group is organized on their own initiative, and if their mutual compassion outweighs the destructive effects of anxiety. It is essential to refrain from delving into the members' personalities any more than is required by the elucidation of problems with patients and the facilitation of the group's work. If such is indeed the case, there is little reason to fear that the group will be rent asunder by enmity or drift into increasing detachment and alienation. Rather, we found it to be a unique experience of the deepest intimacy.

Notes

1. Supervising Psychiatrist, Educational Clinic, College of the City of New York, N.Y.
2. Faculty member, William Alanson White Institute of Psychiatry, Psychoanalysis, and Psychology, New York, N.Y.
3. Clinical Instructor in Psychiatry, Albert Einstein College of Medicine, New York, N.Y.
4. Thompson, C. (1955), Personal communication.
5. Kubie, L. S. (1959), Personal communication.
6. Hinckley, M. W. (1955), Personal communication.
7. Searles, H. (1955), Personal communication.

Reference

Searles, H.F. (1955). The informational value of the supervisor's emotional experiences. *Psychiatry*, *18*, 135–146.

Part III

In Ghent's words

Chapter 8

Relations

Introduction to the first IARPP Conference[1]

Emmanuel Ghent

It's a great joy to be welcoming you all to this celebration of Stephen Mitchell, to this conference, and to the inaugural meeting of the International Association for Relational Psychoanalysis and Psychotherapy. My only wish is that Stephen would be here among us today and standing right here in my place, welcoming you.

I'd like to say a few words about Steve's vision for this organization. Above all, his dream was of an association of psychoanalysts, wherein it would be possible for analysts of all persuasions to meet and share their experiences and ideas, a place where institutional and political concerns would survive only as a memory, a relic from former times. As Steve put it, "its ethos was to be a love of learning, not a consolidation of any particular discipline or any particular interest group." Why then call it "relational"? I hope this will become clear as I go on.

The term, relational, was first applied to psychoanalysis by Greenberg and Mitchell back in 1983 when they abstracted the term from Sullivan's theory of interpersonal relations and Fairbairn's object relations theory. Common to these models of psychic development was the notion that psychic structure—at the very least, those aspects of psychic structure that were accessible to psychotherapeutic intervention - derived from the individual's relations with other people. This, of course, was intended as an alternative to the prevailing view that innately organized drives and their developmental vicissitudes were, at root, the basis of psychic structure.

There is no such thing as a relational theory, but there is such a thing as a relational point of view, a relational way of thinking, a relational sensibility, and we believe that it is this broad outlook that underpins the sea change that many of us recognize as breathing fresh life into our field. Many of the people who will be speaking over the next two days will flesh out something of the range and scope of matters relational. And, as you will see, there are those who identify as Freudian, or Jungian, or intersubjectivists, or interpersonalists, or so called "relational analysts."

I see the Association as having three goals: first, a venue for open discussion of all species of psychoanalytic thinking; second, a forum wherein ideas that broadly fall under the rubric of a relational sensibility have a chance to be heard and to develop in the marketplace of ideas, and third, a place where the meaning and compass of the very term relational may be explored. I would like to enlarge on this briefly. In their original usage of the terms "interpersonal relations" and "object relations," both Sullivan and Fairbairn were focused on the role of human relations in development. They each, in their own way, forged theories of psychic development and the origination of motivational structures that were based essentially on the idea that structure formation arose out of the complexities of interhuman activities. From this point of view what has come to be called the intrapsychic was in fact a dynamic structuralization of the interpersonal. Loewald (1978), too, basically saw the intrapsychic as a condensation of the interpersonal as, for example, when he says, "Thus I conceive instincts…and the id as a psychic structure, as originating in inter-actions of the infantile organism and its human environment (mother) … ." (p. 495), or again (1972), "Instincts, in other words, are to be seen as relational phenomena from the beginning and not as autonomous forces seeking discharge" (p. 242). In this usage, the term relational was essentially conceptual in meaning, rather than descriptive. It referred insistently, although seldom explicitly, to a conception of psychic structure as being largely constructed—the resultant organization of experience, primarily interhuman experience. This conception allows room for both well integrated organization of experience as well as for non-integrated or poorly integrated organizations of experience some of which may be inaccessible to ordinary consciousness, as we see in the phenomena of dissociation. Notice again that we are here speaking of "relational" as a conceptual term that underpins a way of thinking about development, about psychic structure, about psychopathology, and ultimately, about psychotherapeutic interventions.

Unfortunately, and confusingly, a much more superficial usage of the term relational has cropped up and has all but coopted its meaning. In its purely descriptive usage, relational has come to mean anything that refers to activities going on between people, mostly current activities. Thus we hear, "Mr. X has many relational difficulties," meaning not much more than that Mr. X has personal difficulties in relating to other people. If one reads that "a patriarchal culture … lauds strict autonomy [and] denies relational needs," or if one comes across phrases like "fantasy elements are often linked to real relational experiences," it becomes clear that the term is being used to signify something like human contact or connection. What concerns me about this superficial usage is that it won't be long before we hear patients saying "You're not responding to my relational needs." But much more important, it completely obscures the far more radical significance of the term, in which usage, for example, fantasy is relational; it is the outgrowth and condensation of relational experience of all sorts. I emphasize "all sorts" to remind you that relational is not confined to interhuman relations, although they play an enormously important part in matters having to do with psychotherapeusis. We must not neglect the role of emergent self-organization.

Also troubling to me is that in tending to limit the scope of the term relational, to relations between people, we exclude all manner of other relations from consideration. To my mind, relational psychoanalysis is almost ideally suited to make use of insights from the dynamic systems perspective that in the last decade or two has begun to radically change the way we think in science. Poincaré, the father of this outlook once said, "the aim of science is not things themselves, as the dogmatists in their simplicity assume, but the relations among things; outside these relations there is no reality knowable" (Kelso, 1997, p. 97). Money, at one level, is merely a thing; at another level it is a complex relational concept, at root an expression of claims on the labor of others. When with cash we buy food at the supermarket we are not aware that we are redeeming claims, sometimes highly exploitative claims, on the labor of many people all along the food chain, often on a global scale. Using the model of dynamic systems we come to appreciate the significance of history, context and ecology—all of which are expressive of relations, and relations among relations—at all levels from the cellular, to the level of organs, to perception, action, cognition and memory, to the interhuman, and on to the level of societal relations, not to mention the highly complex relations that exist between these different levels. Psychoanalysis until recently has confined itself to the narrow band of the psychopathological, where interhuman relations play an enormous role. In recent years interest has spread down one level to study the relation between brain and mind and up one level to the societal, although we have not yet seriously engaged a concept of a social unconscious.

I do hope that by Sunday evening you will have a new appreciation for the complexity and compass of the relational and by the vistas it offers.

And now to begin … .

Note

1. New York, January 18, 2001.

References

Kelso, J.A.S. (1997). *Dynamic patterns: The self-organization of brain and behavior*. Cambridge, MA: MIT Press.

Loewald, H. W. (1972). Freud's conception of the negative therapeutic reaction, with comments on instinct theory. *Journal of the American Psychoanalytic Association*, *20*, 235–245.

Loewald, H, W. (1978). Instinct theory, object relations, and psychic structure formation. *Journal of the American Psychoanalytic Association*, *26*, 493–506.

Chapter 9

On Relational Psychoanalysis

An Interview with Dr Emmanuel Ghent/ Interviewer: Lewis Aron

Emmanuel Ghent and Lewis Aron

L: Hi, it's Lew Aron and I'm interviewing Mannie Ghent on Monday, December 14th for the online symposium on the development of psychoanalysis. The development of *relational* psychoanalysis. We'll just deal with that. Hi Mannie.

M: Hi.

L: Mannie, we're just going to speak for a few minutes and the purpose really is that since this is going to have people enrolled from all over the world we hope, there are going to be many people who have not had a chance to meet you or get to know you personally and we thought that having a chance to at least hear what you sound like and speak for a few minutes would add to reading your article and discussing it in a more academic way.

M: Okay.

L: So I'd like to start by asking you if you could say something about what got you involved in psychoanalysis and how you ended up being an analyst.

M: Well that goes back a long way. That goes back to when I was in college and I think the first person that influenced me was the work of Erich Fromm. I was first interested in society I would say before I became interested in psychology. And then ran across that wonderful book, *Escape from Freedom*, way back in the 40s. Early 40s. And then that developed an interest in the psychological side of things that he began to speak about in that book. And then from there I discovered that he was at the White Institute and I found out about Harry Stack Sullivan, and I found that very different type of reading because Sullivan's language is rather tortured at times but at the same time it was extraordinarily illuminating. And in many ways, much to my mind, much more exciting than much of the Freud that I had read at that time. The Freud was I guess during my college years was a great time of excitement but when I came across Sullivan I was really thrilled to find out that there were different ways of looking at things that didn't quite sounds so mechanical as a lot of the Freudian theories sounded to me at that time.

L: Mannie, you've been at the forefront of the development of relational psychoanalysis and certainly one of the founders of the relational track at NYU and very active in *Psychoanalytic Dialogues* and the whole relational thrust. Can you say something about the changes in psychoanalysis over the years that you've been practicing?

M: Well, I can say something about my own experience with it. You know, I graduated from the White Institute where, as I mentioned before, Fromm and Sullivan were preponderant thinkers and theoreticians. But even back then I was very much interested in what the British Object Relations people were working on, particularly in Winnicott and I remember reading Milner's work way back in the 50s and was very much taken with that.

One of the things that I was interested in was some of the work that Jane Pearce was doing at the time which felt like an extension of some of Sullivan's work that made it a little bit, I thought, richer. But then the group that she founded and started, the so-called "Sullivanians," went on a very different trajectory and I was not terribly keen on what happened there although I thought that she herself had a very fine mind and had a very creative mind.

L: Let me get into that a little bit more because I haven't heard you speak about that. Can you say, what was it that you felt Jane Pearce was really adding to Sullivan? Before the whole Sullivanian group went its own way, what was being developed?

M: Well, you know, when I was a student at White it was rather strange. Sullivan had died not long before and his name was spoken reverentially but at the same time there was very little actual teaching of Sullivan. I was very struck with how the emphasis was more on saying what was wrong with Freud than what was right with Sullivan. And so when I came across Jane Pearce, which was somewhat by accident, I was a psychiatric resident at Hillside Hospital where we had very long-term, severely disturbed schizophrenic, obsessional patients sometimes, and the supervision I got there was just perfectly dreadful. On the other hand, I came to Jane Pearce who introduced me to Sullivan's actual work with schizophrenic patients and suddenly my work with these patients catapulted into a whole new dimension. It was just wonderful because I discovered ways of working with these people which were not only enlightening to me but made an enormous difference in terms of their therapeutic experience.

Then I got to know something more about her work and she was one of the few people who not only had worked extensively with him but had really thought about it and wanted to extend it. One extension, for example, was the idea of extending. See the problem with the self-system that Sullivan had brought into being was that it was essentially designed as a kind of anti-anxiety system and it left out all the aspects of the self, you might say, that didn't have to do with ways of containing anxiety. And so what she did, and I must say I was instrumental in helping out with that, was develop an extension which spoke of an additional system, you might say, which we called the integral system, and the idea was that the experience people had in their developmental years and throughout life was organized simultaneously along two lines. On the one hand it was organized into the self-system, which was very much like Sullivan's self-system, which was that which was acceptable, you might say. Which was conceivable, which was thinkable by the person and in a certain sense corresponded to what might be called preconscious. It involved everything but the "not me." It involved, what did he call it—I forgot the terms that he used—the "good me" and the "bad me" were Sullivan's terms. The "not me" was what Sullivan referred to as the dissociated system and the line of thinking that we developed was that rather than thinking of it simply as a dissociative system—we conceived of it as another line of integration that took place within the person. Something along the lines, much more current today when you think of multiple personality, multiple personality organization with any given person, the idea being that the integral system was integrated along the lines of a totality of experience rather than that which was acceptable to the relatively accessible self and so on. So that you might say, the way it was thought of after that was that there was constant pressure from the integral system to extend the self-systems. And that was one way of looking at where therapy could be helpful because it was really a way of trying to locate those aspects of the self that were what we would now call in dissociation. And try to make them more accessible. But the way of thinking of it was that these were two parallel systems, one of which was almost totally out of awareness.

L: It's very interesting to me because it really sounds like this is some of the origins or at least antecedents of where you went in later years. I mean, a lot of the focus on multiple self-states but also the constriction and expansion of the self, the polarity there which you've written about, and I guess I want to lead this in to one of your major ideas which has to do with surrender and it sounds like this idea of an integral self also anticipates some of that.

M: Well I think so. I think that, you see surrender in one sense can be thought of as the opposite or the other side of resistance, the inverse or the obverse of resistance. And what I mean by that is that we're all very familiar with processes of resistance in psychoanalysis, we encounter them all the time. But we very seldom talk about those forces which I think exist in many of us, if not most of us, that incline us to want to undo the defensive structure that we are heir to, that we have developed. One way of thinking would be to say that we have some sense of that integral system that was organized and that there's some kind of longing to open that up and make that accessible to one's being, to one's conscious being. And now surrender, that's one route to surrender. Surrender of course has more roots in meditation and Buddhism thinking and there I think I came to have that influence because of my interest in Buddhism and my interest in meditation. And, it seemed to me that one of the sources, I guess when I first came across the usefulness of the concept of surrender was in relation to understanding that there may be other sources of understanding the nature of submissive and masochistic behavior. And it seemed to me, as I began to study this more, that in some people, at least on some occasions, that underlying the impulse to submit or surrender was another impulse, more deeply buried, that was closer to the quality of giving up one's defensive structure, of in a certain sense, coming clean, of divesting oneself of all the false self-organizations (to use Winnicott's terminology), and it seemed to me that it was a useful way, and I have found it a rather useful way of thinking of many of the phenomena that we encounter in submission and masochism.

L: Mannie, we just have a couple of minutes but I want to ask you before we got off the phone, can you say anything about what you think the most current issues are for psychoanalysis? Where do you see the field going? Where do you think we are at this point?

M: Well, that's not so easy to say. I think that we're at a bit of a crossroads in psychoanalysis. Psychoanalysis has had something of a downward spiral in the last twenty or so years from the highpoint in the 50s down to the low point in the 90s. But I have a feeling that there's new fresh blood coming into it, not necessarily with new people, although partly that's so, but I think that there's a kind of vitalization in psychoanalysis that's coming into being now, and my sense is that the general trend towards everybody taking refuge in medication and drugs is going to come to something not exactly of a dead end but its limitations will soon be found or recognized by large numbers of people, and I think that the interest in much deeper kinds of self-examination as a means towards healing will come back into the foreground again. So I think that we're coming down towards the nadir of psychoanalysis and I think it's going to start climbing up again.

L: That's probably a good note for us to end. Mannie, thanks so much. It's always a pleasure and it makes me want to spend more time talking with you.

M: Okay.

L: Okay

M: Good.

L: Bye bye.

M: Bye bye.

Part IV

Reminiscences

Chapter 10

A fragment of an analysis with Mannie Ghent

Ron Balamuth

I thought I was calling Mannie to seek a consultation about a patient. He gets on the phone and greets me with his deep sonorous voice. "Mannie, I'd like to meet with you for a consultation about a patient," I say tentatively. "Sure," he says, "Let me go and fetch my book and see what times I have open." In the brief moment that he speaks, an urgent sense of now or never takes over and I say, "In fact, Mannie, I am the patient—the consultation is about me." I catch my breath. "I will still need to get my book to see when we can meet," he says calmly, without missing a beat.

That was how my analysis with Mannie began.

Between the phone call and our first consultation, I had a dream. I am riding my bike somewhere in Greenwich Village or SoHo, and I get a flat tire. I see a small, grungy storefront with an old sign "Bike Shop" on top. I enter a dark and dank place that smells of a tinkerer's workshop—there's machine oil, old wood, and a faint workman's body odor.

Mannie stands behind the counter, wearing a workman's greasy overalls. He takes my bike and puts it on the bike stand to examine it. I check out the shop, which turns out to be very deep, extending far behind the counter. All kinds of bric-a-brac are filling every shelf. Every possible imaginable type of machine, old and new, is there. Oscilloscopes, speakers, computer hardware, disassembled musical instruments, but also every tool, drills, mechanical saws—you name it. It strikes me that no one would ever have imagined that behind this very humble façade there is a whole secret universe, an inventor's haven.

A main axis of our work together, transformative and healing, revolved around the sudden loss of my father, with whom I had a profoundly ambivalent relationship. He died exactly a week after I turned thirteen, right after my Bar Mitzvah.

Of the many hours and years spent going over this formative and traumatic experience and all its ramifications, none strikes me as capturing more of Mannie than the following episode.

Leading up to this moment with both of us at his recording studio, we spent many months at his office, with me crying with rage and sadness about the lifelong absence of my father. At some point during a particularly painful phase in the analysis, when I was flooded with doubts about how to parent my young child in the absence of a father to raise me, I reached out behind the couch, searching for Mannie's hand. It was right there, just where I conjured it up, and it felt exactly as I expected, warm and fleshy, surprisingly large and strong for his small stature. Calloused, a craftsman and worker's hand. For the next couple of months, I held his hand through long periods of stupor, silence, then rage and longing for my absent father. His hand remained strong and present, just as I needed it, holding me in the face of feelings I could barely contain.

It was during one of these sessions that I mentioned the recordings. My father, who founded an importing business for office machinery, had a large service department in which I used to work each summer, making service calls with the technicians. I recalled that a couple of times a year, an engineer would come to Israel, sent from the manufacturer in Germany, to train the technicians in servicing the year's new models. The engineer spoke German, and my father simultaneously translated. I casually mentioned that these training sessions were recorded on a reel-to-reel tape machine, which, in the early sixties in Tel Aviv, was quite a novelty.

Mannie perked up. "What kind of a machine was it, do you remember?" "Yes," I said, "it was an Italian Geloso reel-to-reel tape recorder, which had a vacuum tube amplifier. I brought the reels with me from Israel, and I have most of them in storage. This is useless," I said, "as the machine with which the recordings were made no longer exists."

"Well, why don't you bring them in and we will take a look," said Mannie.

The next session, as I arrive with a box of small tape reels, Mannie leads me into his studio, across the hall from his office. It is not the first time that I visit this space—I have been in classes and seminars there before; however, now it feels like a new place altogether. Mannie and I and all these electronic gizmos—tapes, speakers and devices; it feels uncannily like my father's shop, minus the machine-oil smell.

Mannie loads one of my reels onto his Akai six-head tape (yes, I recall the brand, as I was always lusting for these super-expensive professional recorders), and attaches the loose end of the tape to an empty reel. Mumbling to himself or me, he muses, "Well, it's not clear whether it was taped on a 0.4" per second machine or a faster one, but we can adjust the speed as needed. Recording speeds have more than tripled since this one was made." Pointing to a slider on the control of this huge tape deck, he shows me how he can adjust the speed of the machine. He looks like he is really enjoying this, and is all business. "This is not analysis," I think to myself.

We stand next to each other, as I look over his shoulder and watch how quickly and naturally he sets the machines up. He gives me a sideways glance, and with a questioning look asks, "Shall we?" I nod.

He presses play. The reels begin to turn, the large speakers crackle, there is a background hum, and then sounds of a room with ambient street noises, chairs sliding on a floor, and a man's voice in German suddenly comes on, crisp and clear. A voice I immediately recognize, without a second of hesitation. It is my father's voice, which I haven't heard for forty years. It is now vibrating in Mannie's studio in SoHo.

"Is that him?" He asks. Now doubt creeps in. "Yes and no," I say, "Something is not right. It sounds like him, but not quite. My dad's voice sounds like this, but for some reason it appears wrong in pitch or something. I am not sure what it is." Mannie responds calmly, "We can experiment with the speed, as it is not clear what speed it was recorded at." He begins to make some adjustments to the recorder's speed slider. The strangest thing happened. I can try and put words to this, but words do not quite capture what happened. As Mannie accelerates the tape's speed, and my father's voice gains in pitch, sounding higher than his initial basso, which just broke through, my whole physical experience of standing in front of my father as a young boy, hearing his booming voice high above my head, often terrifying and overwhelming, melts away. As Mannie slightly adds pitch to the voice, I feel my body rapidly stretching, growing taller. Now eye-level with my father for an instant, and then towering over him with my 6'2" adult body. All of a sudden, like waking from a dream, I am hearing his voice coming at me, bouncing off my chest, where his mouth would have reached if he were with us in the studio. Mannie's voice breaks through my reverie, "Is that about right now?" he asks. He notices the tears in my eyes and smiles. My father's voice, now pitched higher, sounding almost pleading, vulnerable, still expounding in German about technical specs of the newest model, is coming from the right place. I seem to have a new body, a longer and stronger spine. The commanding, exacting, and often frightening voice of my childhood is now the voice of a man vulnerable, needy and seeking my attention and my love. From my new height, I feel safe to hold him, my arms, literally around him, as he rests his head with its gray receding hair on my chest. Mannie turns from the recorder and says to me softly, "I guess this is it. I will transfer it all to cassettes so you can play it at home."

We spent a couple of weeks going over what took place in the studio. In some ways, my grief and sadness over not having a life with my father intensified during that time, and Mannie's hand, present, warm and reliable, grounded me.

One day I took my place on the couch, and, unthinking, reached out for his hand. It was not there where I had come to expect it. "I need your hand, Mannie!" I said with some irritation. There was a pause. I think I knew what comes next. "No," I hear him behind me, "you don't need my hand anymore."

His voice is clear, confident and definitely not inviting or leaving any space for negotiation or a tantrum. This was the moment I dreaded most, from the first time I entered his office and laid on the couch. I did not feel abandoned, pushed away or rejected. As if the room where these feelings were living in me for so many years was no longer there. It was such a clear sense of strength and height, and an ability to stand tall with the scaffolding removed. I recall how the couch felt too short as my feet pushed against the wall. I suddenly felt proud and strong, not deprived, angry, or cheated, not having his hand in my hand. He saw it first and called it.

In the weeks and months that followed, our sessions became more of an exchange and sharing of interests. As we engaged in discussions about Buddhism, our shared spiritual practices, meditation and such, the emotional intensity, the passions, around my father made room for a filial feeling of tenderness and affection. He was preparing his Buddhism and Psychoanalysis reading list for his first class, and we have discussed some of the readings with the understanding that when therapy ended I will see him in class. The prospect of our staying connected in the Buddhism seminar diminished my need to keep my tight grasp on him and fear of losing contact. Sessions had become quite flat, almost purposeless.

One day—by this time I was sitting up—he asked me as I took my seat, "So what did you come for today?"

Again, that dreadful sinking sensation, yet feeling that he just put words to a question I was having and dared not to speak. As if he knew that I just want to be there with him, not to say anything. Silence.

"There is really no point in your coming here just to make sure that I am still alive, you know. If something was to happen to me, you'd find out." So clear, so simple, and so unsentimental. Again, the same shock of not finding any of my old dread. Instead, a sense of total freedom. I no longer need to keep my vigil. I am free, tall, strong, and profoundly grateful to this short man who has just set me free.

Again, the same sonorous, rich and knowing voice was there. It left no room for debate nor doubt. Life was there to be lived, and my children were there at home, waiting and ready for their father.

Chapter 11

Reminiscences of Mannie as a clinical supervisor

Lewis Aron

I had studied object relations theory with Mannie years earlier, and then sought him out because he was the guru of the relational movement as the track was being launched at New York University. I had already had supervision with numerous of the program's leading supervisors, but thought I should get to know Mannie's ways of working first-hand. What I remember about my supervision with Mannie is how totally present he was, and the intensity of his listening and really getting my patient. I recall sitting at a lunch with him some years after the supervision, when he asked me how the patient was doing. He clearly had a sharp memory of my patient, even years after the supervision. Mannie also worked with a different method than I had become used to, even among interpersonal and relational supervisors. He was much more likely to purposefully ask questions that seemed to come out of the blue, or to interrupt a patient's flow with what at first seemed like a non sequitur. Mannie did this purposefully, especially to break up an obsessional or overly linear mode of thought. These questions also focused on affect, feeling, and relationship, and so highlighted emotion over obsessional or intellectual rationality.

Chapter 12

The years with Ghent

Victoria Demos

In *The Years with Ross,* James Thurber (1957/2001) describes Harold Ross, the founding editor of the *New Yorker*, as "a visionary and a practicalist, imperfect at both, a dreamer and a hard worker, a genius and a plodder, obstinate and reasonable ... wide-eyed and world weary" (p. 8). Upon reflection, I suppose something similar could be said of Ghent, or that one could easily substitute Ghent for Ross in the above passage. Mannie was a complex person. An idealist and an iconoclast, compassionate but tough-minded, deadly serious about the analytic work but not without a sense of humor. Writing a portrait of one's analyst is a tricky endeavor, and I'd like to start with a disclaimer. My goal here is not to go into details of my analysis with Mannie, nor is it to paint an idealized or overly sentimental view of him. Instead, I'd like to provide a descriptive snapshot of Mannie so that he may come to life for the reader of this volume. The following snapshot is only one person's portrait of a man who touched the lives of many.

As I call Ghent to mind, my first vision is of walking into his waiting room, a narrow hallway where I would wait my turn on an antique, carved, walnut wood bench. At some point, a curtain leading to the consulting room would part and the patient before me would exit, invariably sobbing (I was initially alarmed by the unrelenting stream of sobbing patients to exit Mannie's office, but soon this became commonplace and I too would leave the office emotionally spent). Eventually, the curtain would part again and Ghent would appear, like the Wizard of Oz. I would step behind the curtain into a four-foot-long anteroom, the walls of which were lined top to bottom with books. Only then would I walk through the door into a very small consulting room, also lined with books from floor to ceiling. Ghent sat, dwarfed in a large, red, leather chair and in front of him was a futon, covered by an Indian print fabric, sitting on a wooden platform. This was "the couch." This small, simple room belied the richness, seriousness and humanity of the work that was accomplished here. This was a place of substance, a place to uncover the past, a place to feel things, and a place where people connect.

Ghent was a warm, emotionally connected person, yet it was always clear that we were there to do serious work. He was disciplined, and his standards for "the work" were very high. It was clear he wanted to work in the transference, and very little work was done in displaced form. He consistently encouraged a return to earlier, deeper affective states. He would use his voice to resonate with affect and would even lean over in his chair to speak right next to my ear. Any retreat from affect was met by silence. There was always the sense that the sadness that emerged would be contained by his optimistic presence. I once skeptically asked him if anyone in a training analysis actually did surrender, or "let go," and without missing a beat, he replied, "Only the lucky ones."

I would often see Ghent going about his daily life in the West Village—grocery shopping, picking up dry cleaning, walking his dog—and this was always a comfort to me. He would wave or greet me warmly, like an old friend. Clad in a Norwegian sweater, Birkenstocks with socks, and khakis, Ghent walked at a very brisk clip, so that one might only catch a flash of his bright, woven cap as he made his rounds. And off he would go, perhaps to exchange news of the neighborhood with the owner of Vesuvio Bakery, a New Yorker to the last.

Reference

Thurber, J. (2001). *The years with Ross.* New York, NY: Harper Collins (Original work published 1957).

Chapter 13

Impressions of Mannie

Jessica Benjamin

What first impressed me about Mannie was the way he let me abide in and muddle through my confusing emotions, yet responded to the feelings directly. He had the ability to convey his resonance and yet sit still with the muddle and my own obvious wish to get out of it, without jumping in to make sense prematurely, and somehow I knew this was going to take me into as yet unknown places. More generally, in comparing him with others, his depth of empathy was quite the exception, and I knew of no one with his intelligence, warmth and complex understanding. Once I arrived at Postdoc, I found, by comparison with Mannie, the other interpersonalists appeared bossy and shallow; and, of course, the contrast with the Freudians was just as great—they seemed chilly and withholding. Neither group seemingly had any sense of how to reach the baby or small child within, which was Mannie's obvious focus and strength.

As to style, Mannie was uniquely able to express his feeling responses, with his musical voice as well as poetic imagery. He could also be very present in silence. He was good at matching both vitality/excitement and grief. He once told me that his analyst Clara Thompson had said, you don't have to tell the patient what to do, but there is no harm in applauding when they get it right. Then again, he had a way of doing the opposite when you got it wrong: He signaled his impatience or even boredom; he conveyed the idea rather clearly that long discursive explanations were useless; and, by use of this negative feedback, he entrained us (I say us, because others related the same experience) to skip the narrative and get to the feelings. However, he himself could seemingly retreat in the face of anger or fear, both feelings he later confessed (more or less) to having difficulty with. Sometimes he was frustratingly uninterested in symbolizing affect (e.g. he cared about the music, not the lyrics). He never knew the words to songs, even though he encouraged me to make use of my frequent associations to them. He thought 'On Top of Old Smokey' actually was 'On Top of Spaghetti'. He would stay up all night composing at Bell Labs, and was occasionally too tired to be his usual relentless self. I'm not sure how I knew this, so he must have told me. This was back on West 9th, before he got his loft in Prince Street, where he had his own computer.

When Mannie came back from India wearing orange, he told me a bit about his experience with Rajnish, and even suggested I go to his center and try the active meditation (I found it way too jangling). I was relieved when he switched to Buddhism.

I had the impression that during the time I knew him as an analyst, Mannie made some important changes—for instance, becoming more involved with Winnicott's thinking. Somewhere along the line, he introduced me to Object Relations and told me what to read. Mannie clearly supported and inspired my dissertation on recognition and object relations theory, his confidence in me was contagious and probably made all the difference, in that I could trust and enjoy my own thinking and connect it to my emotional reality.

Chapter 14

Heart melts forward

Emmanuel Ghent (1925–2003)

Adrienne Harris

Preparing to write this memorial essay, I have found myself on the lookout for some Buddhist saint or Eastern mystic who somehow escaped the treacly soft sanctimony of holiness. I was looking for gurus with edge, not ego—sages with humor and grit. A friend suggested the siddhas—masterful guys who metabolized huge amounts of arcane knowledge but were not necessarily very obedient, docile pacifists. Muriel Dimen suggested Boddhidharma. I Googled "Boddhidharma" and found myself face-to-face with a martial artist, a sage, a trickster, a questioner.

What am I trying for here? When Mannie died, there was an enormous outpouring of feeling: expressions (in so many forms) of his deep kindness, his quiet power, his quite subtle magic, mostly inflected through gentleness. In the days and weeks after his death, and at his funeral, stories unfolded, told in many different styles and from different points of reference. Mannie's life encompassed practice in psychoanalysis, as a teacher, supervisor, and analyst. He had a rich history in contemporary music, playing and composing. He was involved in Buddhism. He had an active writing life. Wherever one looked or listened, there was one overwhelming conclusion: this was a good life, fully and well lived. One could feel happy about Mannie and for Mannie, and connected to personal and professional networks of people who held and were held by Mannie.

All true, but I kept wanting something more—something more piquant, more gritty. In his wonderful celebratory essay on Mannie, Adam Phillips (2001) manages to use the words "ferocious" and "mild-mannered" in the same sentence, trying to capture the paradox, the dialectic—of tone and intent, style and content, depth and infrastructure—that constituted Mannie's unique way of being.

Mannie in Battle

Accompanying Mannie's great personal courtesy and gentleness, his capacity to create for others a place of calm and centeredness, was a very well-developed capacity to do battle. In internecine struggles within postdoc,[1] and battles with New York University on postdoc's behalf, Mannie was quite a joy to watch and to join. For one thing, he matched a will to win a battle with a passion for prodigious hard work. I never went as a foot soldier in one of his skirmishes where Mannie was not incredibly equipped with papers, charts, evidence. Mannie's forms of soldiering involved the mastery of staggering detail and preparation. I like the spectacle and adrenalin in fights, but Mannie was actually interested in deploying the skill it took to win and to achieve results.

But he could do something else in the aftermath of battles. In this regard, I am thinking particularly of the creation of the Relational Track, carved out in a difficult, contentious situation. Mannie could build on struggle—he could turn around and focus his prodigious attention on a creative future. He could imagine generativity after the revolution. We could say that he had the kind of character it takes to make circumstances bloom after a good hard struggle.

I feel sure that Mannie would have insisted, at this point, that I note the powerful effect of Steve Mitchell, Jim Fosshage, Bernie Friedland, and Phillip Bromberg. All of their strong presences went into the creation of the track. Perhaps it is relevant that it was in this period—the late 1980s through 2002—that Mannie, so supported by and engaged with these colleagues, did his most powerful writing.

Mannie had spent many years in the trenches at postdoc and became the first director of the Relational Track. There, he was instrumental in opening a field of opportunity for my generation. We were encouraged to speak and write and teach, and therefore allowed to grow and to flourish. Encouraging highly individual evolutions of teaching, drawing on new topics and new ways of approaching old standards, Mannie made the creation of the relational curriculum an enterprise that occurred in conditions of freedom and authorizing. It has been very easy for many people to say how much they cared for and loved Mannie. But what is so precious is that, in the way that the new faculty and students of the Relational Track were held by Mannie, it was clear that he loved us.

It's a dazzling combination: grit and generativity. In ways I cannot begin to understand, I think this was connected to the various forms of Buddhism that Mannie involved himself in. His practice, to construe that term very broadly, involved words, actions, sitting, moving, silence, and speaking, enabling him to be in the world with a great and quietly held discipline.

Mannie as Montrealer

I shared with Mannie a complex, ambivalent history, as a fellow Canadian. We had a Canadian moment at the Toronto IARPP conference, which took place on a kind of deeply frigid January day that left one breathless and headachy. Thank God, we congratulated each other, we had gotten out of that icy, strangling country. But when I think of Mannie in Montreal, I remember what an amazing and sophisticated and intensely alive world it was. Montreal in the 1940s and 1950s was cosmopolitan and exciting. The Montreal of Mannie's youth, particularly McGill University where he studied, would have been an intense crucible of ideas and experiences. I often think of the novels of Mordecai Richler when I think of Mannie in Montreal, although the Canadian writer I associate more acutely in relation to Mannie is Robertson Davies. Davies' novel *Fifth Business* (Macmillan Company, 1970) weaves a story of a life altered by a chance moment in the youth of the protagonist. There are circumstances, unbidden but potent, out of which lifelong choices emerge, leaving a sense of loss and a shadow cast across one's personal life. Perhaps we can credit this Montreal childhood as Mannie's first acquaintance with chaos theory, with the unpredictable—the sudden, slight shift in a moment that alters everything that follows. Chaos theory has a beautiful metaphor for this process: the flap of a butterfly wing in the Amazon and then, in a few iterations, a hurricane in the Pacific.

Mannie's Writing

If you look back at the essays Mannie wrote, you see that the central publications cover a period of 12 years, from 1989 to 2002 (Ghent, 1989, 1990, 1992a, 1992b, 2002). Looked at in toto, there is a method, a practice of being and of writing, present from the beginning. In surveying his work within that grouping, there are five absolute jewels: original, moral, creative, clinically astute works.

In the first of these, "Credo" (1989), even its title is instructive. Mannie made sure that the reader understands that this paper is not as much about thought as it is about love. He leads with his heart, his belief. "Credo" is an instruction to young analysts to allow the heart to melt forward, to breathe. Rather amazingly, in this essay Mannie called for each *student* to begin training by writing a manifesto of his or her beliefs. But (and it is a crucial *but*) ... he cautions his readers, that this manifesto will have a pretty short shelf life. "Credo" contains a lot of personal biography, and Mannie talks about how the college kid who thought psychology was "moosh" morphed into an analyst in training at White who entered a state of fascinated engagement with Sullivan. Listen to the precision with which he extracts Sullivan's deep view of the interpersonal from its mainstream reductions:

> Sullivan's eschewal of structure in favor of relation had some far-reaching consequences. It certainly made it difficult to diagram psychic phenomena in a manner analogous to what was possible with classical metapsychology, so difficult in fact that it led to the belief among classical analysts that there was no theory (i.e., metapsychology) in Sullivan's system. More importantly it was a stringent effort at ridding the field of the fetishistic structures that had come to be the shibboleths of psychoanalysis. Although Sullivan was anything but a Marxist, I believe it is fair to say that he was trying to build a non-fetishistic psychology (Ghent, 1962). Let me explain what I mean by this. Marx (1867) put it this way: "[In commodity production, and this includes the production of ideas], the social relation between men assumes ... the fantastic form of a relation between things" (p. 83). Things like money or rent, are fetishes in that they obscure the relations between people, even though those relations may not be at all visible. We almost never think of money as an interpersonal or relational concept, at root an expression of claims on the labor of others. When with cash we buy food at the supermarket we are not aware that we are redeeming claims, sometimes highly exploitative claims, on the labor of many people all along the food chain, often on a global scale. In classical analysis such concepts as instinct, id, ego, superego likewise obscure and mystify the underlying relation between people. They are fetishes. One might say that the id is the fetishistic

> formalization of early experience. It is seen as inhering in "nature," so that the result (the id) of a process (human interactive experience) is, instead seen as its cause.
>
> (Ghent, 1989, pp. 178–179)

Now, to be sure, "Credo" is both a new voice and an essay engaged in serious dialogue with many ancestors: Sullivan, Fromm, Winnicott, Fairbairn. The tone of Mannie's next publication—"Masochism, Submission, Surrender" (1990)—is freer. His interlocutors are from the East; he is engaging with new partners for psychoanalytic work.

Mannie was able to sit with many ways of moving toward truth: American pragmatism, Eastern thought on embodied cognition, Sullivanian psychoanalytic theory, British object relations, chaos theory, information-processing models of the most dazzling technical precision, and the plainspeak of Winnicott. Perhaps because he could embed himself and be permeated by all these modes of thought, Mannie could tolerate a decentering of his own authority. He could speak of the self as an aspect of being from which you hear "momentary bulletins" (Phillips, 2001), always as a truth to be made, not a bedrock to be preached from. Certain ideas are so good and so useful that they lift right off the page and live inside you, in your work, animating what you see and what you say. Mannie, I would say, had three such insights in his classic (1990) paper.

First, Mannie worked out the theoretical and clinical relevance of a certain, perhaps surprising, but deeply familiar, clinical moment. It is the moment when good experience is lost, when change is turned away from, when a potential mutative transformation is instead downshifted to something dead and inert and self-punishing. You can hear echoes of Winnicott (1971, 1974). Going beyond the conventional conception of masochism and the often subtle analytic superego disdain for masochism, Mannie found masochism's unsettled edge, the place where the dynamic of masochism (self-reflections or self-lacerations) can go either or any way. He made a wonderful, previously unthought-of distinction between surrender and submission, and instantly made sense of a volatile protean clinical moment when a structure might be on the move. When such a moment occurs, a fork in the road opens up. You can turn the big-heartedness of giving yourself over to change into something crabbed and frozen and hurtful, or you can let go and let change happen.

In this essay on masochism and surrender, Mannie works out many of the barriers against surrender. One interesting problem arises when a person is faced with the disorganizing effect of meaning and conflict. As so often is the case, his example is from daily life, clinical and personal:

> We encounter, daily, in our practice the phenomenon of a patient who can say, "My mother was sadistic," and describe events to nail down the assertion, and yet one has the impression that the patient ends up with the feeling of "but somehow I can't believe it's true." The patient seems not to have been able to "take in" the perception of what he or she has witnessed. It is as if the perception would shatter the prevailing belief system and induce chaos were a complete perceptual letting-go to occur, a surrender to the experience. A total revision of one's perception of, in this case, mother, would have to happen in which the image of mother being sadistic would reside alongside and integrated with other images of mother.
>
> A brief illustration. Many years ago, while vacationing in the country, my 3-year-old niece noticed that my knee was scratched and bleeding slightly. She immediately said, "Oh! Blood! You have a cut. (slight pause). I'll go get you a Band-aid. (slight pause). How did it happen?" I, jokingly: "We were playing in the sand and your mom pushed me!" She: "There's no cut. I don't see any blood." I: "That was just a joke; your mom didn't push me; I fell." She (greatly relieved): "That blood needs a band-aid." She immediately went off to fetch a Band-aid. The story well illustrates that if a perception is threatening to a belief, either the belief or the perception has to go. In this case the idea that good mommy could cause harm to someone was so unacceptable that the perception, as long as it carried significance that would be disorganizing, had to be denied. In other words it could not be "taken in."
>
> (Ghent, 1990, pp. 126–127)

This distinction—submission versus surrender—was a subtle one, but once made it was also obvious. This moment—dialectical, conflictual, multifaceted—has added and aided many relational ideas: vulnerability in the face of another (Mitchell, Hoffman); kaleidoscopic identifications (Davies, Bromberg); use of your own countertransference (Maroda,

Ehrenberg, Davies); facing mortality (Hoffman). Facing mortality was something Mannie knew a lot about.

Second, in connection with this work on masochism and surrender, Mannie worked out another idea, also deeply useful clinically. The idea that a sadistic attack was also an object probe opened a world of clinical complexity. Poke until you make someone bleed figuratively, or actually. It is a staple of marital battles, family scenes, family therapy scenes, and it is often the act of last resort on either side of the couch when the other seems dead, inert, and unavailable. Whether metaphorically or actually, being struck marvelously focuses your attention. What was central to Mannie's way of thinking and working was the notion that amid the hate and wish to destroy and hurt there is the conflicted compromised wish to find and connect.

A third important concept for me is Mannie's development of Winnicott's concept of the use of the object. I have the very strong acoustic memory of sitting in Mannie's class when he talked about the difference between object use and object relating. He described the clinical moment when you have been brave enough to live through some ice storm or heat wave of experience to discover that being of use must predate being in an evolved subject–subject relation. In many clinical contexts, it is Mannie's voice—as supervisor, as mentor, as colleague—that sounds quietly in my ear, and in my mind. It is the kind of experience of thirdness that is personally regulating, calming, solacing, directing.

Over time, Mannie's thinking about the dialectic of masochism and surrender evolved. There are fewer polarities and more intimate partnerings; the interrelationship became more subtle. Masochism could be a trial of surrender; surrender was buried deep inside masochism. Masochism was deeply implicated in the struggle to face human vulnerability.

Mannie as Theorist

One of the aspects of Mannie's work that matters a great deal to me is his utter pleasure in theory. I spend a lot of time rather resentfully thinking that our field is theory phobic. We often idealize the clinical situation and distrust that theory, which is really simply a kind of mind–body work, in which our clinical choices are constructed and sustained. Mannie, who had a million clinical ideas and insights, loved theory. For all the theory geeks who despair when someone tells them that clinical work is intuitive, we can look to Mannie: techie before there were techies—techie with paper ribbon, not floppies; madcap inventor—the playful intellectual wizard of the world of Bell Labs; meaning-maker in psychoanalysis. And for that, I (and many others) have loved him.

In the last major paper he completed, which was written in the 70s (Ghent, 2002), he opened a huge theory vein, setting in play and in place a set of ideas about motivation, about need and desire. Mannie's work on motivation identifies three elements in Edelman's (1987) model: (a) initial values or biases, (b) recategorization and reentry of experience to make for unique and complex internal processes, and (c) a system of mapping. The boundaries and contours and contents of experiences will be variable and unique to any individual in context. Mannie also makes the point that, at the experiential level, the building up of "categorization on value" and mapping will draw on affects, anxieties, and bodily states. All internalized representations are sinew and muscle, feeling and thought, sensing and desiring.

In this final paper on need, wish, and drive, Mannie weaves back and forth between developmental theory, the work of Esther Thelen (Thelen and Smith, 1994); Gerald Edelman's (1987) theory of neuronal group selection; many advances in neuroscience (work on mirror neurons, for example), and nonlinear dynamic systems theory. All these disparate areas are filtered through Mannie's deep understanding of psychoanalytic theory across many perspectives. Here, perhaps, is one of his bottom lines:

> What appears to be a regularity in development, a maturational sequence of prescribed stages is, instead, the resultant of a vast number of individual microcosmic solutions and achievements, leaving room for a great range of variability from one individual to another in the acquisition of capacities and achievements.
>
> (Ghent, 2002, p. 782)

I love that word *microcosmic* and its suggestion of tiny and vast, large scale and small scale.

Within this multidisciplinary framework, Mannie does some very heavy lifting, taking up the great old problems in psychoanalysis. For instance, how are we to thread our way in a theory of motivation between cause-and-effect explanations, on one hand, and the psychoanalytic focus on the growth and evolution of meaning-making and reasons, on the other hand? What model of health or illness threads through motivational theories? In exploring, opening but not resolving, these questions, Mannie pays attention to how we have used words and terms, how these uses are changing and evolving, how to be true to structure *and* process.

What ties Mannie's last preoccupations with chaos theory to the earlier work on submission and surrender? This summer and fall, I gave myself the task of trying to imagine the linkages. Mannie commits to a view of motivation that has an amazing potential for freedom without giving up pattern, reliability, coherence. It's a curious paradox. The chaos theorist Stuart Kauffman (1995) calls it "order for free." You don't build a theory where outcomes are already in lockdown from the very beginning. Motivation emerges; it is not preset or given. You—the analyst, the thinker, the theorist—have to surrender yourself to a process you cannot predict.

The moment when an experience could transform into surrender or submission is a kind of strange-attractor, edge-of-chaos moment. The complexity of any experience, its protean multilayers, offers an unpredictable but nonetheless patterned choice. Which way the die toggles, how the cards fall out, what the unique cascade and integration of experiences turns into, arises in certain conditions. Opening the potentials for freedom as clinicians do in many different ways is an attempt to load the dice toward surrender. But both in ourselves and from our patients we see the strange, emergent troubles and the unexpected successes and failures of an open system.

There is a signature Ghent clinical moment. It is often an impasse in which you sense that a change might be taken, something new attempted. But the odds are uncertain. The dialectics of submission versus surrender, hate versus love, use versus relating, destruction versus survival, all circulate, assemble and reassemble into a kind of strange attractor. These constructions are fractal, complex and unpredictable, unstable; but perceptible, in that chaos, there is pattern. These volatile, protean processes are the engines of change, the production of motivations, not the reified product or drive. This is as true for Mannie's clinical acumen and his ideas of theory as it is of his wonderful performance piece *Phosphones*, in which light, movement, and music arrive into and depart from coherence in an experience of unpredictable pattern.

I end this essay with a quote from T. S. Eliot's "Little Gidding" that Mannie used at the end of his own "Credo:"

> Last season's fruit is eaten
> And the fullfed beast shall kick the empty pail.
> For last year's words belong to last year's language
> And next year's words await another voice.
>
> (quoted in Ghent, 1989, p. 208)

It is this capacity, this willingness to let things move, to surrender to change that cannot be fully under control, that characterized Mannie's work as an analyst, as a supervisor, and as a writer. It's a wonderful legacy.

Note

1. New York University Postdoctoral Program in Psychotherapy and Psychoanalysis.

References

Edelman, G. (1987). *Neural Darwinism: The theory of neural group selection*. New York, NY: Basic Books.

Ghent, E. (1962). Scarcity: A governing principle in man's functioning, *New York University Postdoctoral Program in Psychoanalysis*: Colloquium, September 26, 1962.

Ghent, E. (1989). Credo: The dialectics of one-person and two-person psychologies. *Contemporary Psychoanalysis*, *25*, 169–211.

Ghent, E. (1990). Masochism, submission, surrender: Masochism as a perversion of surrender. *Contemporary Psychoanalysis*, *26*, 169–211.

Ghent, E. (1992a). What's moving, the train or the station? *Contemporary Psychotherapy Review*, *7*, 108–118.

Ghent, E. (1992b). Paradox and process. *Psychoanalytic Dialogues*, *2*, 135–159.

Ghent, E. (2002). Wish, need, drive: Motive in the light of dynamic systems theory and Edelman's selectionist theory. *Psychoanalytic Dialogues*, *12*, 763–808.

Kauffman, S. (1995). *At home in the universe.* New York, NY: Oxford University Press.

Phillips, A. (2001). On what we need: A celebration of the work of Emmanuel Ghent. *Psychoanalytic Dialogues*, *11*, 1–21.

Thelen, E. & Smith, L. (1994). *A dynamic systems approach to the development of cognition and action*. Cambridge. MA: MIT Press.

Winnicott, D. W. (1971). *Playing and reality*. New York, NY: Basic Books.

Winnicott, D. W. (1974). The fear of breakdown. *International Review of Psycho-Analysis*, *1*, 103–107.

Afterword

On what we need: A celebration of the work of Emmanuel Ghent

Adam Phillips

Until Muriel Dimen asked me to give this opening address, I had never really known what people meant when they said, as they often do, that they felt honored by an invitation. So I wondered, as I rarely do, why this particular invitation, this special event, mattered to me quite as much as it did. I have to confess—though I realize in the circumstances that this is rather unfortunate—that I'm not very interested usually in why I feel things. I am more interested, when I'm interested at all, in quite what it is I happen to be feeling. As I thought about rereading Emmanuel Ghent's papers and about what I might write, I realized, with a different kind of clarity, just how important to me a particular group of American psychoanalytic theorists had been. Having trained as a child psychotherapist in London in the 1970s—and having had a Middle Group analysis, and a training that included, and tried to combine with some unease, the work of Winnicott, Klein, and Anna Freud—I had come to New York and browsed the journals and books that my friends had. In blissful ignorance of the history and of the psychoanalytic politics—with very little sense of the institutional issues involved—I had read things by people called Eigen and Boris and Levenson, and Benjamin and Bromberg and Hoffman, and what was then to me a composite figure called Mitchell and Greenberg, and, of course, Ghent. And as I had read this stuff, it was as though I had found something that I hadn't realized that I had been looking for. I had found, I thought, a new Independent group—one impressed by different deities. Instead of being haunted (and daunted) by Melanie Klein, they seemed inspired by Sullivan and Ferenczi; instead of melodramatic and sentimental metaphysics, American pragmatism; instead of the dogma of the Depressive position, the dogma of pluralism. In short, put less abstractly, they could all write. Even though, like the Middle Group writers I most admired, they had their own ferocious, well-mannered convictions; they did not seem hellbent on telling me the truth about human nature, so much as producing interesting descriptions of what they thought was going on. The emphasis in these papers—unlike that in the papers by the demonized Freudians and Kleinians—was quite explicitly that no one in the analytic encounter was in a position of inner superiority (one might say that, in the ideal form of the encounter, equality between patient and analyst wasn't the aim of the treatment; it was the assumption on which the treatment was based). And what was perhaps most striking, and most of a piece with what I wanted an Independent group to be—that is, as genial and congenial as possible—was that these writers were keen to celebrate their so-called patients, and not unwilling to celebrate themselves. In other words, the pleasure of the work was being promoted, not its moral and intellectual superiority to other kinds of work. If to have Sullivan instead of Klein avoided what was for me a peculiarly coercive moralism, to have Ferenczi instead of Winnicott was to make explicit that the mutuality of the psychoanalytic encounter was integral to the work, and not an unfortunate consequence of it (Winnicott, I think, is akin to a Ferenczi-inspired and intimidated Klein). If this sounds like the naïveté of the tourist—one of those idealizations that makes us wonder—for me it was one of those growing recognitions that Mannie Ghent has shown us how to notice. And this preamble is by way of saying that Mannie's work, it seems to me, invites us to have something far more interesting than the courage of our virtues, which is to have the courage of our affinities. That, properly described, what we are drawn to is what can draw us out. To recognize Mannie's work, in other words—which I do here—is to recognize something startling about recognition itself.

The best thing psychoanalysts do is clinical work. But the second-best thing they do, which is not unrelated to this work, is to come up with descriptions of what they believe people need—that is, need in order to live what they consider good-enough lives. This is usually referred to as psychoanalytic theory, but the basic structure—the argument, as it were, and it is always an argument—is quite simple. A need or a set of needs is posited—more or less proved if the theorist is scientifically minded, more or less eloquently asserted if she is not—and more or less adequate responses to these needs are described. The needs have consequences, as do the responses to them. If to call an inclination a need is a rhetorical way of stressing its importance—at one end of this imaginary spectrum we have needs, at the other end we have, say, whims or fashions—then psychoanalysis can be seen as adding to the cultural description pool accounts of who we are in terms of what we need. In the "need-narrative," a need is something that, should it go unmet, disfigures the person bearing it. There is, that is to say, nothing more essential to or about a person than his needs. But in a time, like all times critical of previous essentialisms, and unlike all times critical of the whole notion of essences, needs become a kind of test case. People's needs, like their instincts, are up for grabs. Any of us might be able to come up with a new need, or alternatively might start working out the consequences of doing without words like need (or instinct, or passion, or any of the other Old World nicknames that we and God used about us). And even when we thought we could at least settle for a baseline of eating and breathing (with sex as an optional extra), psychoanalysis showed us that there is no registered need that is not exploitable, no officially sanctioned need that is not adaptable to alternative uses and pleasures. We may need to eat and breathe in order to live, but we may not need to live. If we are, as most versions of psychoanalysis agree, divided against ourselves, in conflict, then our so-called needs become just as precarious, just as puzzling, as any other of our wished-for essentialisms.

Instead of stating what people need, it might be more revealing to say something like: If we agree or decide that people need X, then these are the consequences we can imagine, and we can find out more of the consequences by hearing from people who live as if this need is true (so-called perversions are not a problem for people, but their consequences can be). What we think of as our needs are intimately bound up with what we think of as our options, our opportunities, and our ideals. "The value of our ideals," John Dewey (1972) wrote in *Art as Experience*, "lies in the experiences to which they lead." And the same is true of the value of what we are moved to call our needs. Because what we call our needs leads us into certain kinds of experiences, it matters what we call our needs. To say something is a need is to say that there is no way around it. And to say something is a need from a psychoanalytic point of view is to say that for every need, we are likely also to need to believe we can find a way around it.

I am especially glad to be giving this address because I so much like what Mannie thinks we need, and his remarkable account of how needing works, which includes, of course, an account of how it can go wrong. I want to say what Mannie thinks we need—in his words as much as possible, which means in my words, too—and then try to answer the thornier question of why I think we should value the things that Mannie, in his writing, is persuading us to take seriously. I want to think, in other words, about the experiences to which Mannie's ideals might lead. There is not necessarily any discernible connection between the writer and the person we meet. So I want to emphasize that this is Mannie the writer, the man on paper, who I am talking about. Or, to put it another way, I'm worried and delighted that Mannie is here this evening. And I want to signify all this by calling the writer Ghent to distinguish him as a writer; I have always hated the formality of second names, because it speaks of the strange distances and obediences of adult life, but here, suffice it to say, I use Ghent for a purpose. And as well as calling him by this name, I want to read him backward, in reverse chronological order, so that his remarkable writing seems to unravel rather than progress; to accumulate retroactively is, after all, the psychoanalytic way. If we believe in deferred action, if we believe in dreamwork, even if we believe in development—or growth, as Ghent is also prone to call it—we can read only backward. Or rather, reading backward is the best way of seeing how things have turned out and turned up.

I think that, just before we start working backward, we need to bear in mind, as a kind of epigraph, one of the credos mentioned in passing in Ghent's (1989) "Credo: The dialectics of one-person and two-person psychologies": "It became clear that whatever I might say about what I believe, can at best only be true at this moment" (p. 171). This is at once a truthful and a disarming remark. It acknowledges that we cannot be held to our beliefs, that to foist a consistency on ourselves is to freeze time. But if what Ghent says about what he believes "can at best only be true at this moment," when was that? It seems to me correct that the truth is in the moment, that what we can say about what we believe is always of the moment, and that our beliefs, such as they are, are only what we can say about them. I want to make a meal of this for two reasons. First, Ghent writes a psychoanalysis of the proliferating self, in which what we might refer to as truths or beliefs are momentary bulletins from a continually evolving project; in which the medium in the to-and-fro between development and arrested development is the unstoppable time of a life; in which, in short, Ghent's psychoanalysis is committed to transformations and not resolutions, not so much to the exploration of states of mind but to the sense that states of mind are themselves exploratory. We are always seeking our possibilities even when, or especially when, we are most deadlocked. What he refers to as "yielding the defensive superstructure, being known, found, penetrated, recognised" (1990, p. 117) is all breakouts and breakthroughs. To yield is to let something happen.

Second, and perhaps less obvious, Ghent's credo about momentariness, about the momentary truth of his believings, is also a more oblique allusion to something that Ghent has been quite explicitly exercised by throughout his writing—the nature of need. If we were crudish Freudians, we might say that a belief is the sublimation of a need, or a reaction formation against a need. Whether we think of our beliefs as informed by our needs or as disguised statements about our needs, from a psychoanalytic viewpoint needs and beliefs are linked if not actually inextricable. If we rewrite Ghent's sentence, replace belief with need, we get: "It became clear that whatever I might say about what I need, can at best only be true at this moment." That seems to be a radical innovation in psychoanalytic thinking, and is of a piece with what Ghent has been working on and working out about need—that needs, like beliefs, are not essences that are fixed and develop inside a person, not a prearranged repertoire, not a set of Platonic forms, but rather are essentially circumstantial, inclinations of the moment and the context; and therefore needs have no known essence. They are not urgencies waiting to happen, personal imperatives ready to go off, but artifacts made in relationship. Needs are more like personal experiments in living than designs for a life. The novelist E. M. Forster (1927) famously said, "How can I know what I think until I see what I say?" (p. 43). Ghent says, "How can I know what I need until someone responds to something I do?" I do something either knowingly or unwittingly; someone responds in a way that might seem simply right, or at once apt and surprising, and then I realize, in retrospect, that what I had been doing was needing. I had been, as it were, caught in the act. I had wanted something without knowing what I wanted, or even perhaps that I was wanting. There is, in other words, to adapt Winnicott's formula, no such thing as a need; there are always a need and its correspondent. We are full of indeterminate possibilities, Ghent implies, that require suitable recognition in order to make us start talking about them as needs. They are not so much in-built projects to be exercised or thwarted; they are rather reconstructed after the transformative event of a sign being read or acted on in a certain way. As we shall see, what Ghent calls neediness is the baffling of this experience. From this point of view, dependence is not on another person to gratify our needs but to create them through their response. So what Ghent adds to the more familiar psychoanalytic story about needing in development is the extraordinary and paradoxical idea that a need, as it were, is something you didn't know you had until someone happened to gratify it, or validate it. In short, recognition is constitutive.

Of course, there is by now a genre of psychoanalytic vignette in which either the analyst or the so-called patient does something that is either utterly mundane or a bit out of the ordinary and yet is vividly transformational. Balint's patient did a somersault, Sandler passed a tissue, and Winnicott did many such things, making this particular genre of analytic writing his signature tune. The emphasis is usually on doing instead of or as well as saying, so Kleinians, orthodox Freudians, and Lacanians tend not to go in for these plays within the play. In "Interaction in the Psychoanalytic Situation," Ghent (1995) presents an unusually interesting clinical vignette, which is in itself impressive given that it is the point of the genre to make the reader wonder what is being shown here—a new shareable technique or an astonishingly talented therapist at work. When, in psychoanalytic writing, a transformation scene is offered—and especially when the epiphany is prompted by a gesture—the demand on the reader is perplexing. We may, for example, wonder what we are supposed to do with this. What I think is remarkable about Ghent's vignette is that his gesture is at once unaccountable and straightforward. Claims are not being made for his genius, but for there being something by definition inexplicable in the nature of recognition. Indeed, if it were explicable, it wouldn't be what he thinks of as recognition; it would be a species of proselytizing. "Many years ago," Ghent (1995) wrote,

> I had an office on the ground floor of a Greenwich Village brownstone. As it faced out on a large garden and much open space, the office was quite susceptible to chilly drafts on windy winter days. One such day a woman patient was haltingly recounting, as was her wont, the details of some event that had recently occurred; I cannot now recall the content. She was sitting in a chair at right angles to me, about fifteen feet from the windows. Suddenly, but not abruptly, I got up, went over to where a Scottish throw was folded on the couch, picked it up, covered her lap and legs with it, and returned to my chair. As I

> sat down I noticed, *to my surprise*, that she was sobbing silently. It was the first time in our work, by then over two years in duration, that there was an indication of distress, pain, or even sadness. After some time her first words were, "I didn't even know I was feeling cold," and then she wept profusely. The event was a turning point.
>
> (p. 483)

It is characteristic of Ghent that he should then follow this with two similar accounts, from Irwin Hoffman and Darlene Ehrenberg. Clearly, something other than a unique clinical sensibility is being spoken up for here. And there are two overall points he wants to make. First, he is pointing out that, in these examples, there is no "question of demand, the shibboleth of the neediness that often masquerades as need but in actuality is organised as a defence against—a blackwashing of—the need for caring responsiveness" (1995, p. 485). Second, he is pointing out that "the phrase 'to my surprise' was part of the therapist's reaction. It is as if the therapist's attention has been claimed by something unexpected, a loud hint that a new vista, a new insight is brewing" (p. 485). In other words, the patient has not, to all intents and purposes, asked for anything, and the therapist has been surprised by what he's got to give, at that moment. Neither the patient nor the analyst is acting on, or speaking about, their ostensive beliefs.

Ghent's patient didn't know she was feeling cold until he covered her; she could only recognize what she was feeling after he had, however unknowingly, sensed this, and acted on his imagining. It is the kind of thing a parent might do with a young child, such is its touching and wholly convincing ordinariness. Ghent's passage seems to be a wonderful piece of writing re-presenting a remarkable moment of therapy. The patient had expressed her unhappiness, could do so only after Ghent had recognized it, and gone some way to meet it. It is virtually true to say that, from her point of view, she had not needed looking after until Ghent had looked after her. At that moment, she had not apparently wanted anything; Ghent had given her something and then was surprised, not by what he had given her, but by her response to it. His ordinary recognition prompts her recognition, which surprises him. What had been missing in her—an expression of her unhappiness—was made possible when Ghent satisfied her unthought need. It would be misleading, I think, to say that Ghent's gesture released something in her, because that would imply that a something, say, a pain, had been pent up in her until that moment. Ghent's account leaves this instructively ambiguous. Perhaps it would be truer and more useful to say that, through Ghent's enacted recognition, this woman could construct an unhappiness for the first time. Either a need had been lurking in her all the while, or, at that moment, a need was crystallized. In one sense, the need to be looked after could never be a new need, but it would be a description of this woman's unhappiness to say that she was so unhappy because it felt as if it was a new need. Ghent (1995) wrote, "Of special moment in each of these examples"—and "moment" is the word—"is that along with the old pattern of behaviour, something new was happening." (p. 485) The repetition—"a woman patient was haltingly recounting, as was her wont, the details of some event that had recently occurred; I cannot now recall the content" is "mixed in," Ghent wrote, with another need, and the mixing, as we shall see, is as important as this other need that is "usually much weaker and less developed; it is an expansive rather than a conservative system; one whose tendency or need is either to seek out a new quality of experience, or to destabilise the smooth functioning of the old, constrictive system" (p. 485). There is, Ghent is saying, a need for the new, and, if it is genuinely new, of course, neither the therapist nor the patient could know beforehand what it might be. And if the need for the new is mixed in—that is, to use another of Ghent's good fusional words, blended, or even inextricable from each other—then it has to be part of the analyst's skill to see both happening at once, to acknowledge the mix and do a bit of disentangling. The need for the new, I am suggesting Ghent is suggesting, is also the need for new needs. And when Ghent in this paper says that there is "a need in the patient for a quality of experience in the analysis without which therapeutic effect will be minimal" (p. 489), he is saying that the patient depends on the therapist's not being too knowing about the patient's needs. To acknowledge the need for new needs is to acknowledge, by definition, not knowing what they are. The so-called repetition compulsion, one might say, stabilizes the proliferation of needs.

Two years earlier, in a commentary on a paper by Peter Shabad, Ghent (1993) was keen to show what kind of meanings the word *need* "has taken on" (p. 499). Wanting to "illustrate the range of attitudes about the question of encountering the patient's need" (p. 497), Ghent distinguished what he called "at least two quite different meanings that attach to the word 'need'" (p. 497). The distinction he went on to make might be described as need looked at from the inside (from the point of view of someone feeling what he or she calls a need) and from the outside (a kind of cultural consensus about what human beings fundamentally consist of). "Is need," Ghent asked, "to be regarded as expressive of a requirement for the healthy welfare and development of the person, or should it be employed on the basis of the feeling of need, its urgency, peremptoriness, demand?" (p. 497). This is an interesting way of putting it, because it pits my freedom as a patient to define anything felt as urgent, peremptory, or demanding in myself as a need, and therefore as something to which I am entitled, against the analyst, as expert on human nature, who knows beforehand what I as patient am entitled to regard as a need. And this, of course, has consequences for the responding analyst. To put it schematically, the analyst will respond differently to what she might believe is conducive to "the healthy welfare and development of the person" than she will to the patient's every whim. And yet, as Ghent intimates—though I'm not sure he would endorse this—in a pragmatist vein, things may be only the way we describe them. I am free to call anything in myself, any inclination in myself that particularly matters to me, a need. Indeed, by describing it as a need, in this culture, I am more likely to get it attended to. If needs, in my culture, tend to be defined by the qualities of urgency, peremptoriness, and demand, and needs are given priority over wants, it would be the intelligent policy of, in Nietzsche's phrase, "a clever animal" to describe his own priorities as needs. This is what language is for: language makes us, in a sense, the cleverest animals; language is to persuade people. In the clash and collaboration of the patients' and the analysts' rhetorics, the drama of who has got the best line on need is enacted.

But in order to make a good case for a better life, it is useful to distinguish, as Ghent does, between qualities of need—between need and neediness, in Ghent's language. For me, Ghent has one of the best lines going in psychoanalytic writing on need, though in asserting this I have nothing to offer by way of justification except my unwilled agreement (the affinity and assent induced by his writing) and my knowledge that more knowledge about myself wouldn't give me any better grounds for valuing what he has been keen to say. Ghent (1993) proposed that we should distinguish

> between appropriate and legitimate need and neediness. By legitimate needs I include the needs for recognition and affirmation—to be treated with empathic responsiveness, to be understood—as well as the need

> to use the object, the expression of which may present substantial difficulty for the analyst in that it is likely to spill over into object abuse. (p. 501)

Because of this spillage—because of the blending and mixing of these apparently contradictory projects—Ghent's distinction allows both the patient and the analyst a remarkable margin of freedom in the analytic encounter. It must be part of the legitimate need for recognition and affirmation that the patient could be recognized and affirmed as somebody who, for good reason, might want to call any urgency in himself a need. Paradoxically, in distinguishing need and neediness, Ghent legitimates the value of both. It may be one of my needs to perform my neediness. Neediness, one might say, is the best form the patient has found for his needs so far. So, as we go backward with Ghent, we go from need and neediness (1993), through "Paradox and Process" (1992), to "Masochism, Submission, and Surrender" (1990). Prospectively, of course, this project had no inevitability to it. Retrospectively, it can be construed as a remarkably inspired and persistent account of something that by his standards (and there is no attitudinizing in Ghent's writing) was strongly stated in 1994: "I find it distressing when I encounter Procrusteanism in any form" (Ghent, 1994, p. 481). Just as there is no attitudinizing in Ghent's work, there is also remarkably little mythology. Procrusteanism is, as it were, a well-known analytic approach. Procrustes, in the words of Lempriere (1984), "was a famous robber of Attica … He tied travellers on a bed, and, if their length exceeded that of the bed, cut off part of their limbs to make their length equal to that of the bed; but if they were shorter he stretched their bodies till they were of the same length" (p. 562). What Ghent calls Procrusteanism in any form—which is itself amusing and amused, as Procrusteanism is about keeping forms down to a minimum—is about cutting people down to size and making them fit. Ghent has embarked on the peculiarly and paradoxically difficult task of finding an alternative, in psychoanalysis, to Procrusteanism—the possibility that in the theory and practice of psychoanalysis there may be something other than the Procrusteanism of everyday life.

If Ghent is often asking, one way or another, if there is anything besides perversion in so-called perversion, then the image of Procrustes, tailoring his victims to his bed, is telling in its sexual starkness. It is at once a story about what theories and theorists can do to themselves and others, and what people can do to themselves and others. It is an image of how people can disfigure one another for what seems like the sake of convenience or necessity. Procrustes is, rather too literally, persuading the bodies of his victims to fit the bed. It is, in other words, another transformation scene, a malign one. So it is not incidental, I think, for Ghent to have included Procrustes in passing, and it is not unrelated to this that there are two pieces of psychoanalytic writing that Ghent quotes more than once in his own writing that are about this essential matter of how people go about changing one another—what Ghent (1993) called "the larger question of what makes for personality change and emotional growth" (p. 506). Because Ghent quotes other people so well —which is itself an exemplary instance of the use of an object—it is striking when such an uninsistent writer keeps going back to something. We must all have passages of psychoanalytic writing that we are keen to quote or reread or determinedly avoid quoting—passages that elicit a strong transference because they reveal simultaneously an affinity and a dilemma that are close to our hearts. There are two passages that recur in Ghent's writing—a famous one from Winnicott and one no less intriguing from Arnold Cooper. And, perhaps unsurprisingly, they are linked. They are both questions from the bed of Procrustes. Ghent (1992) quoted from Cooper's (1992) paper entitled "Psychic Change: Development in the Theory of Psychoanalytic Techniques":

> It is less than clear that cognitive aspects of insight are essential for psychic change. … Stanley Greenspan … has shown that better mothering or removal from an abusive situation produces powerful and lasting changes in the child, even though the child is not helped to develop insight into what is going on. … This also brings up the question of non-analytic change, and the importance for analysis of our better understanding of conversion experiences—whether St. Paul or Malcolm X—and the importance of peak affect.

What Cooper referred to might be thought of as a triangle of alternatives for transformation—a change of external environment, the revelation leading to conversion, or changing the internal environment through insight. The psychoanalytic position, Cooper intimated, is uneasily poised between the other two (the patient does, of course, change his external environment by going into the analyst's consulting room), and insofar as the analyst and her patient share a language, something akin to a conversion experience might have occurred. Or, to put it another way, if analysts don't describe themselves as being converted to psychoanalysis, how would they rather put it? In the same way that Ghent's work works for an alternative to the so-called perverse solution of sadomasochism, it is to alternatives to conversion that he pays attention. Cooper's suggestion of the importance, for psychoanalysis, of "non-analytic change" also links up with the tactful and rather understated references in Ghent's writing to meditation.

A quotation from Winnicott's (1969/1971) paper is equally evidently at the heart of Ghent's preoccupations. Ghent (1990) called Winnicott's passage "an almost diagrammatic example":

> Two babies are feeding at the breast; one is feeding on the self in the form of projections, and the other is feeding on [using] milk from a woman's breast. … The change does not come about automatically, by maturational process alone. … Mothers, like analysts, can be good or not good enough; some can and some cannot carry the baby over from relating to usage. [This transition] is the most difficult thing, perhaps, in human development … and the most irksome of all the early failures that come from mending … the change [from relating to use] means that the subject destroys the object [as subjective object] and the object, if it survives destruction, is now real.
>
> (p. 122)

All psychoanalytic writers write about change, but the stronger theorists (or, rather, the theorists who tend to attract more of our attention) tend, either explicitly or implicitly, to tell us the difference between good change and bad change. They specify, in other words, the direction in which change should take place. Lacan says that bad change for the patient is the illusion of an improved adaptation to the environment, or a greater mastery over the self; good change, Klein says, is entering into the depressive position. Good change, Winnicott says here, is what the self can become in the process of making the object real. What Cooper raises more openly—and I think this might be part of his appeal for Ghent—is not merely the question of how good change might be affected, but the thornier question of what makes us think of any particular kind of change as good. Winnicott's rhetoric of true selves and real objects, for example, lures us away from the more vulgar questions like, what's the big deal about relating to a so-called real object? Why is that self-evidently a good life project—indeed, such an essential life project that, in Winnicott's words, inability to achieve this is a "failure that comes for mending?" Of course, we could all give a good answer to these questions, but the answers won't rescue us from the predicament that I think Ghent's work has always been looking at—that no story about change is exempt from a whole range of prior judgments about what we consider, more or less tacitly, a good life to consist of. Our sense of direction is always at stake. When we say it is bad for adolescents to take drugs, or good for adults to become parents, there is always a trawl of values in the wake of these statements. When Ghent (1962) invites us to put our money on paradox and surrender, on acceptance as opposed to resignation, on what Cooper calls non-analytic forms of change as well as, or complementary to, psychoanalysis, he is both asserting his own sense of value and persuading us to value the kinds of experience in which we might be able to find out just what it is we do value, however momentarily. What Ghent calls paradox and surrender—which are, as we shall see, related phenomena—I also want to call experiments in personal morality. In entertaining a paradox, we are free of mutually exclusive options; in surrendering to an experience, in Ghent's version, we abrogate our previous sense of what our possibilities are. Ghent says that the best direction change can take is the direction in which we cannot know where our change will take us. This, to put it mildly, has radical moral and political implications. I should also say—by way of a second and last personal confession—that Ghent is for me an exemplary psychoanalytic writer by being at once plain and straightforward and wonderfully oblique. Just as his "Masochism, Submission, Surrender: I: Masochism as a Perversion of Surrender" (1990) is the best thing I have ever read about listening to music (even though listening to music is not mentioned), by the same token Ghent's writing seems to me ferociously political by being mild-mannered and making only the odd glancing reference to something we might think of as politics. Wittingly or unwittingly, or wittingly and unwittingly, Ghent is an artful writer, and we should take this to heart. And nowhere is this more evident than in what are for me his two finest papers, "Paradox and Process" (1992) and "Masochism, Submission, Surrender" (1990). Everything I have ever come across by Ghent is worth reading, but for me these two papers are inexhaustibly interesting. Having, as he once put it, "contributed to the cause of slaying the one person dragon" (Ghent, 1995, p. 479), and having worried away about the connection, if any, between information and transformation, Ghent really starts something off in psychoanalysis, in his account of paradox and surrender—even as he fairly and squarely acknowledges his debts to certain strands of the psychoanalytic tradition. We don't have to overvalue this now overvalued commodity of originality to notice that these two papers both bring to light, in an unusually vivid way, much that had been latent and lurking in the British Independent group, in relational psychoanalysis, and in Kohut—without doing anything as banal and tiresome as making a synthesis. Ghent doesn't bring all this together; he brings out something of his own in bringing them together. I don't want to paraphrase these unsummarizable papers, because they are too good for that. I just want to, by way of conclusion, pick out a few highlights—when Ghent simply tells us what we need in a way that makes us wonder about what we need and how we go about doing this odd thing.

When Ghent wants to talk about paradox, he starts talking about need. This is strange in a sense. What, after all, could be less paradoxical than a need? It would seem as though, by definition, something is either a need or it isn't. "Among the questions to be touched on in this paper" (Ghent, 1992), he writes, one of them is "How can there be both need and no need at the same time?" (p. 135). It's like the children's joke: When is a door not a door? (When it's ajar.) Except that Ghent is proposing not a synthesis, or a resolution, but a third thing that isn't exactly a third thing—a paradox. Paradox, Ghent wrote, "lives in the world of the aesthetic; it points the way to insight without laying an interpretation upon us" (p. 136). Pointing the way is a direction, not a prescription; it is the difference between my saying "Go in the direction of London." If I say, "Go to London," we both know where you are going. Needs, it is intimated, may be more akin to directions than destinations. And so we might say, paradoxically, that needs get distorted when destinations are privileged (the person with a so-called perverse desire knows exactly where he's going). That needing is a process—to use the other term of Ghent's title—that involves a paradox (to lay an interpretation on a process would be unpromising). What Ghent proposes instead is that the thing about need—the point of needing—is that we can't tell the good need from the bad need. If we can tell, then it's not a need.

"How, then, to understand," Ghent (1992) asked,

> the relation between neediness and need, between "bad need" and "good need"? As with most paradoxical and ambiguous situations, our intellect and our scientific imagination wish to choose between alternatives, to come down on one or the other side. It is either this or that. But in real life we are often in an intermediate zone, where ambiguity occupies centre stage and requires of the analyst a remarkable capacity for living in uncertainty. The likelihood is high that in the clinical process, particularly with some patients, both real need is expressed, and along with it, a curious species of camouflage, the blackwashing of need—neediness.
>
> (p. 141)

The relation between good need and bad need is interanimating; they each at least sometimes require the other to make themselves viable. When is a need not a need? When it's a need. If needs require camouflage, then to all intents and purposes what you see is what you get; the actor seems identical to his part. There is, though, Ghent makes clear, "genuine need," but something has happened in the early relationship that has, as it were, formed and fashioned this need in a certain way. Ghent's language is theatrical: "The neediness by being easily confounded with genuine need, is well designed to keep the real need from being known by the analyst, let alone the patient. It is often expressive of true self, whereas neediness, garbed in protective coloration, is the impersonator" (p. 141).

This combination of military and theatrical vocabulary is instructive. We might have thought that there was an original pure thing called a need, or a true self, and this got disguised by neediness or a false self, for reasons to do with early relationships. And this is certainly one clear implication of Ghent's (and Winnicott's) position. And yet, an actor impersonating Hamlet, dressed as Hamlet, is only in a paradoxical sense impersonating him, because there is no original. The actor on the stage is Hamlet and not Hamlet; he is as much Hamlet as anybody is ever going to be, and he is not Hamlet at all. For some people, or for all people at some times, need will take the form of neediness, but there is no other form it could take. It exists, like an actor, only in the parts it plays. When we see Hamlet, we don't ask ourselves if he is really Hamlet. We ask ourselves how effective, how persuasive, is this actor, this performance of Hamlet. This, Ghent implies, is what the analyst should be asking about the so-called needs of her patient. "My reason for using the word 'paradoxical' here," Ghent (1992) wrote,

> is that two equally valid but contradictory statements apply; there is no need; what looks like need is a manipulative, at times vengeful demandingness, which is, in large measure, an expression of rage at lifelong deprivation of one form or another ... on the other hand there is need—genuine longings for human warmth, empathic responsiveness, trust, recognition, faith, playful creativity—all the ingredients we think of when we speak of love.
>
> (p. 142)

You will notice that sexuality is not mentioned by name in this list of genuine needs, though it may be entailed by all the things Ghent does mention. Perhaps it is worth suggesting that there is nothing more paradoxical, to use Ghent's term, than sexuality—no area of human experience in which need and neediness are so successfully blurred and blended. And that is exactly why it should be celebrated. Is sexual desire true or false? Is it need or neediness? Is it good or bad? These are always the wrong questions to ask. Like the actor who plays Hamlet, sexual desire is both elements in each pair because it is neither. Our sexuality may be the ultimate artifact of our being. So we might say that it has been the attempt among psychoanalysts to distinguish the good sexuality from the bad sexuality that has been so divisive—and that sexuality should be acknowledged to be a paradox rather than resolved as a contradiction. And this too would have consequences for the practice of psychoanalysis. Ghent, I think, is on to them. "It is difficult," Ghent (1992) wrote,

> to maintain the tension of appropriate response to these opposing expressions of need. One attempts to respond to what one feels is genuine need, especially when one senses the need emerging in forms that the patient is unaware of. I think of this type of response as validation of real need, rather than as "gratification," which I look upon as belonging more to the area of demand.
>
> (p. 143)

To validate is to acknowledge as significant, to gratify, and so to defuse and placate and thereby perpetuate the failure of recognition. You might say that psychoanalysis is the relationships in which validation and its consequences are explored, as opposed to gratification and its consequences. One may not need to have very sophisticated or elaborate discussions about the role of the analyst; one might just say that this is the place where we do this and not that. We may think and feel and say all sorts of things, but it is that form of recognition that Ghent calls validation—and that might also be called acknowledgment—that we have agreed to work at. When Ghent (1992) is doing what he calls "separating meanings" that "in practice … often blend" (p. 154), he also, of course, implicitly invites us to blend any of his proposed oppositions. If a bit too sternly we want to separate validation from gratification, we might also wonder what their blending might entail. If good need and bad need can be inextricable, so too sometimes can validation and gratification. Ghent allows us such thoughts, even when he doesn't explicitly promote them. "This capacity for tolerating and living with paradox," he writes, "is closely related to what I think of as acceptance. Resignation, by contrast, is the impersonator of acceptance" (p. 155). This may be a comment addressed as much to the analyst's relationship with himself as practitioner, and his colleagues, as it is a developmental aim for the patient. How much acceptance is going to be possible from a psychoanalytic point of view, when psychoanalysis itself depends on the category of the unacceptable? Perhaps this is also a covert critique of the more dogmatic schools of analysis? Perhaps certain versions of Freudianism and Kleinianism are a schooling in resignation rather than acceptance?

It would not be merely provocative to say that Ghent's great "Masochism, Submission, Surrender" (1990) is, among many other things, a paper as much about psychoanalytic training as about psychoanalytic treatment. It's about whether it is possible to conceive of a psychoanalytic training that is not, in however liberal a way, a Procrustean bed, and whether it's possible to conceive of a psychoanalytic treatment that is not a cramping of the patient's personal style. There is a sense in which what is being fought over here is the nature of need and needing. Do the members of a psychoanalytic training institution or the practicing analyst need to know what people need, or is that the problem masquerading as the solution? A lot of infant research is a quest for the grail of basic human need—suggesting as it does that needs can be discovered if only we can find the right research methods. It may be the case, after all, that what people have suffered from as children is too definitive a decision about what they needed—negatively as deprivation, positively as impingement.

"The term interpersonal relations," Ghent (1989) wrote in his credo

> in its deeper meaning refers to the non-fetishistic analysis of character, and only in a superficial sense to the colloquial "what goes on between people." Sullivan and Marx held in common the concept that consciously or unconsciously everything of value and importance in human life has meaning only in terms of man's relation to man.
>
> (p. 178)

Nothing about people has been more fetishized than the nature of their needs. A fetish, Ghent wrote by way of clarification, "obscures the relations between people … in classical analysis such concepts as id, ego, superego, likewise obscure and mystify the underlying relation between people. They are fetishes. One might say that the id is the fetishistic formalisation of early experience" (p. 177). Needs, one might say, in certain descriptions, can be like the fetishes inside the fetish—their mystification being in the way they seem to clarify so-called human nature. In my reading of Ghent's paper, it is through what he calls surrender that a person can discover the personal nature of his own need (and that needing is an ongoing process and therefore not subject to finalized formulation); it is through submission that a person reinforces the fetishization of his need.

Volumes can be written about this paper, but, in order to make good use of this object, I have to be selective. But it is not incidental that, as Ghent struggles to get at what he is getting at in this paper, he has recourse to the notion of need. "I have already hinted at the notion," Ghent (1990) wrote,

> that these phenomena I am encompassing as surrender are not mere descriptions of a particular way of functioning, but are as well characterised by a quality of need, mostly operating out of awareness, yet seemingly with a relentlessness that is not easy to account for in traditional psychoanalytic terms. By "need" I am not implying that there is something like an inborn instinct for the integration of the self. My view is rather that in normal development the most primitive needs and functions of the infant, when adequately responded to and interacted

> with by the environing others, give rise to ever more sophisticated and complex conative structures, which later we recognise as having the valence or motivational quality of the need.
>
> (p. 113)

Our fundamental need, Ghent says, is to be able to live in a way that enables our needs to come to light. It is notable that when Ghent gives, as he quite often does, his own list of basic needs—to be known, penetrated, affirmed, recognized, nurtured, et cetera— they all describe facilitation, not prescription or foreknowledge. These are not instrumental actions to known ends; they are like passive, uncertain hungers. A need for Ghent is an experiment rather than a fetish. He is keen to emphasize that by need he does not, as he says, mean that there is "something like an inborn instinct for the integration of the self." After all, what could be more fetishistic than the whole notion of integration? It would be like knowing beforehand that all the parts could be fitted together (it would be possible to say that, if there were such a thing as integration, there would be no such thing as psychoanalysis). One's need as an infant, Ghent suggests—and it is, perhaps, the only need he reifies—is to interact with an environment that allows for and encourages the discovery, as a continual process throughout life, of what one will call one's needs. "Surrender," Ghent (1990) wrote, "might be reflective of some force towards growth for which, interestingly, no satisfactory English word exists. Submission, on the other hand, either operates in the service of resistance or is at best adaptive as an expedient" (p. 109). Submission, that is to say, is another word for the fetishizing of need. It is the imposition, or self-imposition, of a fixed description of one's need. "The main hypothesis of this paper," Ghent wrote with his characteristic clarity,

> is that it is this passionate longing to surrender that comes into play in at least some instances of masochism. Submission, losing oneself in the power of the other, becoming enslaved in one or other way to the master, is the ever available lookalike to surrender. It holds out the promise, seduces, excites, enslaves and in the end, cheats the seeker turned victim of his cherished goal, offering in its place only the security of bondage and an ever amplified sense of futility. By substituting the appearance and trappings of surrender for the authentic experience, an agonising, though at times temporarily exciting masquerade

> of surrender occurs; a self-negating submissive experience in which the person is enthralled by the other. The intensity of the masochism is a living testimonial of the urgency with which some buried part of the personality is screaming to be exhumed. This is not to be minimised as an expression of the longing to be healed, although so often we bear witness to its recurring miscarriage.
>
> (pp. 114–115)

That is, I think, an astonishing piece of writing. So much can be written on those few sentences. We might differentiate psychoanalytic theories (or theorists) according to whether they require of us our submission or our surrender. And, of course, Ghent shrewdly counsels us to distinguish things in order to better acknowledge that nothing lives in a state of such stark distinction. We are likely to see submission and surrender together. I think Ghent's paper has a paradoxical effect that is integral to its subject matter. I can't help but surrender to this paper; I don't feel I am submitting to anything, because it is inspiring rather than informative, and, yet, there's something enthralling about it. But then it may also be part of the preconditions for surrender that one is moved to work out just what it might be that one is enthralled by—and this, one could say, is where psychoanalysis comes in. That we have a sense of being buried alive in our lives ("some buried part of the personality is screaming to be exhumed"), and that masochism might be a self- defeating performance of the wish to surrender—these are descriptions and propositions it would have been a great shame to have missed.

Nowadays, everybody in psychoanalysis says that no one has access to ultimate truth. But Ghent (1992) said that he believes that "no one has a lien on ultimate truth" (p. 139). Ghent is full of surprises: "Even as I portray the difference of viewpoints in this paradoxical way, I am aware that further complexities abound." Mannie's paradoxical way, which actually wants further complexities to abound, is more than cause for celebration.

Note

1. Adam Phillips is a child psychotherapist in London. This paper was first presented at a conference in New York City on May 12–13 entitled "For Mannie Who Will Be 75 in the Year 2000!" to celebrate the work of Emmanuel Ghent.

References

Cooper, A. M. (1992). Psychic change: Development in the theory of psychoanalytic techniques. *International Journal of Psycho-Analysis*, *76*, 245–250.

Dewey, J. (1972). *Art as experience*. New York, NY: Berkley Publishing Group.

Forster, E. M. (1927). *Aspects of a novel*. London, UK: Edward Arnold.

Ghent, E. (1962, September). *Scarcity: A governing principle in man's functioning*. Presented at a Colloquium of the New York University Postdoctoral Program, New York, NY.

Ghent, E. (1989). Credo: The dialectics of one-person and two-person psychologies. *Contemporary Psychoanalysis*, *25*, 169–211.

Ghent, E. (1990). Masochism, submission, surrender: Masochism as a perversion of surrender. *Contemporary Psychoanalysis*, *26*, 108–136.

Ghent, E. (1992). Paradox and process. *Psychoanalytic Dialogues*, *2*, 135–159.

Ghent, E. (1993). Reply to Shabad. *Psychoanalytic Dialogues*, *3*, 495–507.

Ghent, E. (1994). Empathy: Whence and whither. *Psychoanalytic Dialogues*, *4*, 472–486.

Ghent, E. (1995). Interaction in the psychoanalytic situation. *Psychoanalytic Dialogues*, *5*, 479–491.

Lempriere, J. (1984). *Lempriere's classical dictionary*. London, UK: Brecken Books.

Winnicott, D. W. (1971). The use of an object and relating through identification. In *Playing and reality* (pp. 86–94). London, UK: Tavistock (Original work published 1969).

Index